LANGUAGE AND LEARNING TO READ

What Teachers Should Know About Language

Edited by
Richard E. Hodges
E. Hugh Rudorf

UNIVERSITY
PRESS OF
AMERICA

LANHAM • NEW YORK • LONDON

FOREWORD

For anyone in the teaching profession today, particularly at the preschool and elementary levels, no topic is of more enduring concern than how to help children in mastering the arts of language. The veteran teacher with years of experience, no less than the teacher-in-training, probably thinks more about this responsibility and devotes more time to study and preparation in this field than he gives to any other aspect of his work. For parents, no question seems more crucial in education than whether their child is learning to read in the best possible way. Even for the child himself, this is a matter of prime concern.

Regrettably, the state of the art is less than satisfactory, and both teachers and researcher-specialists seem on the whole agreed that significant improvements are necessary. Happily, as this important new book amply demonstrates, there is now a great deal of solid material to guide practitioners; and within this dynamic field there are emerging (or maturing) very sound theories of the reading process and of efficacious reading instruction. As the editors and the authors frequently remind us, there are disturbing gaps between what we must eventually know and what is already known, but the progress that has been made over the past decade or so is nothing short of remarkable.

This volume has unusual timeliness and great breadth in the scholarship on which it draws. Though not encyclopedic, it presents the work and ideas of nineteen people including the editors, whose skill in assembling and interrelating the sixteen essays deserves special mention. The authors have a variety of backgrounds, as the editors explain, and their papers are not only fresh but, thanks to the editors' introductions, a cohesive collection. When, as editorial adviser, I first read the papers I was struck not only by the good overall balance but also the uniformly high quality of the essays. Not always in a multiauthor project is this achieved, and for the reader this is a notable bonus.

Each reader, of course, will have his own needs and interests, and certain sections will therefore have more appeal or utility for him. For the typical reader with a general interest in the topic, my advice would be to read *first* the editors' own contributions; the Preface, the Introduction, the opening paragraphs for each of the eight sections, and the Summary. Thus given a capsule view of the available material, the reader can make more informed decisions about his further approach to this wealthy volume. It will help him to see why the editors identify the Goodman papers as the heart of the volume, and it will provide easier access to the chapters most related to his own role.

Although graduate students and reading specialists will find abundant scholarly material, the chief audience will be students enrolled in methods courses on reading and language arts. Not only is this recognized in the chapters by teachers about teaching applications, but throughout the scholarly material (e.g. Sarah Gudschinsky's analysis of writing systems) there are cues and suggestions for classroom practice. Some of these suggestions, such as Rebecca Barr's advocacy of linking oral language strengths with the reading task, or Frank Smith's final two paragraphs about teacher response to error, will seem particularly valuable. No teacher, I should think, can read this book without finding at least a few ideas that will lead to new resolves—and better teaching!

In view of the scholarly progress this volume illustrates, one cannot but agree with the editors in their concern for radical improvement of teacher education. Methods courses in language arts, usually the backbone of preparation programs, clearly must become a laboratory for testing new approaches and examining in greater depth the knowledge (and the good guesses) now available. This book can be a valuable resource in any such enterprise.

Robert H. Anderson
Harvard University

PREFACE

   This book constitutes a report of an invitational conference held in May, 1970 in conjunction with the annual meeting of the International Reading Association. This conference was sponsored by four organizations: the Psycholinguistics and Reading Committee of the International Reading Association, the Tri-University Project in Elementary Education of the University of Nebraska, the National Conference on Research in English, and the Center for Applied Linguistics. Its participants were individuals whose work relates to reading instruction. Its goal was to provide these individuals with an overview of the important advances being made in language study and the consequences of such information for reading instruction. In pursuing this goal, the conference tried to demonstrate that theory and research can be practically applied even though there is a diversity of views about the nature and function of language.

This book was written by teachers, linguists, psychologists, and reading specialists. They elucidate the relationship between reading and language, and explain why reading should be regarded as a language-based process. We feel that the information provided is necessary to understand reading properly and to make effective decisions about its instruction. The authors have admirably condensed a great deal of material with clarity and comprehensiveness; and we are indebted to them for their contributions to this volume and their willingness to help the conference achieve its aims.

We would like to express our deepest appreciation to the organizations who sponsored the conference. The Psycholinguistics and Reading Committee promotes the development, application, and dissemination of knowledge from linguistics, psychology, and psycholinguistics, as these domains are related to reading and reading instruction. The Tri-University Project of the University of Nebraska—now a TTT Project in Elementary Education supported by the U.S. Office of Education, Bureau of Educational Personnel Development—is particularly concerned with teacher training. It is designed to bring together prospective teachers, experienced elementary school teachers, university and college educators, public school administrators, predoctoral English students, and community residents in a joint effort to make schooling relate to the societies and cultures of which it is a part. The National Conference on Research in English is an organization of invited membership that has among its purposes the stimulation and encouragement of research in the teaching of English. The Center for Applied Linguistics is an independent, nonprofit institution that lists among its concerns the application of the results of language research to practical language problems, particularly those of dialectal and foreign language origin.

Acknowledgements are also due to the many individuals who supported the conference in spirit and with their time and energy: Ronald Mitchell, Associate Executive Secretary of the International Reading Association; Professors H. Alan Robinson, Hofstra University; James Fleming, State University of New York, Albany; Marvin Glock, Cornell University; and Dr. Terry Graham, Virginia Polytechnic Institute; and to the conference leaders and recorders. Special thanks are due to Professor William Durr, Professor Robert Anderson, Professor H. Alan Robinson, and Dr. Arthur McCaffrey for their critical reading of this manuscript and for the many useful suggestions they offered.

Richard E. Hodges
E. Hugh Rudorf

CONTENTS

INTRODUCTION

This book is about language and reading. Its purpose is to show that effective reading instruction is based upon an understanding of language and the way children use it.

It should be noted that the term *linguistics* has not been used in the title of this book. Unfortunately, many people consider linguistics to be a dirty word. Linguists, according to a popular opinion, are scholars who say that "anything goes" in language and, therefore, are undermining language "standards." Yet, most of the newer textbooks in reading and in the language arts are advertised as "linguistic," or as having had a linguistic consultant. Despite this controversy, linguistics has emerged as a science that is influencing language-related subjects in schools.

Since this book is about language, it may be useful to review briefly the history of linguistic science in this country and to describe its recent influence on the school curriculum.

WHAT IS LINGUISTICS?

Linguistics, as used throughout this book, is a twentieth century term. Although thinking men since the time of Plato have been interested in language, the impersonal "scientific" methods of language analysis did not develop into a major disciplinary effort in this country until the early part of the twentieth century. Up to this modern period, English teachers relied upon the "traditional" grammars—grammars that were developed by seventeenth and eighteenth century English scholars. These scholars attempted to describe the English language with certain presuppositions that still affect our attitudes about language and the teaching of grammar. Some of the more important characteristics of traditional grammars warrant brief review.

TRADITIONAL GRAMMAR

Traditional English grammar was based upon the model of Latin. Latin was the language of all Western scholarship—and of the Church—throughout the Middle Ages and up to the rise of the vernaculars during the Renaissance. It was assumed that all languages should be based upon the same universal "model"; and it was believed that Latin best exemplified that model. For this reason, seventeenth and eighteenth century English grammarians attempted to describe the English language according to paradigms of Latin structure.

Traditional English grammars were prescriptive. Since Latin was the model, any linguistic change away from that model was considered to be degenerative. People *should* talk and write according to the rules of English established by these early grammarians and their interpreters.

Traditional grammar relied upon definitions which were often linked with meaning, and often were contradictory. For example: (1) A noun is the name of a person, place, or thing; and (2) An adjective is a word that modifies a noun. Given these definitions of noun and adjective, what part of speech is *brick* in "the brick wall"? Both definitions appear to fit. The dilemma over which definition applies to *brick* lies in the fact that the noun definition is based upon semantics (the meaning of the word), while the adjective definition is based upon function (what the word does). Thus, confusion results when two different criteria for definition are applied to the same lexical item.

THE STRUCTURAL PERIOD

Linguistics emerged as a modern science during the first quarter of the twentieth century. In 1921, Edward Sapir's landmark publication *Language: An Introduction to the Study of Speech* attempted to show that linguistic notions are more than "the private pedantries of idle minds [p. v]." Then, in the late 1920s, Leonard Bloomfield published several of the articles which served as the basis for his classic volume *Language* (1933). Both language scholars were instrumental in removing English from under the shadow of Latin-based grammars.

Description Versus Prescription The "school" of linguistics to which Sapir, Bloomfield, and others belonged is generally referred to as the *structural* or *descriptive* school. Both terms indicate the direction in which linguistics was moving during this period.

The first men in the United States who might be described as "linguists" were, for the most part, anthropologists, who, in their attempts to study and understand other cultures, realized the importance of understanding the language of that culture. Much of their motivation came from an interest in American Indian languages. When they began to look at these languages, they soon discovered that they were quite different from English and Latin. While it had been possible, with considerable effort, to force a description of English into the Latin mold, it was impossible to even come close in the case of these exotic languages. It made no sense to study Hopi with presuppositions as to what that language *should* be like and how it *should* be structured. The only thing that they could do was describe the language as it was used by native speakers, and try to show its structure. Hence the terms "structuralist" and "descriptive."

For approximately the first half of this century, the same rationale caused the prevailing mode of investigation of English grammar to be descriptive rather than prescriptive; that is, the scholarly study of English proceeded without preconceptions of its structure. Thus, the structuralists began to explore language on three different levels: phonology, morphology, and syntax. They considered sentences to be the largest units of language capable of scientific analysis. Then, they systematically broke sentences into their smallest components—sounds. Phonology evolved from attempts to describe these minimal units of sound, or *phonemes.* Morphology is roughly analogous to the study of "words." It investigates the way sounds combine to form units of meaning, or *morphemes.* The way morphemes combine to form phrases and clauses —and the study of these formations—is called *syntax.* In the course of their investigations, linguists also attempted to separate meaning from structure. These efforts led to the creation of generative-transformational grammars, which are discussed below.

Language Is Speech Another important tenet of structural linguistics was the view that speech held primacy over writing. Traditionally, it was assumed that *writing* was primary and that the spelling of a word determined its pronunciation (e.g., the pronunciation of *often* as "off-ten" because of the letter *t*). Likewise, dictionaries were seen as containing the "correct" meanings of words; and the rules for "correct" writing were viewed as the rules for "correct" speech.

However, as was stated earlier, much of the impetus for descriptive language study was derived from the investigation of languages which had no writing system. Thus, the role of writing in language description assumed secondary importance. Many, if not most, of the structural linguists became convinced that language *is* speech. This led them to the conclusion alluded to above: language can be described as a system of arbitrary *vocal sounds*. In turn, the history of the development of writing, and some analyses of the relationships of the English writing system to speech, led most structuralists to conclude that English orthography was primarily based upon the principle of representing one sound (phonome) by one letter-symbol (grapheme).

Structural linguists also had an influence on the teaching of other language-related subjects, particularly grammar. However, a discussion of this impact is beyond the scope of this book.

THE MODERN PERIOD

As structuralism may be considered a reaction to traditional grammars, so may *transformational grammar* be considered an expansion of, if not a reaction to, structural grammars. It is Noam Chomsky whose name is generally associated with this "new" grammar. The publication in 1957 of his monograph *Syntactic Structures* is generally considered to be a turning point in contemporary linguistic study.

At the risk of oversimplification, the following statement characterizes a major difference between structuralists and transformationalists in approaches to the study of language.

Underlying meaning is an integral part of linguistic analysis. The structural analysis of English sentences could not explain certain seemingly mysterious features of linguistic behavior. Two of these features are *ambiguity* and *surface similarity*. Two classic examples taken from transformational literature illustrate these phenomena (see Chomsky, 1964, pp. 50–118).

The sentence "Flying planes can be dangerous" is ambiguous. It can mean two quite different things. Yet, descriptive surface analysis of this sentence into lesser parts, such as subject-predicate, parts of speech, words, and sounds, gives no clues as to *why* this ambiguity exists.

An example of surface similarity is seen in the following: *John is easy to please* and *John is eager to please.* On the surface, the two sentences seem identical. Both contain a noun, a verb, an adjective, and an infinitive. However, one *cannot* say, "It is eager to please John," while one *can* say, "It is easy to please John." Logically, it would seem that if two things are composed of identical elements, one ought to be able to transpose or rearrange these elements with equal ease and with equal results. But these two sentences show that this is not possible. When one changes the elements of these two sentences in identical ways, we get an acceptable English sentence in one instance, but not in the other. Structural grammar was adequate to describe these sentences, but it could not adequately explain them.

Language, Speech, and Writing Transformational grammar can explain the difference between the two sentences mentioned above. This is because it does not consider language to be synonymous with speech. In transformational grammar, language is considered to be an underlying form that can be expressed *through* speech and *through* writing. This is a major shift from the structuralist view that language is really speech and that writing is only a representation of speech (Reed, 1965).

Indeed, transformational grammar makes it clear to us that even though a deaf mute, for example, cannot speak, he does possess language. He expresses language through writing or through physical movements, that is, sign language. Like any other user of language, he possesses an understanding of language and its relationship to meaning and form. To reiterate, underlying meaning is an integral part of linguistic analysis; and language is the medium we use to convey meaning. These tenets comprise our "understanding of language." This understanding enables us to recognize the similar structures possessed by *John is easy to please* and *John is eager to please*. It also enables us to know that these sentences have different meanings, and that *It is eager to please John* is nonmeaningful.

The importance of this transformationalist view of the relationship between language, speech, and writing cannot be overemphasized: language is the *framework* for ideas expressed through speech and writing. When reading this volume, it will be helpful to keep in mind that a transformational view of language underlies most of the papers. The viewpoint of the authors is explicit in some instances, and merely assumed in others.

THE IMPACT OF LINGUISTICS ON THE SCHOOLS

Up until the mid-1950s, linguists did not consider the implications of their work for schools, or *vice versa*. But at least one linguist—Leonard Bloomfield—was concerned with the teaching of reading. Out of concern for his own child's mastery of this important skill, he developed a system of initial reading instruction. This system was based upon the implications of his own explorations into the relationship of language to reading.

Bloomfield's work was published posthumously under the title *Let's Read* (Bloomfield & Barnhart, 1961). It was the first of a series of attempts by linguists to apply language principles to reading. Bloomfield was soon followed by Charles C. Fries and Henry Lee Smith, Jr., who published their own versions of "linguistic" readers. In accordance with the one-sound–one-letter principle mentioned earlier, these books considered that learning to read consisted of "cracking the code" of symbol-sound relationships. They emphasized that the teacher should be careful to use words that have consistent patterns of symbol-sound correspondence (e.g., a child should not be confronted with the word *couple* or the word *group,* until he has learned the major sound-equivalent of *ou* as it is pronounced in *loud, cloud, ground, found*). Yet, even though such disciplines as mathematics and science were making considerable inroads into both elementary and secondary school curricula during the period of the late '50s and early '60s, linguistic application to reading instruction met considerable resistance for a number of reasons, some of which have already been briefly mentioned.

MEANING IS UNIMPORTANT

Concomitant with the structuralist view of the relationship between language, speech, and writing was the view that meaning was largely irrelevant in initial stages of learning to read. This did not mean, of course, that linguists were interested in developing readers who could not comprehend what they read, even though they were often accused of this. Bloomfield justified his reading program's use of nonsense words on the ground that patterns were being learned which were often parts of real words (e.g., *san,* although not a word, does appear as a syllable in a word like *sanforized* or *insanity.*) Other linguists pointed out the often ignored fact that children just starting school already have a large store of words. Moreover, they have the ability to use these words in sentences, and to comprehend many more sentences than they, in fact, use. According to these linguists, children know what words mean if the content is kept at their level and if they do not need to be taught the meaning of printed configurations. They only need to learn that such configurations represent speech sounds, and that these sounds are meaningful words.

ATTACK ON TRADITIONAL METHODOLOGY

Prior to these linguistic approaches to reading, reading programs were generally characterized as either "whole word" (look-say) approaches, or "phonics." For the linguists of this period who became involved with reading curriculums, there was general agreement that both methods of instruction were poor. The alphabetical nature of orthography was a strong argument against the "whole word," basal reader type of approach; and the language of the basal readers did not come very close to approximating children's speech patterns. Thus, it seemed to some people that the linguists were supporting the old phonics approach. Indeed, they were often accused of promoting phonics with new labels. Actually, they were just as critical of phonics as they were of the "whole word" approach. The key difference between the old phonics and the new "linguistic" methods was the concept of sound patterns. Combinations of letters were supposed to be pronounced as words or syllables— without the isolation of individual sounds for each letter. To have a child sound out the word *clan* as though it were pronounced *cuh-ul-a-n* does not help him learn realistic associations between sounds and symbols.

Structuralists performed a great service in asserting the primacy of speech over writing and destroying some of the mythology that still prevails about the role of writing in human communication. Most of the authors of this volume—and certainly the editors—agree that the theories of structural linguists were invaluable contributions to our understanding of language and reading. Nevertheless, as this volume illustrates, reading is a more complex linguistic and psychological process than has previously been supposed.

THE STAGGERING MAGNITUDE OF LANGUAGE STUDY

As is usually the case, as knowledge in a scientific field increases, specialization becomes the rule. The study of language is a project of staggering magnitude. Language enters all fields of human relationships and many new domains of study have been spawned by its investigation.

For example, the relationship between language, thought, and the learning process has developed the new discipline of *psycholinguistics*. The study of language differences in relation to such factors as social class, regional differences, and educational levels, has given rise to the specialization of *sociolinguistics*. The study of meaning—*semantics*—has been rejuvenated, and has become an increasingly important area of linguistic study.

This book, then, is intended to provide an overview of language in relation to reading as observed from different areas of scholarly endeavor. It does not purport to be a textbook in theoretical linguistics, language variation, or the psychology of language learning. One cannot, for example, learn phonemics, become a dialectologist, or totally comprehend how language is acquired by reading this text.

In order to facilitate the overview presented here, the papers appear in pairs. The first paper of each pair presents the theories and research findings of a particular area of study. The second indicates the consequences of this knowledge for teaching. For the reader who is interested in pursuing a particular aspect of language study further, each section of this volume provides a brief annotated bibliography.

While the emphasis of this volume is upon reading as a critically important skill, we strongly maintain that the implications of linguistic research are vital tools for understanding *all* the language skills used by children and teachers in educational enterprises. Indeed, they may even be vital to our understanding of mankind. Our language and culture are so interrelated that it is inconceivable that one could exist without the other. Thus, as well as being a scientific endeavor, linguistics may be the most humanistic of all the humanities.

REFERENCES

Bloomfield, Leonard   *Language*. New York: Henry Holt and Co., 1933.

Bloomfield, Leonard and Barnhart, Clarence L.   *Let's Read: A Linguistic Approach*. Detroit: Wayne State University Press, 1961.

Chomsky, Noam   *Syntactic Structures*. The Hague: Mouton, 1957.

Chomsky, Noam "Current Issues in Linguistic Theory," in Jerry A. Fodor and Jerrold J. Katz (Eds.), *The Structure of Language: Readings in the Philosophy of Language.* Englewood Cliffs, N.J.: Prentice-Hall, Inc., 1964.

Reed, David "A Theory of Language, Speech, and Writing," *Elementary English*, 1965, *42*, 845–51.

Sapir, Edward *Language: An Introduction to the Study of Speech.* New York: Harcourt Brace Jovanovich, Inc., 1921.

ONE · THE NATURE OF LANGUAGE

In the opening paper, Ronald Wardhaugh discusses the differences between the layman's view of language and the linguist's. Professor Wardhaugh is Director of the English Language Institute at the University of Michigan, Ann Arbor. His essay defines language, and then uses that definition to describe the role of the linguist and the characteristics of linguistic study. This overview of linguistics provides a helpful frame of reference for considering the more specialized papers of the other contributors. Moreover, after completing this book, a rereading of Wardhaugh's essay will help tie together many of the ideas presented by these other authors.

One need not be a linguistic scholar to use linguistic principles for educational purposes. Carolyn Burke, author of the second paper in this volume, bases her judgments upon continuous contact with teachers, prospective teachers, and elementary school pupils. She is an Assistant Professor of Education at Wayne State University and Associate Director of their Reading Miscue Research Center. Professor Burke's essay is about preparing teachers to teach reading. It presents an enlightened view of the interrelationships between different areas of linguistics, and illuminates the problems of providing prospective and experienced teachers with a basic understanding of the implications linguistic study has for reading.

Professor Burke's work concerns *applied* linguistics. She is interested in applying linguistic principles to the solution of educational problems. Dr. Wardhaugh is primarily a *theoretical* linguist. He studies language for its own sake—to understand what it is and how it operates. While he is acting in the role of the theoretical linguist, he is not concerned with the implications of his findings for people other than linguists. Nevertheless, as his book *Reading: A Linguistic Perspective* (New York: Harcourt Brace Jovanovich, Inc., 1969) and other numerous writings suggest, he is very much interested in the application of linguistic principles to the field of education. We have stressed this distinction between applied and theoretical linguistics because it is often ignored by the layman.

THE STUDY OF LANGUAGE

Ronald Wardhaugh

To the best of our knowledge man has always been interested in language, in its origin, its nature, and its various uses in persuasion, poetry, and prayer. Language has also been something of a mystery to man, not unlike the mysteries of creation, the origin of the sun, and the coming of fire. Language has provided man with such a rich source of myth that even today much of the mystery and myth of language still prevail. One important difference that distinguishes linguists from nonlinguists lies in those aspects of language that the two groups consider to be mysterious, and secondly, in how they choose to investigate apparent mysteries.

We are assailed on every side by language; yet very few of us know what language is. We are told to think positively, constructively, or imaginatively, but there is little agreement on how language is to be used in such thinking. Even when well-intentioned philosophers attempt to come to grips with the nature of language, they sometimes create such absurd statements as the following: "Thus language is not only being. It is also becoming existing anterior to the split between thinking and thought." If a philosopher can claim that such a passage "makes sense," a linguist must wonder whether that philosopher really inhabits the same world as he does. Certainly, it is not the same intellectual world as the one in which the linguist has chosen to work.

LINGUISTICS IS A SCIENCE

Language is all around us just as are comments about language. We encounter very few other phenomena as important to us as language. Towards many of these phenomena we have adopted a more or less scientific attitude, for example, in the matters of health and well-being. Generally too, astrology has given way to astronomy. However, linguists would observe that, for most men, the study of language more closely

This paper is based on material that is included in the first chapter of *Introduction to Linguistics*, New York: McGraw-Hill, 1972.

resembles primitive astrology than it does the sophisticated astronomy necessary for the scientific space travel and exploration of the 1970s.

However, we should observe that science itself does not have the same meaning for all people. There are widely differing views concerning the nature of scientific inquiry and the status of scientific theories. Each science is concerned with a body of data; that is, with certain phenomena that may be related within a theoretical framework. The necessity of a theoretical framework is vitally important; for, in a real sense, that framework determines the data that will interest the scientist and sets the limits for the science. Matters that fall outside the limits are not regarded as the concern of the science, although, eventually, it may become necessary to recast the framework to include previously excluded data. Consequently, a linguistic scientist, or linguist, has certain notions about which phenomena are relevant to his discipline because these phenomena can and must be handled within the theoretical framework within which he has chosen to operate. He may be tempted to look at any one of a variety of linguistic phenomena: word origins, phonetic features, ambiguities, or linguistic variation in time and space. He can also approach each of these sets of phenomena in a variety of ways and ask questions about them. Above all, though, he will be concerned with how useful the answers to the questions are in shedding light on important theoretical matters. However, what are regarded as important theoretical matters are likely to change from time to time. For example, the problem of the origin of language is no longer regarded as being important because it is regarded as insoluble, linguistic theory having nothing of significance to contribute to an answer. On the other hand, the problem of finding the best set of phonetic features with which to describe all natural languages is currently regarded as very important. A linguist may be distinguished from someone who has a dilettantish interest in language by the fact that he is concerned with examining serious theoretical issues, rather than with making random observations, or flitting from one linguistic oddity to the next.

The scientific method makes further demands on the linguist. It requires him to develop a disciplined interest so that tight rein is drawn over wild speculations. Theories must be testable; that is, they must make some empirical claims. From time to time, there will be changes in what is regarded as testable, since questions which appear to be answerable empirically no longer appear to be so answerable, and vice versa. It is only comparatively recently that scientists have been able to describe some of the characteristics of the planets in the solar system. Previously, it was possible only to speculate about such characteristics. On the other hand, the question as to how many angels can stand on the point of a needle is no longer regarded as being of any great interest, and not merely as a result of advances in theology. It will become obvious to anyone who reads widely in the linguistic literature that a similar state of affairs exists within linguistics: various kinds of treatment of data, and various attitudes towards empiricism and scholasticism are apparent from time to time.

Linguists are in broad agreement about some of the important characteristics of human language, even though they do not all agree on how these characteristics are to be accounted for in their theorizings. One definition of language which is widely associated with linguistics may be used to illustrate some ideas on which linguists agree and some on which they disagree. This particular definition states that *language is a system of arbitrary vocal symbols used for human communication.*

LANGUAGE IS SYSTEMATIC

The term *system* in the definition is the key term. First of all, we can observe that a language must be systematic, for otherwise it could not be learned or used consistently. However, it is also necessary to ask in what ways is a language systematic. One of the first observations we can make is that all languages contain two systems rather than one—a system of sounds and a system of meanings. Only certain sounds are used by the speakers of any language, and only certain combinations of these sounds are possible. A speaker of English can say *I saw the bank,* but he cannot say either *[1]I saw the banque* without sounding partly like a Frenchman, or *I saw the nbka* without feeling that he is saying some kind of tongue twister, rather than a well-formed English sentence. Likewise, he can say *I saw the bank* but not *I bank saw the,* which is nonsense; and if he says *I bank the saw,* it means something quite different. All languages have two such systems; and linguists concern themselves not only with the characteristics of the systems, but also with how the two systems, those of sound and meaning, relate to each other

[1] * is a linguistic symbol that is used to signify a non-English sentence.

within one overall linguistic system for a particular language. The nature of this relationship in all languages is very important and constitutes one of the most interesting problems in linguistic science.

A related problem has to do with the description of the total system; that is, with the kind of phenomena that must be accounted for, and with the principles to be used in deciding which phenomena are relevant and how relationships are to be expressed. One kind of coverage would demand of a linguist nothing more than the making of a catalogue of observations of certain kinds of linguistic phenomena according to some preconceived plan. A dictionary is such a catalogue of observations about words and their meanings, with, of course, different lexicographers having different plans about what is to be included and how these included items are to be accounted for. It would not, however, be possible to make a dictionary of the sentences in a language in the same way as one can make a dictionary of its words. Consequently, linguists have searched for satisfactory ways of describing sentences, parts of sentences, sounds, and combinations of sounds. Some have tried to devise sophisticated descriptive techniques, but problems always arise in such endeavors.

We can appreciate what difficulties can occur if we ask what kind of system can account, at the same time, for the multiple negatives of *He ain't got none now, and he ain't never had none neither;* the ambiguity of *What annoyed John was being ignored by everyone;* and the superficial similarity between *John is eager to please* and *John is easy to please.* It would be quite possible for a linguist not to concern himself with a dialect in which multiple negation is normal, or with resolving ambiguities syntactically rather than situationally, or with any notion of more than one concurrent level of linguistic structure. In fact, many linguists have done good linguistic work without ever having become concerned with such problems. However, other linguists will insist that all of these sentences contain phenomena that must be accounted for within a unitary theory. The result, of course, will be that the goals of linguistics will vary widely among linguists themselves. In still another case, a linguist might quite happily explain how words such as *name* and *night* have had different pronunciations at different times without excluding certain kinds of sound changes from his explanation. For example, in the foreseeable future, *name* might be pronounced like *foot*, or *night* like *lamp*. However, this theory does not exclude the possibility that *name* might also, one not too distant day, be pronounced as *neem* or *nime*, or *night* as *nah* or *nigh*. Theoretical linguistics is very much concerned with the question of comprehensiveness; that, is, just how inclusive any system should be. It is also concerned with why the system must have the form proposed for it.

Linguists also study the units and processes within the system. An utterance is not a continuous phenomenon. It is broken into discrete units of various sizes; and these units are arranged by various processes. Linguists are concerned with trying to understand what these units and processes are. Very likely, they are not the units and processes that the educated public hold dear to their hearts, or, at least, not as these are defined by that public. For example, such units as letters and words, and such processes as sentences, are thought to be constructed according to some "sense-making" formula. Linguists postulate the existence of units such as phonemes and morphemes, and of such processes as phrase structures and transformations.[2] The linguist's search is always for the units and processes which best account for the data that interest him.

LANGUAGE IS ARBITRARY

The term *arbitrary* in the definition does not mean that everything about language is unpredictable. Languages do not vary in every possible way. It means that it is impossible to predict exactly which specific features one will find in a particular language if one has no familiarity with that language or a related language. There will be no way of knowing what a word means just from the sounds of the word; and there will be no way of predicting whether nouns will be inflected, or whether pronominalization will take one form or another. Likewise, there will be no way of saying what sound-types will be found; or how many consonant and vowel sounds there will be, or how many nasals; or whether there will be both oral and nasal vowels.

If languages were completely unpredictable, it would not even be possible to talk about nouns, verbs, pronominals, consonants, and vowels. However, languages are not completely unpredictable and all

[2] Editors' note: For brief explanations of these and other terms used throughout the papers in this volume, the reader is referred to the Glossary beginning on pg. 228.

of the above phenomena are in any language one chooses to examine—taking different forms in different languages. For example, the phenomenon of *deletion* may be illustrated by the particular ellipses in a series of English sentences: *I could have gone and Peter could have gone too; I could have gone and Peter could have too;* and, *I could have gone and Peter too.* This deletion phenomenon will be found in all languages but the particular variation will depend on the language. There will be negation in all languages, as in the example of *The boy ran* negated to *The boy didn't run.* In this English example, there is an inserted *n't* and a change in the tense carrier from the verb *run* to the verb *do* after the introduction of that verb. However, no linguist would ever expect to find a sentence such as *The boy ran* negated by such sentences as **The boy ran the boy ran,* **The boy ran ran boy the,* or **The boy ran boy the*—that is, through some system of total sentence repetition or total, or partial, inversion.

Language is unpredictable only in the sense that, within certain limits, it employs certain processes. It seems to be the case that certain very simple logical processes are never employed, as in the above examples with negation; but that certain seemingly illogical, and obviously complicated, processes are preferred, as with the genuine English negative above. The linguist is interested in what determines the preferences and, therefore, what makes so many things about language predictable while, at the same time, allowing for a vast range of unpredictability within the limits of these preferences.

LANGUAGE AND SPEECH

The term *vocal* refers to the fact that the primary medium for all languages is sound—no matter how well developed are their writing systems. All the evidence we have, from the continued existence of preliterate societies, through the knowledge we have of language acquisition, to the existence of historical records, confirms the fact that writing is based on speaking. Writing systems are attempts to capture sounds and meanings on paper; and, although certain characteristics of writing systems originated to inform people how to recite correctly, particularly to recite certain religious texts, the primary purpose of writing is to lend some kind of permanence to the spoken language—not to prescribe that spoken language in any way. In attempting to describe a linguistic system, a linguist keeps this fact in mind. Therefore, he is not free to ignore the sounds a speaker makes in favor of studying the writing system, nor is he free to invent some kind of abstract pseudomathematical system which makes no reference to sound in order to describe a language. The facts that languages are used by speakers and that language is speech are central to his work; consequently, only very few linguists have ventured to claim that language can manifest itself through either speech or writing, and that the two manifestations are, somehow, "equal." All this is not to deny the importance of the study of writing and writing systems, nor that mass literacy has been without its effects on language systems and linguistic usage, because, undeniably, writing has affected speaking. The insistence on the vocal nature of language is an insistence on the importance of the *historical* primacy of speech over writing, and a denial of the common misunderstanding that speech is a spoken, and generally somewhat debased, form of writing.

LANGUAGE IS SYMBOLIC

The term *symbol* refers to the fact that there is no connection, or only, in a few cases, a minimal connection, between the sounds that people use and the objects to which these sounds refer. Language is a symbolic system, a system in which words are associated with objects, ideas, and actions by convention so that "a rose by any other name would smell as sweet." Only in a few cases does there appear to be some direct representational connection between a word and some phenomenon in the "real" world. Onomatopoeic words like *bang, crash* and *roar* are English examples of this phenomenon, although the meanings of these words would not be at all obvious to speakers of either Chinese or Eskimo. More marginal are words like *soft* and *harsh,* or *slither* and *slimy,* in which the connection between sound and sense is controversial among native speakers. Some claims have been advanced that words beginning with the sounds *s* and *sn* in English are more often than chance used to denote a variety of unpleasant things; in much the same way as the vowel in *little* and *bit* is said to be associated with small things, and those in *huge* and *moose* with large things. However, once again, it would appear that we are in an area of subjectivity, for counter examples are easy to find and no more than a statistical trend can be established. Under the circumstances, then, there is little evidence to refute the claim that languages are systems of arbitrary symbols.

LANGUAGE IS UNIQUELY HUMAN

The term *human* refers to the fact that the kind of system that interests linguists is possessed only by human beings, and is very different from the communication systems possessed by other forms of life. Just how different, of course, is a question of some interest, for it can shed light on language to know in what ways human languages are different from systems of nonhuman communications. The differences may be ascribed to the process of evolution that man has gone through and be the result of the differing genetic characteristics man has from other species. No other communication system, unless it is derivative from human language, makes use of the duality feature, that is, of concurrent systems of sound and meaning; and few other communication systems are either discrete or noniconic. Moreover, none allows its users to do all that language allows human beings to do: speculate about the future, reminisce over the past, tell lies at will, and devise theories and a metalanguage about the language system itself. Dolphins are not next-year oriented, bees do not discuss last year's supply of food, jackdaws do not deceive each other with their calls, and dogs don't bark about barking.

LANGUAGE IS A MEANS OF COMMUNICATION

Finally, language is used for *communication*. It allows people to say things to each other and express their communicative needs. These needs are strong, whether they are the needs of a Robinson Crusoe for a parrot to address his remarks to before Man Friday came along, or of the Trappist monks who devise sophisticated signals to avoid breaking their vows of silence. Language is the cement of society. It allows people to live, work, and play together; to tell *the* truth, but also to tell a lie, or lies. Sometimes it is used merely to keep communication channels open so that if there is any need to say something of importance a suitable channel is available. This last function is met through the conventions of greeting and leave-taking, by small talk at parties, and in the chatter of secretaries in a large office. It is conspicuous only when it is absent, as witnessed by the image of the tall *silent* stranger in the movies, or by the phrase *He didn't even speak to me when we passed in the street.* Language also functions, then, to communicate general attitudes towards life and others, creating what Malinowski called a phatic communion, a type of speech in which ties of union among speakers are created by a mere exchange of words. We need only notice how absurd it would be to take each of the following expressions literally: *How do you do! Where have you been all my life?* and *What have you been up to since we last met?*

THE TASKS OF LINGUISTS

This definition of language as a system of arbitrary vocal symbols used for human communication still allows for a wide range of scientific inquiries into language and its functions. At this point, therefore, it would be useful to return to a discussion about what it is that a linguist claims to be describing. Should a linguist merely describe what he observes, or should he attempt to filter out some important principles from these observations? He can, for example, report that so many people of such and such a social or regional background use expressions like *He be wise* and *He asked did John go;* and he need make no attempt to explain these constructions or relate them to the appearance of other sentences like *He wise,* or to the almost certain nonappearance in the same speaker of the second expression above of *He asked if John went.* The linguist's interest in what constitute the data which need to be described and explained will therefore control what he has to say. It will also in a very important way control the actual selection of the data.

It is essential that the linguist set up some kind of formal model for his data, so that he can have a theory into which he can fit his data. This is so because science is concerned with theory building. One very simple theory, though, would be a rudimentary catalogue of observations constructed according to an elementary scheme of classification. A simple dictionary is such a catalogue; however, it must be remembered that large modern dictionaries are rather sophisticated catalogues, as any examination of one of the major unabridged dictionaries will show. The most appropriate theory for language will share all the characteristics of any good scientific theory. It will be an abstraction in the sense that it will make reference to idealized units and processes. It will, of course, acknowledge that these abstractions are realized in the world in which we live in various ways, just as the physicist's gravitational system and the economist's monetary system are abstractions realized respectively in real falling bodies and price fluctuations. It will attempt to relate apparently diverse phenomena within a single theoretical framework; it will provide a terminology for making observations about those phenomena; and it will stimulate interesting investigations. A theory must do all of these things if it is to be of any scientific value; and the usefulness of any theory must be judged by how well it does all three.

Various kinds of relationships can be shown to hold among apparently unrelated phenomena. Sentences like *John kissed Mary* and *The boy chased the dog* can be related to each other as exhibiting the same "pattern"; words like *Mary* and *dog* can be considered to be "nouns"; *Mary was kissed by John* and *The dog was chased by the boy* can be regarded as "transformations" of the first two sentences; and both **John Mary kissed* and **The the boy dog chased* can be regarded as "ungrammatical," either because they do not apparently occur in real life, or because they violate certain "rules" described by the grammarian as a result of his research.

The diverse phenomena are related through a set of terms in the above examples. This set of terms should not be an ad hoc set devised to describe a particular language; rather, it should be a set that can be used to describe phenomena in any language. It is precisely for such a reason that attempts have sometimes been made to describe all languages within a particular system of terminology. For example, attempts have sometimes been made to describe English as though every word must belong to one of eight parts of speech; or in terms of phonemes or morphemes which could be discovered by following a prescribed set of procedures; or in terms of possibilities and impossibilities of occurrence, for example, the possibility of *Be quiet!* but the apparent impossibility of **Be tall!* Each set of terms arises from a theory; and together, the theory and terminology predispose the linguist to look at a language in a certain way. It would even be true to say that the linguist does not just fit data into a theoretical framework using the terminology he has at his disposal; rather, that framework helps him to delineate just what are the data with which he must be concerned. It is for this reason that, at various times, certain questions about language have been held to be answerable but at other times not to be answerable; for example: how many parts of speech are there in all languages, how many cases, and what are the essential meanings of certain words. A good theory also leads to the formulation of interesting questions so that gaps in a conceptual framework may be explored and new linguistic evidence used to confirm or deny basic assumptions.

The points made in the previous paragraph are extremely important. Linguistics is a science only insofar as linguists adopt a scientific attitude towards their subject. A scientific attitude requires objectivity: the investigator must not deliberately distort the evidence, but must try to see it clearly and as a whole, all the while admitting that how he sees the data is influenced by his theoretical predispositions. Moreover, these theoretical predispositions should be quite uninfluenced by the scientist's emotions. A scientific statement should also be verifiable, and the techniques and experiments used should be replicable; for, one scientific goal is explicitness. A scientist must also be thorough in his treatment of problems and refuse to adopt ad hoc solutions: he should be prepared to generalize his solutions to similar problems by being prepared to say something of significance about general problems. In such circumstances, it is not surprising that, at any one time, there are different theories in existence, each claiming adequacy in covering what purport to be the same data; that there is sometimes bitter conflict among supporters of the various theories; and that new theories appear to come upon the scene with revolutionary impact, rather than evolutionary slowness.

If we examine certain statements about English which were current at one time or another, we can see how these are unscientific when judged by the standards of science that prevail today. A statement such as "A noun is the name of a person, place or thing" is quite inexplicit; and we know from experience in parsing English sentences that the degree of replicability in using it is fairly low, because it clashes with other definitions in the same system. Statements about how to discover phonemes likewise often lack explicitness; nor do they deal adequately with certain problems such as the "correct" phonemicization of words like *here* and *there* in English, a difficulty which must therefore be regarded as "marginal" or be resolved by an ad hoc rule. Relating a passive sentence such as *The cat was chased by the dog* to an active sentence such as *The dog chased the cat* by a transformational process may also appear to be theoretically justifiable. However, when one stops to ask what *transformation* means in this sense and what this transformational relationship tells us about either the linguistic abilities of speakers or language in general, a whole new set of theoretical concerns emerges. When a linguist makes a revolutionary change in his linguistic theory rather than an evolutionary one, in order to accommodate these concerns, beliefs about the proper scope of linguistic inquiry will also change quite drastically.

SOME FUNDAMENTAL LINGUISTIC CONCEPTS

Language, as we have defined it, is uniquely human, just as is the activity of studying language and languages. Languages, however, do appear to share some universal constraints. It can be assumed that these constraints exist because of human limitations or predispositions. Languages are apparently learned universally in the same way no matter how different are the cultural traits. Such universal learning is of interest to psychologists as well as linguists. Language is also probably the most creative system possessed by man. Psychologists and linguists, therefore, have an interest in linguistic phenomena; the former, the better to explain behavior in general, the latter, to explain linguistic behavior in particular.

Finally, languages are learned but must also occasionally be taught, or taught about. Linguists can be expected to contribute some understanding of language to this teaching. They may also occasionally offer advice about the substance of what must be taught. Occasionally, they venture statements about how this substance should be taught. When such statements are made with full understanding of the complex process of teaching and learning, they should be listened to with attention. However, too often they are not made with such understanding. For, linguists are just as prone as any other professional group to offer gratuitous advice in areas outside their realm of competence. Nor are linguists always completely objective in their own use of language; but, then, no more is to be expected. Language is heady stuff; and not even the strictest linguistic disciplinarian can entirely resist being captured now and again by some of its more mysterious attributes, nor avoid being trapped occasionally during actual linguistic performance.

THE LANGUAGE PROCESS:

SYSTEMS OR SYSTEMATIC?

Carolyn L. Burke

Language involves a series of interrelated systems—a system of oral and/or written symbols, a system of grammatical structure, and a system of meaning. To the extent that these are discrete systems, we can examine and define them apart from the whole that is language.

Special areas of linguistic study have, in fact, emerged as a result of treating these systems discretely. The development of phonetic and phonemic alphabets, and of the concept of suprasegmentals (the stress, intonation, and juncture features of speech) resulted from concern for the sound system. The development of numerous, competing grammars, as well as the concept of the morpheme (a word or word part conveying meaning) reflect thought about the syntactic system.

Meaning, the semantic system, has received the least attention—not because linguists failed to recognize its significance, but because they recognized its complexity. They tactfully agreed to set it aside until language aspects more immediately amenable to their manipulation were examined.

THE INTERDEPENDENCE OF SYSTEMS

Increasing knowledge, or change of perspective, concerning any one of these systems causes developments in the others. As linguists have developed increasingly more inclusive theories—and thus more usable ones—they have found the seeming boundary lines between the systems increasingly blurred.

The rules that describe phonemes (speech sounds) can no longer be kept discrete from those that describe morphemes. And so we get a series of morphophonemic rules which begin to describe the behavior of phonemes within the larger environment of syntax. For example, a-n-d is seen not simply as the spelling for the morpheme and, as in the clause: And *then I really told him,* but also for its allomorphs in the phrases *Dick* an' *Jane, bread* n' *butter.*

An increasing emphasis on the interrelationship of systems in a language is seen in the more recent grammars being developed. The generative-transformational, Tagmemic,[1] and stratificational grammars are the results of conscious efforts to deal with the relationships between semantics and syntactics. Such efforts have pushed linguists into dealing with language units of ever increasing size. If ambiguous structures[2] can't always be handled at the sentence level, can they be explained by contextual and syntactic constraints at the paragraph level?

Many linguistic investigations were initiated around the proposition that language systems could be investigated as discrete units. Now, however, this statement must be added to this proposition: *To the extent that these systems are truly interrelated within language, they are indivisible as functioning processes from the whole.*

Because there is some truth to the old adage that you will "teach as you were taught," the manner in which we choose to pass on linguistic information to teachers in training becomes of critical importance.

THE LINGUISTIC PREPARATION OF TEACHERS

If and when prospective teachers are exposed to linguistic courses, such courses tend to be the initial offerings from a sequence of linguistics courses or are patterned after them. Often then, a teacher's limited exposure to linguistics includes a course in historical linguistics and one in phonemics. Without arguing whether this is the most effective introduction for the novice linguist, I think it can be argued that it is not the most profitable for the future teacher.

What information the teacher receives about language tends to be separated into neat and discrete packages. In many respects it is "dead" information because it has been forceably segregated from the other systems. The fledgling linguist at some future time may put it all together. But prospective teachers may never see either the relevance or utility of what they've learned.

[1] See the article by Sarah Gudschinsky in Section IV for a more detailed description of Tagmemic grammar.

[2] See Introduction, p. 1, and Wardhaugh, p. 12, for additional treatment of *ambiguous structure.*

Figure 1 illustrates the two alternate views of the relationship of language systems about which I have been speaking. In the first view, the respective systems of language are seen as discrete. They each hold a portion of the "pie" that is language. Individual segments of this pie can be examined without disturbing others. In many respects, this is the view under which linguists did operate and from which many linguistic course offerings are still organized.

Figure 1   Alternate Views of Language Systems

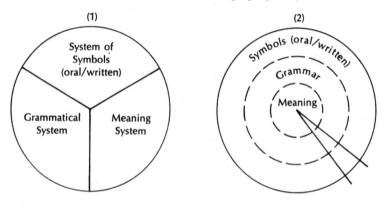

The second view suggests meaning as the core of the language process. It has an inner ring in which grammatical structure is fused to meaning and to an outer ring of oral and/or written symbols which act as the vehicle for displaying meaning. The divisions between the systems are not complete. When you cut a wedge from this "pie" you retain elements of all the systems. This model more closely represents the concept of language with which linguists generally now seem to be operating.

Chemists used to describe materials by their elements so that water was H_2O, a combination of two parts hydrogen and one part oxygen. Their science then went through a period in which the primary accomplishments revolved around searching out and classifying the elemental content of material. With the discovery of the atom, the whole course of their investigation was altered. The concept of the atom holds that the significant aspect of a material is the smallest particle which still retains all of the properties of the whole. They began to treat matter as a *process* and to examine the interrelationships of the elements involved in the process. Scientists were then able to move from categorization of matter to its manipulation.

In many respects, the science of linguistics is in a position similar to that of chemistry a few years ago. The first successful attempts of language study deal with the systems of language as integral parts of a whole. There is the knowledge that language elements, when pulled out of the total language process, do not retain the properties of that process.

LINGUISTICS AND THE TEACHING OF READING

The significance of retaining the properties of the total language process can also be documented from the perspective of the school room. Reading programs have traditionally treated reading as if it were composed of discrete systems. These systems have been called reading skills, and the reading programs which are constructed around them either attempt to treat each of them equally and are called eclectic, or one skill is singled out for special attention and goes under such names as "phonics approach," or "word-centered," or "look-and-say."

We can use the phonics approach as our example. Schools employing this approach usually use instructional material which controls the introduction of sounds and not infrequently provides extra phonic lessons each day apart from the regular reading lesson. They have, in effect, carried the concept of discrete systems to its extremes. Yet, they have always been unable to explain that portion of their students who can successfully complete the phonics tasks which they are given but who are unable to read successfully.

Similar examples can be given for any of the popular reading approaches. In most instances, the students with reading problems have successfully learned what is being taught. And what they are being taught is systematic and well-organized. However, though the difficulties which these students have may differ on the surface due to the different reading approaches being used, the cause of their problems is the same in all instances. The systematic and carefully sequenced procedures which these students are being taught simply do not function within the language process. Their relationship to language was destroyed when they were separated from it. The "whole" of language is *not* the sum of its parts.

Teachers in training do not need to spend their small amount of linguistic training in examination of the historical developments of linguistic science. They need, rather, to be introduced to the most successful tools which linguistic science *now* controls. They will be dealing with language in operation within their classrooms; and they should be brought to examine it in the same way.

THE USE OF GRAMMAR IN READING

Read these two nonsense sentences out loud to yourself.

1. "Er'm muvle chander," rupe narg bloden.
2. "Zasto si cacio flato u moju kastu," nakoga ikari.

Now determine which one is English nonsense. You have, I hope, selected the first one. We can examine the cues which were available for your choice. All of them should revolve around the simple fact that you found the first sentence easier to pronounce. The organization of the letters, their sequence and combination within word units, and their frequency were all familiar to you. Because they were familiar, you were able to associate them with phonemic patterns of your language. It is possible, then, to focus a person's attention upon the sound system while still retaining the natural constraints of the language process.

Here is a longer segment of nonsense material. Some of you who are familiar with Slavic languages might recognize it as Serbo-Croatian nonsense.

Ikari vogao je u ponoti svoje kašte. Od donop čedko caci flato na kašti. "Zašto si cacio flato u moju kaštu" nakoga ikari. "Gomno mi je pok," odvragori čedko. "Djuko mis žolito da tu vi gosoli flato u vašoj kašti." "Molim, Ikriko dali dak vogate u vašoj kašti?"

Like the material in the second nonsense sentence, the phonemic system has been retained. In addition, the function words and the inflectional system have been left intact. If you are not a speaker of Serbo-Croatian, you are now in the position of the linguist researching an unfamiliar language. Look the paragraph over, identify those items that you feel might be function words. Most of you have probably successfully identified *je* and *u* as function words, and have done so on the basis of their reoccurrence in the text and their restricted length.

After this point, your clues become more obscure and less certain. You might note that the last sentence in the paragraph of nonsense material is a question and tentatively mark *molim* as an interrogative, or seeing the repetition of *kašte* in various forms consider two of the words which precede it, *svoje* and *vašoj*, as possible function words. However, only the continued examination of multiple texts will sustain or discredit your initial choices.

If you were to go back over the text now and try to identify the inflectional system, you would again be able to build up only a tentative hypothesis. You might note that *kašte* has both an e and an i ending, then seeing that vowels can be found at the end of a majority of the words, suspect that they form a part of that system. You would be unaware, from this small sample of text, whether any internal word changes are involved in the inflectional system, or whether any of your candidates for the function-word list are, in fact, a part of the inflectional system. To this point, for those of you who speak only English, what tentative choices you have made have been on the basis of your knowledge of your own language. Continued examination of Serbo-Croatian texts will further your theories about its function words and inflectional system only to the extent that you begin to recognize its grammatical structure. *Kašte* has already been identified as having an inflectional ending. Until you determine whether *kašte* is a noun, a verb, or some other part of speech, you will be unable to consider the extent of the inflectional system. Even as you begin to build up theories about one aspect of a language's organization, you must do so on the basis of tentative decisions concerning its other systems.

The final example of nonsense material, created by Kenneth Goodman, is a piece of English nonsense in which all function words and the inflectional system have been left intact. Read the paragraph and then write complete sentence answers to the four questions that follow it.

THE MARLUP

A marlup was poving his kump. Parmily a narg horped some whev in his kump. "Why did vump horp whev in my frinkle kump?" the marlup jufd the narg. "Er'm muvvily trungy," the narg grupped.

"Er heshed vump norpled whev in your kump. Do vump pove your kump frinkle?"

1. What did the narg horp in the marlup's kump?
2. What did the marlup juf the narg?
3. Was the narg trungy?
4. How does the marlup pove his kump?

With careful reading, you should have decided:

1. that the narg horped some whev in the marlup's kump.

2. that the marlup jufd the narg, "Why did vump horp whev in my frinkle kump?"

3. that the narg was muvvily trungy.

4. and that the marlup poves his kump frinkle.

You are able to derive the answers to these questions solely through your intuitive[3] knowledge of the grammatical structure involved.

You are able to determine that *poving* is a verb and that the *kump* gets *poved*. Yet, you are unable to define either the act of *poving* or a *kump*. In this final example, both the symbol system and the grammatical system are operating fully, but meaning is nil and your behavior is not unlike that of large numbers of school children who function successfully in their reading group but who never develop the basic notion that reading must make sense. The method through which they are taught reading is systematic, but it does not retain the interrelationship of the systems which produce language.

[3] In the next section, Frank Smith develops further the concept that a speaker-listener possesses intuitive knowledge of the grammar he uses.

FOR FURTHER READING

Brengelman, Fred   *The English Language: An Introduction for Teachers.* Englewood Cliffs, N.J.: Prentice-Hall, 1970.
   An introductory survey of current findings about the English language which the author regards as having clear application to the teaching of English.

Gleason, H. A., Jr.   *An Introduction to Descriptive Linguistics.* (Rev. ed.) New York: Holt, Rinehart & Winston, 1961.
   An introduction to the principles of structural linguistics which stresses analytical procedures in widespread use until recently.

Langacker, R. W.   *Language and Its Structure.* New York: Harcourt Brace Jovanovich, Inc., 1968.
   An introduction to the principles of generative-transformational linuistics, together with some discussion of historical linguistics.

TWO · LANGUAGE AND

LANGUAGE DEVELOPMENT

In the preceding section, Wardhaugh described the conditions for the scientific study of language, while Burke illustrated how linguistic insights can have consequences for language-based subjects such as reading. Both authors described language in terms of its systematic nature and also acknowledged that a *complete* description of this system is a goal toward which linguistic study strives.

Yet, what linguists still seek to understand about the systematic nature of language is, in fact, performed by all language users. In a very real sense, all speakers are sophisticated linguists whose *intuitive* knowledge of the systematic nature of language is continually demonstrated by the ability to speak and to understand the speech of others. The present section of this book considers the nature of the language user—particularly the young child.

The authors' range of experience ideally qualifies them to discuss the language user in relation to reading. Frank Smith, who is a professor of educational psychology at the Ontario Institute for Studies in Education, Toronto, Canada, has an interest in language that encompasses a career as journalist, novelist, psychologist, and language researcher. A graduate of Harvard University, Professor Smith is coeditor of *The Genesis of Language* (Cambridge: MIT Press, 1966) and author of *Understanding Reading* (New York: Holt, Rinehart & Winston, Inc., 1971).

Mrs. Dolores Mather is a primary teacher in the public schools of Lincoln, Nebraska. She has been involved in the University of Nebraska's Tri-University and TTT[1] Projects in Elementary Education. In her paper, she applies a substantial knowledge of child language development to the problem of learning to read.

---

[1]TTT projects are USOE-financed projects for Training Teachers of Teachers. Each project must contain input from four sources: teacher training institutions, college arts and sciences departments, schools, and the community. They are nationwide outgrowths of the original Tri-University Project (see Preface).

Each contributor emphasizes the naturalness of language learning in the lives of young children. This emphasis belies the commonly held belief that language is something which is learned in school. Smith describes the conditions for initial language *acquisition* and the way language is developed in the natural setting of the home. Mather contends that the classroom should permit the child the same freedom for language exploration that the home provides. She describes the classroom as a natural setting for language *growth*.

As shall be seen, one of the major themes woven throughout Smith's paper is that, given an environment which makes learning possible, children are *compelled* to learn language. Smith shows us that the process of acquiring language skills relies very little on imitation or direct instruction. Instead, it relies on an exposure to language from which inferences about the structure of language can be made. The child, like the linguist, hypothesizes about the nature of the language system to which he is exposed and, in his own speech, tests these hypotheses against those models of language that he hears. Thus, language growth proceeds from having opportunities to test out *incorrect* hypotheses. This basic insight into language learning has notable implications for classroom practices.

Although opportunities to test hypotheses about language—*and to risk being wrong*—are an integral part of child language development, the child's willingness to do so is related to the extent to which his language environment supports his efforts. While the home setting typically has afforded the child a supportive environment for the exploration of language, the school setting usually has not been so flexible.

Mrs. Mather's paper depicts one kind of school setting where the child's opportunities to explore language are maximized. Her personalized account of language activities in her classroom implicitly illustrates how language growth can be nurtured in a supportive environment where child language is viewed within the context of the child's *own* level of linguistic development. Like Smith, Mrs. Mather views reading as a language-based process in which learning to read conforms to many of the same principles that govern language development—although additional principles related to the nature of written forms of language must also be considered. Thus, both authors stipulate that learning to read, like learning to talk, involves hypothesis testing.

THE LEARNER AND HIS LANGUAGE

Frank Smith

Language—as Wardhaugh indicated in his opening paper —is a two-level system. In the case of spoken language, the two levels of the system are sound and meaning; and the task of the language learner is to construct a set of rules that will enable him to translate from one to the other. Many linguists refer to the two levels of language as *surface* and *deep* structure, with syntax, or grammar, as the set of rules that permits the language user to operate between the two.

Similarly, the task of the beginning reader is to construct a set of rules that will enable him to translate the surface structure of written language —the visual symbols on the page—into meaning. To a considerable extent, these rules for reading will include rules that the beginning reader has already acquired in his mastery of the spoken form of language, although other rules are specifically related to the visual aspects of written text. The purpose of the present paper is to discuss briefly the degree to which the beginning reader has already mastered the syntax of spoken language, and, more importantly, to consider the means by which this mastery is acquired.

The attention to the first question, the beginning reader's competence in spoken language, will be relatively brief because to all intents and purposes the process of learning spoken language may be considered to be complete by the time a child's attention is turned to reading. But the question of *how* this competence in spoken language is acquired— of the kinds of information and learning experiences that a child requires in order to acquire a grammar—warrants consideration in a little more detail. An understanding of the manner in which a child develops spoken language skills provides a clue to the kind of information that a child requires in order to learn a complex skill such as reading, and indicates the strategies that he is likely to employ. Acquaintance with the manner in which spoken language is learned also reminds us of the remarkable intellectual potential of a child in his first few years of life, at an age when he is often considered the least attentive and tractable. At such an age, practically every child constructs and verifies a set of rules that summarize the relationships and regularities underlying language, even though adults are far from any understanding of what these relationships and regularities are, let alone how to impart them through formal instruction.

For, as Wardhaugh pointed out, linguists still cannot describe fully the system that is language. The problem is not paucity of data—there is no shortage of language in the world—but rather that there is an inadequacy of theories of language, an inability to construct valid and testable hypotheses for the rules that relate deep and surface structure.[1] There is as yet no theoretical basis that will permit the construction of computer programs to translate from one language to another, or even to distinguish grammatical from ungrammatical sentences in one language, with anything like the facility of a human.

Of course, it would be absurd to suggest that linguists are not able to distinguish a grammatical sentence from an ungrammatical one. They are in the frustrating, but not uncommon position of being unable to explain how they do something which they are, in fact, able to do very well. Fortunately, it is not necessary for a child to be told what the rules of language are in order to acquire them; and few people have the impression that they know enough about spoken language even to attempt to teach a child to talk. This is not the case with reading, of course. And because children often learn to read at the time when a parent or teacher is engaged in the behavior we call instructing, there is a widespread belief that the rules a child develops in order to read must be the rules an adult has verbalized. But, the fact that a child demonstrates some desirable behavior after exposure to a particular kind of instruction does not logically entail that he has acquired a particular kind of rule. Quite coincidentally the instructional situation may provide the child with the information that he needs in order to develop and test unverbalized rules of his own. There can be no other explanation for the fact that so many children learn to speak and to read in such a variety of instructional environments.

---

[1] Editors' Note: In generative-transformational grammar, every message is regarded as having two levels of representation, a *deep structure* which relates to meaning or semantic interpretation and a *surface structure* which relates to the physically observed message, whether spoken or written. The rules that relate deep structure to surface structure are called *transformation* rules, and the complete description of these rules is a major part of current linguistic study. See also Kenneth Goodman's discussion of deep and surface structures in his paper in Section VI, pp. 143–159.

THE NATURE OF CHILD LANGUAGE [2]

The language competence of the beginning reader can be stated very succinctly. Although linguists have been unable to provide anything like a complete description of the rules of grammar, the great majority of children develop a set of these rules within the space of about two years. At the age of about eighteen months a child produces his first two-word sentence, and by three-and-a-half years he appears to have mastered all the important rules of his language. Of course, a child of four does not speak like an adult—his vocabulary is not as rich and his memory is more limited—but he has acquired the competence to produce and comprehend all the possible forms of sentence construction found in adult speech.

First-language learning proceeds in an extremely rapid, smooth, and predictable sequence, indicating that a child is predisposed biologically both *to learn* and to use language. Because of this innate ability, and the fact that all the world's languages have many basic similarities, the view has been developed that the task confronting the newborn infant is not so much to learn what language is, as to discover the idiosyncratic aspects of the particular language spoken in his own community. The child is born ready to start speaking a unique language—which adults denigrate with the name of baby talk—and progressively modifies this language until it comes closer and closer to that spoken by his parents. Some linguists and psychologists use the metaphor that the child learning to talk is "testing hypotheses," literally conducting linguistic experiments, to discover specifically what kind of language is talked around him.

Other sources of evidence support the view that the essential skills of language learning are innate; they concern the idiosyncratic nature of child language and the fact that its progressive refinement into adult language follows an orderly sequence. Thorough analyses of the verbal productions of infants have shown that the language they speak is neither a miniature or deformed version of adult language, nor a random throwing-together of words. Very little language learning is attributable to imitation, because very few of the constructions that children utter are arrangements of words that they could possibly have heard their

[2] Parts of the remainder of this paper are based upon Chapter 4 of my book *Understanding Reading* (New York: Holt, Rinehart & Winston, 1971) and the work of McNeill and other psycholinguists cited in that chapter.

parents speak. In fact, one of the most difficult things to ask a child to do is to imitate either a sound or a phrase that he has not already spontaneously produced for himself. Children change their ways to conform to adult language, but they do this by starting with a language of their own, not by starting from nothing. Their language is always systematic.

THE PROCESS OF LANGUAGE DEVELOPMENT

The baby who starts to babble at the age of three months does not build up from silence to the sounds of his own language; he starts with all possible language sounds and gradually eliminates those not used by the people around him. For those of us who are not skilled polyglots, the only time that we find it physically possible to utter sounds that are not in our native language is when we are a babe in arms.

During the first few years of life children find no particular difficulty in learning *any* language. They are not born more ready to speak one than another. At three months it is impossible to distinguish the babbling of a Chinese child from that of a Dutch child, or an American. At the age of six months, however, this is not the case. A six-month-old baby may not be able to speak a word of his native tongue, but he is "babbling" in Chinese, or Dutch, or English. There is experimental evidence that the "native language" of a six-month-old child can be identified from a tape recording of his babbling. The baby is demonstrating that he has acquired rules for the sounds that are produced around him. But it would be an oversimplification to say that he has learned these sounds by imitating his parents. The baby acquires them the way a sculptor "acquires" a statue—by disposing of surplus material that he originally had available for use if required.

By the age of one year, many children are speaking single words— *drink, mama, bye-bye*. Are they imitating their parents when they produce these words? Again, the answer is that the elements are the result of successive approximation, and not imitation in the sense that the child is aping an adult model. For one thing, many of a child's words are quite unique—the child could not possibly have heard his parent saying them (unless the parent was imitating the child, which is not an infrequent grown-up pastime). Furthermore, the child uses these first words in quite a different manner from the way in which adults use them. While adults put words together in accordance with a grammar, one-year-old children do not. Instead, infants use single words to express entire sentences (*holophrases* is the technical term)—an economy not generally practiced by grown-ups. Underlying the single words of the holophrastic stage may be quite complex meanings: *drink,* for example, might mean anything from "Bring me a drink" or "Look at that drink" to "I did not want that drink and I have just thrown it all over the floor."

Contrary to popular parental belief, the child is not learning words and then finding meanings for them. Instead, he is acquiring or inventing words, which may, or may not, have a close relation to adult language, to meet his own particular requirements and represent quite complex deep structures.

By eighteen months, many children have developed a powerful grammatical rule. At this age, they are producing two- or three-word phrases, like *allgone milk* or *see baby* or *want big truck.* Two aspects of this development are significant: first, these short sentences are certainly not imitated from parents (how many adults would say *allgone milk* or *want big truck?*); and second, the constructions are not random. The child, who may have a vocabulary of two or three hundred words by this time, does not put his words together arbitrarily in his first sentences—he has a system, a rule. *This rule is developed by children for their own use, for it does not occur in adult language.*

The condition for the first rule is that all words of the vocabulary are ordered into one of two classes which some researchers call *Pivot* class and *Open* class. The Pivot class is relatively small and "closed"—new words are not added very frequently—while the Open class, relatively large, is the class to which most new words are added.

The first rule can be represented like this:

$$S \rightarrow (P) + O + (O)^3$$
$$P \rightarrow \text{allgone, see, my} \ldots$$
$$O \rightarrow \text{milk, baby, big, truck} \ldots$$

and interpreted as follows:

[3] Editors' note: The arrow ($\rightarrow$) is a symbol used in tranformational grammar meaning "consists of" or "is to be rewritten as."

A sentence *S* can be formed by an Open class word *O* (e.g., *big*) optionally preceded by a Pivot class word (*P*) (e.g., *see big*) and optionally followed by another Open class word (*O*) (e.g., *see big truck*). Among the sentences that can be produced are *allgone big truck, see milk, my baby* but not—*big truck allgone, milk see* or *baby my*.

The words in each class vary, of course, from child to child; and a word that originates in one child's Pivot class may be in another child's Open class. But, all children appear to go through the same first-rule stage, although no children are explicitly taught it. The development of the rule is one of the universals of language development in children.

From the first coarse-grained Pivot-Open class distinction, children go on to make successive differentiations within each class, progressively making their language more complex and gradually bringing it closer and closer to that spoken by adults. All the time a child is speaking a rule-governed language of his own—at no time does he just throw words together randomly, and at no time can he be said to be slavishly imitating an adult model. Those rules which are productive in the construction or comprehension of sentences in adult language are retained, the others the child progressively modifies.

Sometimes it is very clear that a child is not imitating. One very revealing example of the manner in which children discover rules, rather than copy examples, lies in the highly predictable sequence in which almost all children utter *incorrect* forms of very common verbs after they have apparently learned the correct forms. The phenomenon occurs among "strong" verbs like *come, go,* and *drink* which occur frequently in the language, and which have irregular past tense forms such as *came, went,* and *drank*. Frequently, a child produces these past tense constructions correctly until he discovers the +*ed* rule for the "regular" inflection: *walk/walked, climb/climbed, laugh/laughed*. As a demonstration that he has learned the past tense rule, the child suddenly begins to lose the correct forms *came, went, drank* and to overgeneralize the +*ed* rule and say *comed, goed, drinked*. These are obviously not forms that the child has heard his parents or anyone else utter—he is trying out a new rule, and does not use it correctly until he gets the information that certain words like *come, go* and *drink* are exceptions.

In fact, it can be shown that imitation of adult speech is one of the hardest tasks that can be set. If an adult says to a child at the Pivot-Open class stage, "Say *the milk is all gone*," the child will reply "Allgone milk," or whatever construction has the same meaning to his own rules.

HOW LANGUAGE IS LEARNED

The task of the child is to find out the underlying rules of grammar—to uncover the system that underlies the surface of every utterance and which relates sound and meaning. He never "just repeats" a sentence that he hears an adult utter—what would be the point of that? Nor does he try to learn by rote the sentences that adults produce; that would also be pointless, because almost every sentence we hear and use is novel. The child needs to learn to produce and understand all the *potential* sentences of his language; that is to say, to learn the rules by which the sentences of his language are produced. And of course, that is something no adult even attempts to teach a child. The child in effect performs a detection task—he hears a sentence and tries to determine a possible rule by which it could be produced. Then, he tests whether the rule is correct by using it to produce a few sample sentences, and seeing whether they are acceptable as sentences of the language.

In this light, the responsibility of adults becomes rather clear, although it is quite different from the role traditionally attributed to them. Basically, adults supply the child with two types of information which may be termed *general* and *specific*. They capitalize on the child's implicit knowledge of the way to learn by keeping him exposed to plenty of adult language. This is the *general information* that a child requires. The adult who does not help his child is the one who tries to speak only "baby talk."

Specific information is best given to a child only when he needs it. The child does not want, and cannot use, little snippets of information thrown at him arbitrarily in a formal learning situation. Instead, he needs feedback to tell him whether he is observing the significant differences of his language in a particular situation. The simplest way to provide feedback at the right time is perhaps to regard every utterance made by a child as having a double function, the first being the expression of a need or feeling, and the second the test of a rule.

If the preceding discussion makes the task of the adult sound too vague, there is one simple rule of thumb: a child wants information about a grammatical rule when he uses it. Many parents follow this rule unknowingly when they engage in the game which has received the technical name of *expansions*. In this transaction, parents take a sample of child speech and expand it into adult form. For example, when the child says *want milk,* the parent "expands" the statement into *You want some milk, do you?* or *May I have a glass of milk, please.* An adult expanding child language is providing a specific adult-language surface structure for a deep structure that the child already has in his mind. It is not simply a matter of "correcting," but of giving information so that the child can verify a rule that he has just applied, at a time when he can relate it to the appropriate deep structure.

GENERAL COMMENTS

There are several aspects òf learning to speak and learning to read that are common to many cognitive tasks. One common aspect is that learning cognitive skills is far more complex than we conventionally believe. But the child is able to overcome instructional deficiencies because his learning competencies are far richer than we usually give him credit for.

To take a nonlinguistic example, consider the situation when a child is "taught" to tell the difference between cats and dogs. This type of task, involving the determination of "significant differences" of particular categories of objects or events, is something that a child is very good at accomplishing and an adult very poor at explaining. We never *tell* a child what the differences are between cats and dogs; in fact, it is doubtful whether most adults could verbalize a foolproof set of rules. Instead, we let the child see many instances of cats and dogs, and of objects which are not cats and dogs (this is all *general information*), and leave it to him to work out what the significant differences must be. In order to learn what it is about cats that makes them cats, the child needs to examine positive and negative examples. It is no use exposing him just to cats and saying each time, "This is a cat"—the result may well be that he thinks all four-legged animals are cats. Instead, he needs to see dogs, horses, cows, and so forth, and to be told that these are *not* cats. Only by being shown what the alternatives are will he get any clue about what a cat is.

Having been shown what the alternatives are, a child will draw his own conclusions, which he will test by seeing if he can use the terms *cat* and *dog* in a manner concordant with the way adults use them. The child does not go to an adult and say "Kindly give me a set of rules to commit to memory that will permit me infallibly to distinguish a cat or dog whenever I meet one." Again, what adult could oblige him? Instead, the child tests his hypotheses, plays his hunches, by using the words *cat* and *dog* and looking for the *specific information* of feedback. It does not matter if he calls an occasional Sealyham a cat, or a Siamese a dog, provided he is given the appropriate feedback about whether he should modify his rules. The sure way of preventing a child from discovering what are the distinguishing characteristics of cats and dogs would be to discourage him from using these terms on any occasion when he might be "wrong."

I have come to a critical point in this paper. The time when specific information is most useful to a child is when he is making a response *which could be wrong*. He has got to make some kind of response, to put some kind of rule into practice, otherwise he can never receive feedback. He will not learn by sitting and listening or looking—the brain does not assimilate information in that way. But there is no value in making a response if the child waits for those occasions when he knows he must be right. In that case, he is merely exhibiting rules that he has already confirmed. Instead, the child must test hypotheses that he has not yet confirmed, which means that there must be a probability that his response will be "wrong" by adult standards. He will only learn adult language if he is encouraged to use his child language, and receives the necessary feedback.

We do not usually punish young children for not speaking like adults, and parents who encourage their children to be articulate are generally rewarded by the ease with which baby talk is discarded. Similarly, we are usually not inclined to get emotionally unsettled when a child has trouble distinguishing cows from horses. The situation in reading is rather different; we are far more prone to talk of mistakes and errors, and far less tolerant of the child who is hypothesis-testing. I think a major insight to be gained from the study of spoken language development is that we cannot expect a child to learn simply on the basis of the rules that adults try to feed to him.

THE LANGUAGE LEARNER

IN SCHOOL

Dolores Mather

Given time, encouragement, assistance, and ample feedback, children can learn to read just as they learn to use language, provided we don't give them a sense of failure. I wonder—do we really *teach* them to read?

For the past two years, I have been working in a room into which come six-, seven-, and eight-year-old children. Our classroom is modeled somewhat after the Infant Schools of England, with many activity or learning centers. We have been striving to "let reading happen," letting children discover reading, just as the discovery of mathematics and science is encouraged in today's schools. We are trying to establish for and with the children more of a family setting, that is, a more benign authority system than is often found in classrooms. We let children *use* language. Ours is not a quiet room.

We spend a great deal of time talking with the children, reading stories to and with them, writing chart stories, and letting them dictate stories to us. Thus, beginning reading materials are composed of language that has been spoken and whose flow is natural.

Just as we don't expect all children to learn to walk or to use spoken language at exactly the same age or with the same facility, neither should children be labeled as failures if they don't all read by the end of the first grade. Last year, we welcomed into our room a little girl who had been in a first grade room the year before and who had not had success in learning to read. She was a very quiet child in the classroom —a "nonverbal" child. She didn't want to have anything to do with learning to read. Although she loved to listen to stories we read to her, she rejected all our invitations to read with us. She would tell us, "I don't like to read. I don't want to learn to read." Yet, she was observed spending considerable periods of time in the library corner looking at books.

One day in March, she was observing me read with another child.

She began to supply words the other child didn't recognize. I was extremely curious to know what she really knew but had so far been unwilling to share with us. Within a few minutes she said, "I'll read that next." And she did! She had a way to go, but she had already come a long way.

Confidence, an "I can" belief, as Eleanor Duckworth has said (1968), is important for us all. Give "nonverbal" children confidence, and there will be far fewer "nonverbal" children, and far fewer nonreaders.

DISCOVERING THE JOYS OF READING

The discovery that "I can read!" is a beautiful process to behold. Before she could really read as would be usually defined, another little girl in my class exclaimed, "Gee, I didn't know I could read!" after reading *Ten Pennies for Candy* (Wing, 1963) with me.

For some children from inner-city circumstances, being read to is a new experience. We see them picking up a book, reading stories to themselves, or perhaps to friends, before they are really able to decode the printed words before them, just as we have observed children from other environments do at the age of three or four.

Again, another child who had "turned off" reading, worked his way through plastic design blocks, Tinkertoys, Lincoln Logs, word games, and other such devices, and one day in March finally said, "Where's a book that *I* can read?" With very little help, he was off and running. He was so pleased with this new found success, that he wanted to take a book to the principal's office to read during the noon hour rather than sally forth to the playground. I haven't seen that happen very many times.

It takes courage to read to an adult, and an assurance that you won't be embarrassed for not knowing a word. But, my children last year did attain, I believe, such courage; or, perhaps better, a feeling of trust. Almost all visitors—and there were many—heard children say to them words which became very familiar to those of us who were working with the children: "Come read with me." Complete strangers were being invited to "Come read with me." Reading for these children had become something that was fun and a joy to be shared with others.

As we have long known, most early readers learn to read at home, having been helped by parents or siblings who know little about teaching from basal readers. I can't take credit for the best readers in my classroom; for that is exactly where they learned to read—at home. We have consequently encouraged parents to read to and with their children whenever possible.

We find these children wanting to read their favorite stories with adults again and again. These stories range from *The Bears' Vacation* (Berenstain, S. & J., 1968), where Dad gets his "comeuppance," to *Ten Pennies for Candy* (Wing, 1963), which contains repetitions that children never cease to enjoy. I think that we have perhaps been wrong in thinking that we must have a new story to read each day. Familiarity provides pleasure, security, and a source of pride in being able to do something well. Just as when they are learning to talk, young children enjoy reading and using a new word repeatedly to get the "feel" of it.

THE ROLE OF LANGUAGE IN LEARNING TO READ

Since I seriously began to consider the role which language acquisition plays in learning to read, I have had a number of my pet theories about teaching reading upset. I had believed that children being taught to read would most certainly need the prerequisite of knowing the alphabet, and that using a "linguistic approach" in which letter and sound patterns are carefully controlled would assure success. I now know that mastering the alphabet is not an absolute prerequisite to beginning reading. Children do read without always first jumping that hurdle.

It wasn't until late in the year, after much exposure to Dr. Seuss books in general, and *Green Eggs and Ham* (Dr. Seuss, 1960) in particular, that I saw much transference occurring among words like *at, bat, cat.* I won't deny that this type of material helps the decoding process for some children when used at a particular stage of learning to read, but only after assessing each individual's indications of interests and needs. I can't help but wonder if some of the success that has been attributed to "linguistic" materials has really been because of a considerable amount of conditioning. Real use of "rules" is made only when children have incorporated them into their own system. Then, the "rule" helps the beginning decoder of written language verify some vague generalization that he has begun to formulate.[1]

---

[1] Editors' note: See page 38 ff. of Frank Smith's paper for an elaborate discussion of language development as a rule-forming–rule-testing process.

Generalizations that are "discovered" are not soon forgotten. Often we hear statements about word recognition similar to the one a child made to me after dictating several sentences, most of which had begun with the word *this*: "Oh, *this* begins like *Theresa!*"

I no longer believe that listening is taught, unless it is through the model of the teacher or any adult who listens *to* children and talks *with* them rather than to them. One boy wanted to continue to work with Tinkertoys rather than join the group for story time. When I insisted, he agreed, but with the following condition, "O.K., I'll come, but I ain't gonna listen." How true. I could insist that he come, but I really couldn't insure that he would listen.

We also tend to forget that the deep structure of language may not be the same for the child of age six or seven as it is for us. For instance, what response can be given to the following question posed by one six-year-old youngster who asked, "You mean there really is a Holy Ghost?" (Is it like Casper—with holes?) Because it is important for the children to be exposed to many linguistic forms, I no longer worry about the correlation of vocabulary from one book to another. The motto now is: new words, new contexts, new deep structure.

SOME STORIES DICTATED BY CHILDREN

Let's look now at some stories that were dictated by the children which show the progressions and growth that children make when they are encouraged to *use* language. Although we make use of the tape recorder in our class, these particular stories were dictated after the children had drawn a picture and the language was written down for them as they dictated. Here is Denise's story that she dictated in early September:

> Can you tell what this Indian's doing?
> That's right, he's making a fire.
> Count how many puffs of smoke.
> That's right, there are three.

Denise continued to tell this form of story for two or three weeks. I'm quite certain that this form must, in fact, have been modeled on her experience in kindergarten the year before. I had been well aware that teachers become models for many things, but I had never really considered the impact that a teacher has upon the use of language at this particular age. Denise is a talented child, however; and after hearing a variety of linguistic forms, she dictated the following story in early October.

THE HEN AND THE PEN

Once there was this little hen. He was walking along one day. On his walk he found a pen on the ground. First, he thought it was a little worm. He came running after it and said, "CHARGE!" And then he knew it was a pen. So he picked it up.

He didn't get too far, and he found a piece of paper. First, he thought it was a place where water was at. So he ran over there and licked it. He got it stuck in his mouth. He stuck his big claw in his mouth, and then he got it out.

He started to giggle, because he'd thought it was water. After he stopped giggling, the paper was all soggy by then. He had to wait for it to dry. After it was dry, he tried to make a picture of a chicken. It ripped because it wasn't really dry. And then after while he started to get hungry. After a long time, he died.

Although Denise gave us many delightful stories during the course of the year, I have chosen this next one because it illustrates the rhythm and flow that she often played with, as well as demonstrating the twist she often had at the end of the story. She loved to surprise us with an unexpected bit of humor.

One potato, two potato, three potato, four.
Walking in a line.
The big one says,
"HEZOO", every time he takes a step.
Their names is Spuds.
The line goes from biggest to the littlest.
"HEZOO, HEzoo, hezoo."
Plop, plop, the little one threw up.
Get the sponge!
Wash, wipe, wash, wipe, WHISH!

Sometimes children just aren't inspired to tell a story. In December, Ricky had shared the following with the class:

Once upon a time there was two reindeers.
One was black-nosed and the other one red-nosed.
And Santa Claus came Christmas Night, and he forgot his bag.

So he had to go back and get it.
And he couldn't find it.
And then his reindeer took off with the sleigh,
Without Santa in it.
And he called them back.

But, one day in January Ricky dictated the following in its entirety:

This is a house.
This is a haunted house.
That's all.

The following is a story that was dictated by Doraine in January.

This is a world of candy
with lemon drops and jelly beans
and all the good things
that little boys and girls like.
All the candy in the world was happy.
Every boy and girl loved to eat candy.
The mothers and fathers loved to eat candy.
The people don't have cavities,
because they don't have teeth.
They suck!

The next story by Doraine was dictated in March. At first glance, it may appear to be a regression of sorts, but, in fact, it exemplifies how children do test hypotheses. Here, Doraine, observing her oral language become written language, was exercising a very controlled language play, not only with syntax, but with the morphological and phonological aspects of language as well.

The saucer is creepy.
The saucer is spooky.
The saucer is squincy.
The saucer is silly.
The saucer is landing.
The saucer holds a Martian.
        And I just hate Martians!

The story that Doraine dictated to us in April indicates a more sophisticated plot again, but also another instance of play with phonology.

Once there was a boy named David.
David was crippled.

He had a friend.
He was Mr. Neckwy.
Mr. Neckwy liked David.

Every day David saw Mr. Neckwy.
Every day Mr. Neckwy saw David.
Mr. Neckwy was a policeman.

Then something went wrong.
When David came to school,
     Mr. Neckwy was gone!

Then David walked into the school.
The teacher was not the teacher
That was the other day!

IT WAS MR. NECKWY!

For some reason,
Mr. Neckwy wasn't the policeman after all.
He, for some reason,
Didn't want to be a policeman.
He really wanted to be a man teacher.
Then David got to see Mr. Neckwy every day.

I believe that language acquisition is the most important prerequisite to reading. Surround children with language in books and records; surround them with language that is used in the context of many models; provide them with opportunities to see their own language become written language; provide them with ample opportunities for hypothesis testing, enabling restricted language to become elaborated. From there, it may not be a very long step to reading.

REFERENCES

Berenstain, Stan and Jan *The Bears' Vacation*. New York: Beginner Books, a division of Random House, Inc., 1968.

Dr. Seuss *Green Eggs and Ham*. New York: Beginner Books, a division of Random House, Inc., 1960.

Duckworth, Eleanor "A Child's View of Knowing." Paper read at the Second National Conference sponsored by the U.S. Office of Education, Tri-University Project in Elementary Education, New Orleans, Feb. 1–3, 1968. Published in *Reason and Change in Elementary Education,* Nebraska Curriculum Center, University of Nebraska, Lincoln, 1968 (uncopyrighted).

Wing, Henry *Ten Pennies for Candy.* New York: Holt, Rinehart & Winston, Inc., 1963.

FOR FURTHER READING

Chukovsky, Kornei *From Two to Five.* Berkeley: University of California Press, 1968.

A classic. A Russian poet demonstrates how insights into the manner in which children develop and use language can be achieved quite independently of any restrictive linguistic or psychological theory.

Herriot, Peter *An Introduction to the Psychology of Language.* London: Methuen, 1970.

Herriot provides an eclectic view of language development together with general summaries of psycholinguistic theory at a nontechnical level.

Lyons, John (Ed.) *New Horizons in Linguistics.* Baltimore: Penguin Books, Inc., 1970.

An alternative to Herriot. The chapter on language acquisition by Robin Campbell and Roger Wales takes a generative-transformational perspective but is also critical of its limitations. The chapter on sociolinguistics in the same volume by M.A.K. Halliday also stresses the need to consider environmental and functional aspects of language in any analysis of its development in children.

THREE · LANGUAGE DIFFERENCES AMONG LEARNERS

Frank Smith has discussed language acquisition and argued cogently for the appreciation of children's language. He strongly suggests that the language acquisition process might well provide a model for the process of learning to read. Mrs. Mather, a teacher well-versed in linguistics and psycholinguistics, has described how, as a first-grade teacher, she has approached reading on the basis of her understandings of children and children's language.

If one grants Smith's thesis that children's language is a completely valid form of language with an adequate and systematic grammar, then it follows that the various grammars developed by children from different environmental backgrounds are also valid. The description of this linguistic variation within a given language is the province of the dialectologist; the understanding of the relationship between language variation and social status is the province of the sociolinguist. The present section contains two papers that pertain to language variation and its implications for schooling.

Roger Shuy is Professor of Linguistics and Director of the Sociolinguistics Program at Georgetown University. He is also Director of the Sociolinguistics Program of the Center for Applied Linguistics in Washington, D.C. His paper discusses the way language variation among children from different dialect areas affects the process of learning to read. The dialect of many children—for example, children from inner-city ghetto areas—differs markedly from the dialect of classroom instruction. Instructional materials are almost exclusively written to represent "standard English"; and normally, the teacher's speech is also "standard." Since more children with divergent dialects "fail" reading in the first grade than an equal population of middle-class suburban children, it should seem obvious that differences between divergent dialects and the language of instruction may contribute to reading failure. Yet, an awareness of such a possibility has only recently been recognized.

The schools have traditionally ignored this problem and have usually proceeded to teach all children reading with the same materials and with the same methodology. The tacit assumption has been that language differences can be ignored in reading instruction. In the case of successful students, it has also been assumed that ignoring language differences has resulted in the "standardization" of "nonstandard" language patterns. Shuy discusses this problem and suggests four alternative strategies for teaching reading to pupils with divergent dialects. Each alternative is a logical one; and each has its proponents among educators and the lay public alike. Each solution awaits empirical evidence of its efficacy.

Mildred Gladney, a former teacher in the inner-city schools of Chicago, was a member of a team which applied Shuy's fourth alternative to the dialect and reading problem. Supported by the Chicago Board of Education and the Office of the Superintendent of Public Instruction of the state of Illinois, Miss Gladney and others prepared a series of reading texts that incorporated the experiences and language of the Black child. Whether one agrees with this solution of the dialect problem or not, any serious attempt to resolve this educational quandary can only be applauded. Miss Gladney is currently on the staff of the TTT Project in Elementary Education at the University of Nebraska. Primarily, her work deals with learning problems encountered by children who have backgrounds which are at odds with the middle-class white culture of the American educational system.

SPEECH DIFFERENCES

AND TEACHING STRATEGIES:

HOW DIFFERENT IS ENOUGH?

Roger W. Shuy

In past years linguists have been working diligently in different parts of the country to define the exact linguistic features which characterize people of different social status. The research of the *Linguistic Atlas of the United States and Canada,* begun in the thirties, made some attempt at obtaining socially interesting information along with invaluable data which revealed important historical and geographical insights. The rise of interest in urban problems in the sixties, however, has called for an entirely new strategy. As the interest of linguists shifted from historical and geographical concerns to synchronic social matters, it became increasingly difficult for them to hang on to older ways of operating. They learned more about sampling design, about data gathering techniques, about analytical procedures, about social stratification. Major linguistic research in urban areas has been conducted recently in New York, Detroit, Chicago, and Washington, D.C. These research projects are just beginning to bear fruit for educators.

These projects are not involved in the study of phonetic or grammatical "deficiencies." And they are not saying that the child cannot learn to read because he does not know standard English. They are saying, instead, that the linguistic system of the ghetto Negro is different in a number of identifiable features from that of standard English.

THE NEED FOR LINGUISTIC DESCRIPTION

The theoretical assumption made by the linguist in his study of these linguistic differences is that whatever pedagogical strategy is devised for Black children, whether in reading, oral language, or composition, one of the first stages in the process is a careful delineation of the exact differences.

IN THE DEVELOPMENT OF ORAL LANGUAGE MATERIALS

The earliest applied work which related to the systematic differences between the speech of low socioeconomic Black people and other middle-class Americans focussed heavily on oral language materials. The battles over whether it was better to eradicate nonstandard English (as it was then called) entirely or to teach children to be biloquial (to control two or more dialects) generated considerable heat in the mid-sixties. Toward the end of the decade, some well-meaning white liberals over-stated their dismay concerning the long recognized but uncontrollable intimidation processes involved in language standardization by present-ing strong, if not self-righteous, arguments that it is the standard English speaker who should become biloquial by learning Black English (as it is now called) (Sledd, 1969).

Whatever lack of clarity may exist with regard to pedagogical strate-gies, political alignment, the will of the community, teacher attitudes and the inner motivations of researchers, one fact remains clear. It was good to have isolated, as much as possible, the linguistic features which set off the speech of ghetto children from middle-class norms. It was good because *any* of the pedagogical strategies, political positions, and community pressures require us, ultimately, to specify exactly what it is we are talking about when we say that the speech of ghetto children is different from that of their middle-class peers.

That is, if your position is that Black children should acquire standard English speech, for any reason you might suggest, it is necessary for teachers and materials writers to know exactly where the speech of Black children differs from that of other people. If, on the other hand, you believe that white people should learn Black English, you first have to know essentially the same sort of information.

IN THE DEVELOPMENT OF READING MATERIALS

Likewise, in the field of reading, such specifications are critical, regard-less of whether it is finally decided that the best approach to beginning reading in the Black ghetto is to:

1. first teach them standard English

2. accept their dialect reading of traditional material written in standard English (Goodman, 1965)

3. develop materials in standard English which minimize dialect and cultural differences (Venezky, 1970)

4. develop materials which incorporate the grammar of Black children (Stewart, 1969).

If it is decided that children must be taught standard English before they learn to read, the teachers and the materials must surely begin with an exact account of the differences between Black English and standard English. If the schools decide to accept the oral renderings of the standard English *she goes* as *she go*, the teacher will have to be alerted to the precise conditions in which such renderings are to be expected. If an avoidance strategy is set up to neutralize the mismatch between the written text and the child's oral language, the materials developers will have to rely on this same delineation of the contrast between standard English and the speech of Black children. And, if it should be decided that special reading material should be developed utilizing Black English grammar, it will be necessary to know precisely what that grammar is.

What should be perfectly clear, at this point, is that regardless of the pedagogical task or the proposed teaching strategy, we will not get very far without a rather thorough description of the language of the Black child. Although it may seem to the anxious public that more time should have been spent on developing materials during the past five years or so in which American education developed its belated interest in the language problems of Black children, the simple truth is that it was first necessary to try to isolate the characteristics of the problem. And this was considerably harder to do than anyone would have imagined. The growing literature in the field clearly documents the sorts of problems we faced as we moved slowly toward the goal of developing classroom materials.

THE BACKGROUND OF LINGUISTIC DESCRIPTIONS

The early materials developed for teaching standard English to non-standard speakers clearly suffered from lack of accompanying linguistic analysis. It was fashionable, for example, to be concerned for the future welfare of children who said /pin/ (as in *pin*) for both the instrument you write with (*pen*) and the thing that holds two pieces of cloth together (*pin*). Nor was there much perceptiveness about whether a given feature was grammatical or phonological. That is, the child's use of *jump* as the past tense form was generally thought of as carelessness with the ends of words. The obvious solutions to both problems were to give the students practice in producing a distinction between the two sets of words in question, *pen/pin* and *jump/jumped*, and to develop care in articulating the ends of words rather than "swallowing them."

The next phase through which materials development seemed to pass was that of the audio-lingual stage. In the mid-sixties, TESOL (Teaching English to Speakers of Other Languages) was still held in high regard in most circles; and it suddenly became fashionable to talk about the speech of Black children as a foreign language. And if it was a foreign language, one might well consider the use of foreign language teaching techniques for ghetto kids (Lin, 1965; Stewart, 1964). Some researchers rushed immediately to the task, building lessons filled with repetition drills, pattern practice and long assignments in the language laboratory, despite the early warnings by Lin that such activities seemed to have little effect on the children other than boredom. A recent intensive survey of such materials by the Center for Applied Linguistics managed to identify twenty-eight such sets of materials, only four of which are currently available commercially. Most of the laborious efforts of hundreds of hours of various curriculum revision and materials development committees which produced many of these programs ended in anonymity. Like so many such innovative projects, the materials were used only as long as the funding for the program lasted. In some cases, it is now even impossible to discover where the materials have been stored.

During the development of the foreign-language teaching phase, it became apparent to many people that a careful description of Black speech was necessary in order to determine what features to build lessons upon. It was at this point that the importance of careful linguistic descriptions became obvious. Linguistic descriptions of the speech of Black people began to be made in the second half of the decade of the sixties, especially in New York (Labov, Cohen), Chicago (Pederson), Detroit (Shuy, Wolfram, Riley), Washington (Stewart, Fasold, Luelsdorf),

Florida (Houston) and Los Angeles (Legum). These descriptions vary in scope and philosophy, but they constitute a considerable step in meeting the goal of a large scale description.

THE CURRENT STATUS OF LINGUISTIC DESCRIPTIONS OF BLACK ENGLISH

Several types of information about the nature of Black English are now available. The earlier reports were largely lists of various features, frequently oversimplified, and occasionally inaccurate as far as Black English is concerned (see Wolfram, 1970). As more and more linguistic research was done, a second type of information source developed— the technical report, which, though accurate, made for difficult reading by nonlinguists and generally dealt with only a few aspects at a time (Labov, 1966; Wolfram, 1969). Now a third source of information has been made available—the rather complete, linguistically accurate but relatively nontechnical description of the most crucial features of Black English (Fasold & Wolfram, 1970). This article is of great importance in that it provides the first thorough analysis of Black English while, at the same time, being accessible to the lay audience. Since this information about Black English is now readily available, there is no point in merely summarizing it here. Instead, let us review some of the kinds of problems which such a description is helping to solve. Some educators have been critical of the depth and extent of the linguistic description and analysis which sociolinguists have insisted upon. To some, it has seemed like an unnecessary luxury; and it is now time to assess what it is that these descriptions have brought us.

In brief, five years or so of description and analysis have revealed some answers to the following questions:

1. What role does linguistic environment play in the contrast between Black English and standard?

2. How does one determine a pronunciation characteristic from a grammatical characteristic?

3. How does one tell how much of a given feature a child knows and how much he doesn't?

4. How does one determine which features are most crucial or most stigmatizing?

THE ROLE OF LINGUISTIC ENVIRONMENT

Much of the recent research of Labov, and Wolfram and Fasold, and others has consistently pointed out the importance of being able to determine the exact linguistic environments of the features which are said to contrast between standard and Black English. This particular type of knowledge enables the teacher or materials developer to build lessons with desirable precision. For example, it is important to note that the frequently observed lack of the -ed past tense marker in the speech of Black children is not an indication that such children have no past tense sensitivity. Indeed, their use of irregular verb past tense forms is substantially similar to that of white people of similar socioeconomic status. What must be seen, here, is the working of the word final consonant cluster. Since most regular past tense formations are merely the addition of /t/ to verb bases ending in certain voiceless sounds (i.e., *jumped, picked*) and /d/ added to verb bases ending in voiced sounds (i.e., *pinned, hanged, zoomed, rubbed, begged*), and since /t/ and /d/ tend to be lost in certain kinds of word final consonant clusters whether they are part of a past tense formation or not, this past tense reduction must be interpreted as directly related to phonological environment.

Fasold and Wolfram clearly point out how consonant cluster reduction operates both in Black English and in the colloquial speech of standard English speakers. Both groups reduce the second member of the cluster when the following word or suffix begins with a consonant. Thus, we all normally say *bes' kind* or *wes' side* in casual speech instead of *best kind* or *west side*. The major difference between Black English and standard English, however, occurs when the sound following the consonant is a vowel; thus, in standard English one would say *best one* and *west end*, but in Black English one would say *bes'one* and *wes'end*.

Another aspect of consonant cluster reduction, noted earlier by Wolfram, is that it operates only when both members of the cluster are either voiced or voiceless. Where the consonant cluster is of mixed voicing, as in *jump, cold* or *belt*, this reduction does not take place. These two clarifications of the general nature of consonant cluster reduction in Black speech should prevent future material writers from producing lessons on the nonexistent problems involving clusters of mixed voicing (as in *jump, colt* and *belt*) as well as wasting the time of Black children by trying to get them to produce consonants in positions where even colloquial standard English does not require them (as in *best kind* and *west side*).

Whether the user of this information wants to eradicate nonstandard English, teach biloquialism, or teach standard English speakers to use or appreciate Black English, the data provided by an exact description of the linguistic environment involved will enable him to accomplish his task with a high degree of efficiency.

DISTINGUISHING BETWEEN PHONOLOGICAL AND GRAMMATICAL FEATURES

To indicate how important it is to examine the phonology of Black English in its entirety rather than in bits and pieces, we may observe the often noted pluralization rules of certain Black children. Fasold and Wolfram (1970) point out that in Negro dialect, words ending in /s/ plus /p/, /t/, or /k/ take the -es plural form (-es is also regularly used in words ending in /s/, /sh/, /z/, or /zh/). Because the /p/, /t/, and /k/ are so often removed by the word final consonant cluster reduction noted earlier, the plurals of *wasp, ghost,* and *desk* are formed as though these words ended in /s/ rather than the consonant cluster. Thus, Black children often say *wasses* for *wasps, ghosses* for *ghosts,* and *desses* for *desks.*

It would be pedagogically wrong to assume that Black children who produce words like *wasses, ghosses* and *desses* have problems with rules of standard English pluralization. This, indeed, is only a superficial view of the situation. At the heart of the issue is the consonant cluster reduction rule which induces these children to treat these words, quite regularly, as though they were *spelled* with word final /s/. It is reasonable to assume that a classroom lesson which addresses itself to consonant cluster production will be of considerably more relevance than a lesson which attempts to teach children to produce the past tense.

DISCOVERING HOW MUCH OF A GIVEN FEATURE A CHILD KNOWS

If Black children are completely unfamiliar with a given phonological or grammatical feature, the pedagogical strategy is considerably different from when they are familiar with part of the system, or when they have two systems operating at the same time. For example, Fasold and Wolfram (1970) show that word final consonant clusters are not foreign to the speech of Black children. Their clusters are simply different from standard English because they can undergo reduction in certain contexts where reduction is not possible in standard English (e.g., when the following word begins with a vowel). Unless one determines whether or not consonant cluster reduction operates consistently in Black English, one cannot build teaching materials efficiently. If the students have no word final consonant clusters at all, they will produce utterances like *tes pattern*, *tes in math* and *tesser*. If they are like most Blacks in the North, they will not produce utterances like *tesser* for *tester* or *tessing* for *testing*. These speakers evidence familiarity with the cluster before suffixes beginning with a vowel and, like standard speakers, they reduce the cluster to /s/ before words beginning with a consonant; that is, for example, the /t/ in *most* is likely to be elided in the phrase "most people" since *people* begins with a consonant, but less likely to be elided in "most of us" since *of* begins with a vowel. The specific contrastive environment is before words beginning with a vowel.

Any materials developed to help such speakers to produce full consonant clusters before vowels should most certainly take into account that the speakers are perfectly capable of producing the full cluster in certain environments. We should not fool ourselves into thinking that we are teaching such children something that they cannot already produce. On the contrary, what we are doing is extending the territory in which they are to produce a sound that they are, in other environments, quite capable of producing.

Another dimension of the question concerning how much a child really knows of a given linguistic feature is found in linguistic variability. Labov (1969) has observed that some of the variation between forms of a given grammatical or phonological feature are an inherent part of the child's dialect. That is, a child may produce the /s/ form of the plural part of the time and delete it part of the time. The sociolinguist tries desperately to focus on the exact nonlinguistic environments accompanying this variation and to describe this variation accordingly. He looks for clues in terms of switching based on stylistic requirements, relative excitement, audience interaction, etc. But even after exhausting all such clues, he frequently discovers that a certain amount of variability may exist within the same style, context, and setting.

With respect to the current discussion of potential dialect interference to beginning reading, linguistic variability plays a vital role. Those who are testing the hypothesis that beginning reading material should be prepared in the child's own dialect must decide how to handle this linguistic variability. Should dialect readers use the pure, invariable dialect or should they incorporate this documented variability? Wolfram (1970a) goes so far as to observe: "Some of the beginning dialect materials which start with pure dialect may, in effect, be creating a new type of mismatch between written and spoken language. That is, they have made the dialect to be more divergent from standard English in written form than it actually is in spoken form [p. 28]."

This whole issue of variability, in fact, helps solve the question concerning teaching strategies for nonstandard speakers. As was noted earlier, for several years it was thought that foreign language teaching techniques would be useful to teach standard English to nonstandard English speakers. But a careful assessment of their speech indicated that such speakers actually produce the standard form in some contexts or even variably within a single context. We seldom find a parallel to this situation in foreign language teaching, where it is reasonably clear which language is which and few, if any, English words or grammatical forms creep into a French sentence. If such an intrusion were to take place, meaning signals would start flashing a warning. Between dialects, however, such switching seldom carries with it a switch in meaning, so that *She goes to the store* means exactly the same thing as *She go to the store*.

Thus, it is clear that we cannot call on the traditional foreign language teaching techniques in teaching about contrastive forms when there are no contrastive semantic functions accompanying the transfer. What is at stake is the social status of the speaker, and only minimally is there a problem of communication loss.[1] This recognition of a speaker's variability has caused materials developers to realize what we probably should have known all along: we are seldom teaching the child something new; we are only helping him to realize how and when to switch from one system to another. This task is of tremendous importance and is by no means simplified by this discovery.

---

[1] This is often denied by people who claim that they can't understand a thing their students are saying. This hyperbole can be easily remedied, as I have indicated elsewhere (Shuy, 1970), by simple focussed listening to such children and by learning to adjust to their system.

DISCOVERING WHICH FEATURES ARE MOST CRUCIAL

As linguistic geographers have long observed, it is not enough to point out where the speech of one group differs from that of another. We must also try to discover how crucial that difference is, particularly if we intend to use such information as a basis for shaping classroom activities. It has long been known, for example, that some people use relatively little aspiration at the beginnings of words with an initial *wh* spelling. Consequently, *witch* and *which* are homophonous in their dialects. This minor pronunciation difference carries relatively little social consequence even for those who produce a contrast between these two words. Those who pronounce them the same are often not even aware that some speakers produce a contrast. There are several reasons for the lack of social stigmatization attached to either side of the issue, not the least of which involves the relatively light functional load which the sounds carry. In isolation, there is potential ambiguity between *which* and *witch* but in real-life speech there are obvious syntactic clues which prevent confusion. That is, one seldom utters sentences like, *Look, there goes a *relative pronoun* (witch) *on a broom!* or *This is the story old hag (which) *I heard last night."*

Of late, considerable attention has been given this matter of relative cruciality by sociolinguists who are concerned about which linguistic features are most stigmatized. The most comprehensive treatment of this issue to date is Wolfram's (1970) set of criteria for ranking such features:

1. Sharp Versus Gradient Stratification Since all linguistic features do not correlate with social status in the same manner, it is obvious that those features which show sharp breaks between social classes are more crucial than those which show only slight differences across social status groups. Wolfram's research clearly shows that verb third person singular *-s* absence (*My sister go to school every day*) stratifies sharply whereas pronominal apposition (*My brother he came home late)* has only gradient (gradual) stratification across social class.

2. The Generality Of The Rule "Some nonstandard forms affect only a small subset of words or a single item, whereas others involve general rules that operate on the form of every sentence of a particular structural type" (Wolfram, in Fasold & Shuy, 1970, p. 110). The Black English rule of multiple negation (e.g., *He didn't do nothing*), for example, is a general rule that affects all negative sentences with an indefinite pronoun, determiner, or adverb. On the other hand, the Black English equivalent of the *there is/there are* construction, *it is*, concerns only one item.

3. Grammatical Versus Phonological   It has already been pointed out how important this difference can be to the development of materials. Nonstandard grammatical features, which tend to show sharp stratification between socioeconomic groups, are generally considered more stigmatizing than most phonological features by sociolinguists working in this area.

4. Social Versus Regional Significance   Although some features which are perfectly acceptable in one part of the country become stigmatized in another, other features have negative social values everywhere. It has been discovered that the latter, the generally stigmatized features, tend to be the most crucial for they always display sharper stratification than the regionally distributed items and they do not run the risk of developing regional snobbery.

5. The Relative Frequency Of The Items   Since some Black English patterns occur infrequently, they take less precedence than those which occur often. It is obvious that features which occur frequently are more crucial than those with low frequency.

To be sure, considerably more research needs to be done to refine our current knowledge in this area, but considerably more is now known than ever before about the relative values placed on socially stigmatized differences.

THE IMPLICATIONS OF THESE DIFFERENCES
BETWEEN BLACK AND STANDARD ENGLISH

It is clear from the emerging picture of the contrast between standard and Black English that we have a situation which is unique in the study of language variation in this country so far. Until the mid-sixties most dialect research in America focussed on historical and geographical concerns. It used the data of pronunciation and vocabulary in particular, since these categories revealed reasonably sharp contrasts when plotted on dialect maps. The study of grammar usually pinpointed regional contrasts between different groups of lower-class speakers, most frequently in the verb forms. But very little research before Labov (1966) addressed itself to the most crucial problems involved in sociolinguistic variation or degrees of stigmatization. In depth studies which determined whether a feature was a phonological or grammatical component in a person's language are extremely recent; and comparatively little information is extant, even yet, about the general distribution of Negro speech in this country.

Research has progressed far enough, however, to enable us to say that the speech of most American Negroes is certainly not as different from standard English as a foreign language; and it is certainly more different than the concept of dialect which we most commonly hold. In their treatment of the linguistic features of Negro dialect, Fasold and Wolfram (1970) have written the clearest statement yet about the nature of Negro speech:

> . . . First it should be understood that not all Negroes speak Negro dialect. There are many Negroes whose speech is indistinguishable from others of the same region and social class, and there are many whose speech can be identified as Negro only by a few slight differences in pronunciation and vocal quality. Second, Negro dialect shares many features with other kinds of English. Its distinctiveness, however, lies in the fact that it has a number of pronunciation and grammatical features which are not shared by other dialects. It is important to realize that Negro dialect is a fully formed linguistic system in its own right, with its own grammar and pronunciation rules; it cannot simply be dismissed as an unworthy approximation of standard English. In fact, there are some grammatical distinctions which can be made more easily in Negro dialect than in standard English. Negro dialect, then, as the term is used here, is a cohesive linguistic system which is substantially different from standard American English dialects. It is spoken by some, though not all Negroes, particularly those of the lower socioeconomic classes. Furthermore . . . almost all the features associated with Negro dialect alternate with standard English forms in actual speech. . . . [pp. 41–42]

Within the confines of the preceding qualifications, then, Black English may be said to be different enough from the schoolroom norms to merit special attention. It is different enough from these norms to require specially developed teaching strategies and materials which address themselves specifically to the beginning points of these speakers.

Research has revealed some things about Negro speech that come as a surprise to certain teachers. For example, Black children have neither more nor less difficulty with irregular past tense forms than do standard English speakers (Black or white). But Black English is different enough from standard English (and still more different from the prose of beginning reading materials) to merit serious research into the use of this indigenous system in the teaching of early reading skills. Venezky (1970) dismisses this possibility on the following grounds: (1) there is no proof that it will work; (2) it is too complicated and expensive; (3) the problems of attention span, motor coordination, and cognitive skills usually accompany nonstandard speech, and these may be the real root of the problem; and (4) it has been shown that lower socioeconomic status Negro children do not find educated speech any less intelligible than Negro speech. Not one of these objections is adequate for stopping the ongoing research and testing in this area. To the objection that there is no proof that it will work we must respond that there is also no adequate proof that it will not work. Likewise, there is less than adequate proof that any approach to reading works, at least as it is conceived of by its author.

The objection based on complexity is irrelevant. It is argued, for example, that if native literacy materials were constructed for Hawaiians, this would have to be done for Hawaiian pidgin, Japanese, Chinese, the various Philippine languages, Korean, and so on. This may or may not prove to be true. Whether it is true or not, the issue involves making children literate, no matter how hard it is to do so. The creative American spirit has not yet been stifled by arguments of expense or complexity; and there is no reason to expect it to be stifled here.

The argument that nonstandard speech accompanies cognitive deficit has been rejected by almost all linguists since educational psychologists first presented it publicly (see Labov, 1969); and there is evidence even from psychology that data which appear to show such conclusions are measuring test-taking ability, cultural difference, or something else rather than cognitive ability. Furth (1970), in fact, has clearly demonstrated that children who are deaf from birth have no cognitive deficits whatsoever, despite their total lack of language environment.

That lower socioeconomic Black children find educated white speech intelligible should not be surprising in light of what has been said about the two linguistic systems. Even ghettoized Black children come in contact with standard English on the television set; but it appears that they develop an editing process quite similar to the apparently universal contrast between two kinds of vocabulary. We all have a "use" vocabulary and a "recognition" vocabulary. We can input through either set but we usually output only through the former. Baratz' sentence repetition tests (1969) seem to verify this phenomenon. Given a stimulus sentence in standard English, Black children converted the sentence into their own linguistic system when they "repeated" it. That Black children can do this says little or nothing, however, about what interference a different language system might have on them as they acquire beginning reading skills, especially at the time when heavy emphasis is traditionally placed on developing skills in decoding and when the flow of predictability from what children already know (their oral language) to what they are learning (the written manifestation of that oral language) is of such great significance (see Shuy, 1969).

To dismiss any promising hypothesis on such grounds as those stated above is dangerous business, especially in a field of study which historically and, perhaps, necessarily may be characterized as hypothesis-oriented. The entire tradition of educational research suffers from much the same problem. We are engaged in research which is quite different from that of the hard sciences. That is, we have precious little that can be thought of as a scientific base. Any serious researcher in reading will verify that, in this area, the variables tend to multiply so fast that experimental control becomes extremely difficult, if not impossible. Since we know relatively little about how humans acquire learning, how they process language input or control its output, and how their knowledge and use of language relates to all this, we are probably doing well to operate even at the level of hypotheses. What we are finally beginning to know about is the broad outline of the linguistic system of the target population. It would seem reasonable to try to utilize this small segment of what may be called a scientific base in connection with reasonable hypotheses about the acquisition of reading skills.

To those who claim that nonstandard English speakers should be taught standard English before they are taught reading we can only say that there is also relatively little upon which this hypothesis is based.

But, it probably should be thoroughly investigated with as much rigor as we can marshal for the occasion, despite the apparent contradictory positions of researchers concerning the ability of children to acquire language skills at this age.

Likewise, those who argue for beginning reading materials written in standard English but which avoid the grammatical and cultural mismatch of Black-English–speaking children with the printed page also work from a reasonable but unproved hypothesis, but one which should certainly not be ignored.

It seems likely, then, that the combined effects of our current frustration concerning what to do about teaching Black children to read and our developing knowledge about the linguistic system of such children should work together in a new phase of our research in which these various hypotheses should be given a fair and thorough try, and not necessarily always by those who have been grinding axes for their own hypotheses.

A far more potent reason for discouraging any of the hypotheses noted in this paper may come from the Black community itself. In a time such as this, when it is commonplace to be suspicious of the motives of researchers, it is particularly difficult to address ourselves to the problems of minority groups, whether in reading, economics, family planning, or almost anything else. There is little reason for us to agonize over this situation or to feel sorry for ourselves as a result of it. The fact remains that no matter what route we take toward addressing these problems, we stand a pretty good chance of being called racist, Uncle Toms, Communists, or empire builders. Perhaps this matters; perhaps not. It should be clear by this time, however, that any experimentation in the various teaching strategies which grows out of our descriptions of language differences must have the approval and support of the community in which the experimentation takes place. It is not likely that teaching strategies which grow out of (1) teaching standard English before reading, (2) teaching reading by using dialect materials, (3) developing teaching materials which neutralize dialect differences, and (4) teaching teachers to accept oral dialect renderings of written standard English will seriously harm the students in the experiments. But if the community *thinks* these will be harmful, it has the right to say no. Personally, these approaches seems to me to be no more harmful than the other strategies currently in vogue, including phonics, the whole-word method, and *i.t.a.* (the Initial Teaching Alphabet). But, since a specific minority population is identified, the public relations problem is intensified.

CONCLUSION

In this paper I have attempted to demonstrate the importance of a careful and thorough sociolinguistic description of the speech differences which characterize different groups of people. It has been observed that such a description is at the heart of any pedagogical strategies, whether for teaching standard oral English or reading, and that until such descriptions were made, the teaching materials were frequently based on less crucial aspects of the problem or on features which were not problems at all. Such descriptions enable us (1) to develop materials which relate more specifically to the exact linguistic environment in which the features are found, (2) to devise strategies determined by whether the feature is grammatical or phonological in nature, (3) to assess what the child already knows about given features of language which otherwise we might have overlooked, and (4) to determine which features are most stigmatized by the society as a whole.

During the past five years, when most of the sociolinguistic research concerning Black English was undertaken, various teaching strategies have taken shape. We are currently at that stage of research in which we can best take advantage of our knowledge of the specific differences between Black and standard English. Since there is no known way to determine exactly what it is that keeps children from learning to read, it will pay us to take the next logical approach to the problem— hypothesis testing. This should come as no shock to reading researchers, since hypothesis testing has certainly characterized the work of the profession to date. To be sure, certain aspects have already begun to be tested, particularly with respect to the development of materials written in the Black child's dialect. Now it is time to urge researchers to coordinate their work in such a way that the four models involving potential dialect interference with reading (noted above) are thoroughly examined.

Sociolinguistic research to date has clearly shown that the systematic difference between Black and standard English is great enough to cause people to be clearly marked socially with great consistency (Shuy,

Baratz & Wolfram, 1969). This difference is great enough to be a clear handicap to employers (Shuy, 1970); and, whether desirable or not, it is great enough to enable listeners to achieve 80 percent accuracy in racial identification tasks (Shuy, 1969). Research to date has not clearly established whether or not this difference is great enough to affect the acquisition of reading skills. But, the evidence suggests that every effort should be made to discover which of the four strategies noted in this paper will be most helpful, in what settings, and under what circumstances. The stakes are too great for us not to try.

REFERENCES

Baratz, Joan   "Teaching Reading in an Urban Negro School System," in Joan Baratz and Roger Shuy (Eds.), *Teaching Black Children to Read.* Washington, D.C.: Center for Applied Linguistics, 1969.

Fasold, Ralph and Wolfram, Walt   "Some Linguistic Features of Negro Dialect," in Ralph Fasold and Roger Shuy (Eds.), *Teaching Standard English in the Inner City.* Washington, D.C.: Center for Applied Linguistics, 1970.

Furth, Hans   "On Language and Knowing in Piaget's Development Theory." Paper presented at the Lincolnland Dialect Conference, Charleton, Ill., March 18, 1970.

Goodman, Kenneth   "Dialect Barriers to Reading Comprehension," *Elementary English,* 1965, *42* (8), 853–60.

Labov, William   *The Social Stratification of English in New York City.* Washington, D.C.: Center for Applied Linguistics, 1966.

Labov, William   "Contraction, Deletion and Inherent Variability of the English Copula," *Language,* 1969, 45, 715–62.

Lin, San-su   *Pattern Practice in the Teaching of Standard English to Students with a Non-Standard Dialect.* Monograph. New York: Teachers College, Bureau of Publications, Columbia University, 1965.

Shuy, Roger W.   "Subjective Judgments in Sociolinguistic Analysis." *Georgetown Monograph Series on Languages and Linguistics,* 1969, No. 22, 175–188.

Shuy, Roger W. "A Linguistic Background for Developing Beginning Reading Materials for Black Children," in Joan Baratz and Roger Shuy (Eds.), *Teaching Black Children to Read*. Washington, D.C.: Center for Applied Linguistics, 1969.

Shuy, Roger W. "Speech and Employee Selection, Training and Promotion: Pitfalls of Good Intentions." Paper presented at the C.A.L.–N.C.T.E. Conference, Education and Training in the National Interest: The Role of Language Variety, Washington, D.C., February 14, 1970.

Shuy, Roger W. "Teacher Training and Urban Language Problems," in Ralph Fasold and Roger Shuy (Eds.), *Teaching Standard English in the Inner City*. Washington, D.C.: Center for Applied Linguistics, 1970.

Shuy, R. W., Baratz, J. C., and Wolfram, W. A. *Sociolinguistic Factors in Speech Identification*. Research Project No. MH–15048–01, 1969, National Institute of Mental Health. Washington, D.C.: Center for Applied Linguistics.

Sledd, James "Bi-Dialectalism," *English Journal*, 1969, *58*, 1307–1315.

Stewart, William "Foreign Language Teaching Methods in Quasi-Foreign Language Situations," in William Stewart (Ed.), *Non-Standard Speech and the Teaching of English*. Washington, D.C.: Center for Applied Linguistics, 1964.

Stewart, William "On the Use of Negro Dialect in the Teaching of Reading," in Joan Baratz and Roger Shuy (Eds.), *Teaching Black Children to Read*. Washington, D.C.: Center for Applied Linguistics, 1969.

Venezky, Richard "Nonstandard Language and Reading," *Elementary English*, 1970, *47*, 334–45.

Wolfram, Walt *A Sociolinguistic Description of Detroit Negro Speech*. Washington, D.C.: Center for Applied Linguistics, 1969.

Wolfram, Walt "Reading Alternatives for Nonstandard Speakers: A Sociolinguistic Perspective," a mimeographed report. Washington, D.C.: Center for Applied Linguistics, 1970. (a)

Wolfram, Walt "Sociolinguistic Implications for Educational Sequencing," in Ralph Fasold and Roger Shuy (Eds.), *Teaching Standard English in the Inner City*. Washington, D.C.: Center for Applied Linguistics, 1970. (b)

A TEACHING STRATEGY

Mildred R. Gladney

Many of the ideas discussed here were presented by Roger Shuy in the preceding paper. These ideas concern the development of a reading program for Black primary students in a poor community in Chicago. The group which developed this program included an educational psychologist, three Black primary classroom teachers, and a student of linguistics. I was one of the classroom teachers.

We began our work in 1964 in a search for materials that we hoped would be more effective in teaching beginning readers in a school in a Black community. Although we were influenced by new insights and information obtained from reading the works of linguists, we relied primarily upon our background, training, and experience as teachers for our initial assumptions and direction. We knew, for example, that the children we were working with spoke and used the English language, albeit one of the varieties of that language. We knew that they articulated ideas and feelings adequately and, as a group of learners, were neither verbally deprived nor verbally deficient. We knew that they *could* learn to read, and that their failure to do this was, in part, because of our failure to use the right methods and/or materials. Most importantly, we knew that our negative attitudes toward their learning abilities had a deleterious effect on their classroom achievement. Thus, in many respects we did not communicate with, or adequately understand our pupils.

The following exchange is an example of the kind of communication gap I am talking about. In a conversation with a group of kindergartners, a little girl told us that when her mother had to go out she had to stay with her baby brother and sister. When I said, "You take care of those babies by yourself?"; Robin answered, "No, one of 'em not." (Meaning, "No, one of them is not a baby.") Robin's answer suggests that she was responding to a concern that she (a young child) had a responsibility beyond her years, that of taking care of babies. It also suggests that her reaction was to a negative signal (criticism of her mother), rather than a positive one (you're a capable girl). Fortunately, I understood this, but instead of responding to all of her explanation, I only responded to her words by saying, "Is not a baby?" Robin either misunderstood my "modeling" the "correct" form, or disregarded it as not being relevant, and proceeded to strengthen her original explanation, "They both not." And then after a pause she said, "When my mama come back I could go outside."

In our exchange, Robin and I were voicing different concerns. At first I responded to *what* she said, then to the *form* she used. She, in turn, was responding to what I *implied*.

We determined, therefore, that in order to become more alert to the Black child's concerns, the reading program we developed should reflect his language and life experiences. Thus, we decided to develop reading materials which incorporated the grammar of Black children, Roger Shuy's fourth alternative (*see p. 56*).

We also wanted to help the children learn to recognize other dialects of English, and to show them how to practice these dialects in their own speech. To accomplish this end, we decided to focus on verb form differences between the child's dialect and the "standard" dialect, and to use the labels *Everyday Talk* and *School Talk* to help the child distinguish between the two.

We chose to use regular orthography because the stories we wrote would be taken from the conversations we had with the children, and, thus, differences in pronunciation would not present a problem. Besides, the problems of trying to represent phonological aspects of dialect in print are formidable, and, in accordance with much modern linguistic insight, unnecessary.

We agreed only to use idioms which we felt were common to all speakers who might be using these books. Thus, we did not use "There goes a piece of paper," for "There is a piece of paper."

We were aware that the children understood the concepts of past, present, future, pluralization, and negation; but that their forms indicating these concepts differed from the standard forms. Thus, our approach was to introduce the standard form as an additional way of getting their message across.

As already indicated, we concentrated on verb forms. In our materials, Everyday Talk is characterized by:

1. the lack of /s/ with third person singular verbs

2. lack of -*ed* as a past tense marker

3. elision of *be* forms (e.g., "She my momma.")

4. use of *ain't* (mostly because the children themselves discount *ain't* as "correct")

5. the use of *have* and *do* with third person singular verbs

6. the use of *was* with second person singular and all plural subjects

School Talk uses the standard English forms.

The child is required to recognize one language form from the other, but outside of the lesson period (reading or oral language) is not required to use one or the other.

In one of the reading stories, for example, the child reads, "Yesterday I help my daddy paint." In the standardized version of the same story, the sentence is written, "Yesterday I helped my daddy paint." The child is made to note the printed *ed* and is told that in School Talk this indicates that the action took place in the past. He is encouraged to pronounce it when he reads it; and the teacher acts as his model for pronunciation.

An example from an oral language lesson is the following: The teacher tells the children, "Suppose the landlord comes to your door and asks for your mother, but she isn't home. What do you say to him? How do you tell the landlord your mother isn't home?" At our first use of this question in the classroom we received these responses from the children: "She ain't here"; "She not home"; "She isn't here"; and "She's not here." We told the children that these were all ways of saying the same thing. We then labeled the responses as either Everyday Talk or School Talk. Some were labeled both: "She isn't"; and "She's not home."

THE READING MATERIALS

Our first reading materials were mimeographed pages stapled together and illustrated by the children. The stories were typed with a primary typewriter. As indicated in the following illustration, blank lines for either the child's entire sentence or for his completion of a sentence were part of the "text." The emphasis was upon the child and his language. Our present books have these features also.

The child's involvement in the development of the reading process is emphasized in the earlier books by allowing them to draw their own illustrations as well as to provide their own text. Later, illustrations are

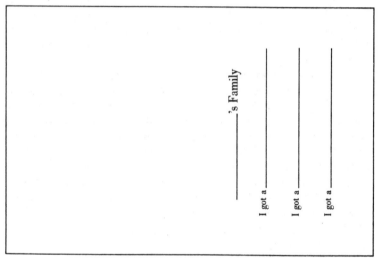

Sample pages[1] from a reader developed for Black primary students.

[1] From pp. 19 and 21 of *All About Me* (Book 1), Psycholinguistics Reading Series. Developed by O. J. Davis, M. R. Gladney, and L. Leaverton. Copyright © 1968 by the Board of Education of the City of Chicago and reproduced with their permission. Note: in the book *All About Me* p. 21 is not illustrated. This is a sample drawing by a five-and-a-half-year-old Black child from a poor community in Cambridge, Mass.

provided by means of realistic photographs of Black families, or drawings by Black artists; and the text is more ours than theirs, while still keeping their speech patterns in mind. The following examples of comparable Everyday Talk and School Talk stories do not appear here as they do in the books, where they would occupy several pages, but are offered for comparison of the different syntactic patterns:

SCHOOL TALK	EVERYDAY TALK
My Family	My Family
I have a mama.	I got a mama.
I have a daddy.	I got a daddy.
I have a mama and a daddy.	I got a mama and a daddy.
I have a brother.	I got a brother.
I have a sister.	I got a sister.
I have a brother and a sister.	I got a brother and a sister.
I have a grandmama.	I got a grandmama.

SCHOOL TALK	EVERYDAY TALK
Stop That!	Stop That!
When I talk, my teacher says, Stop that!	When I be talking, my teacher say, Stop that!
When I run, my teacher says, Stop that!	When I be running, my teacher say, Stop that!
When I fight, my teacher says, Stop that!	When I be fighting, my teacher say, Stop that!
No talking!	No talking!
No running!	No running!
No fighting!	No fighting!
What a school.	What a school.

In the last book, which focuses on famous Black Americans, the child chooses the standardized verb form:

GWENDOLYN BROOKS

Gwendolyn Brooks _____ a famous Afro-American poet.
She _____ in Chicago.
She _____ very good poems.
She _____ prizes.
_____ can read her poems to us.

It is good that the teacher become familiar with the works of those contemporary Black writers who switch from dialect to dialect, and from word form to word form, so that she can point out these instances to her pupils as examples of "funny" patterns in print. For often a child will balk at an Everyday Talk sentence by saying that it sounds funny. The teacher should immediately give the child the School Talk story and have him compare the two stories and determine the difference. By being able to show the child the Everyday Talk forms in print as used by Black writers, the teacher gives dignity and validity to the alternate forms of the language.

THE ORAL LANGUAGE PROGRAM

The oral language activities were developed in the classroom from input from the children as we asked them questions, or told them stories to which they would respond, using the verb form which paralleled the standardized form we wished to introduce.

The oral language lesson follows this procedure: the teacher introduces the School Talk pattern if none is given by the child, the teacher agrees with the child that a standardized form can be Everyday Talk or School Talk, but insists that the nonstandard forms are Everyday Talk alone. (The teacher must be careful not to confuse immature speech or simple mistakes by the children with Everyday Talk.)

Practice activities include drill on what we call *word partners*, that is, pronoun-verb fit. For example, we tell the children that, in School Talk, *I* goes with *am; he, she,* and *it* go with *is*; and *we, you* and *they* go with *are*. They practice saying:

I am	you are
he is	we are
she is	they are
it is	

The teacher makes a game of it, letting the children use various ways of practicing, including using the partners in sentences.

THE COMMUNITY'S REACTION

The community's reaction to the kind of language programs we are discussing here is, of course, of great concern to both educators and linguists. There are varied responses within the Black community to the subject of dialects, the terminology used to describe them (e.g., Black English), and, particularly, to their use in the schools. Many Black people (including children) agree that there is such a thing as a Black dialect. One of the first-graders that we discussed textbook stories with said that an Afro-American child pictured in the illustration was different from Sally (of Dick, Jane, and Sally fame) because "She don't talk like Sally." But the disagreement as to the status of Black English and how it should be treated by the schools is marked. Some comments of Black people illustrating this diversity of opinion follow.

In some, we find a flat rejection of the standardized dialect. Carolyn Rodgers, a poet and essayist says (1970):

> All Black writers in America write in a language that is often called English. It is a lot like English. . . . Because English words have European meanings, writers have a difficult task. The words are a *form* of the oppressor. At an early age, we learn to associate words with various forms of oppression. Thus the college student who left home talking mush-mouth/African tonal, and returns talking "better English," becomes the tool of the system through the sounds he makes which are of an alien oppressive culture. Consequently, you find that many Black people sneer at—or detest—the Black who speaks with the oppressor's accent. That Black has become the Black colonizer. His value system speaks through his tongue. He has erased the tonal range of feeling which speaks in African through English words—not words but sounds, or a reconstructed order of words. Black writers must not use the colonizer's language as it exists [pp. 5–11].

In a somewhat similar vein, we hear from Kenneth Johnson, a Black educator-linguist, a characterization (1970) of the uniqueness of the Black dialect:

> This idea that nonstandard Negro dialect is sloppy (and the way to speak it is with "lazy lips and lazy tongues") has caused some people to think that in order to talk the way many Black people talk, all one has to do is to "mess up the English language" (leave off a few inflectional endings, don't have subject-verb agreement, etc.) and pronounce the words. This is false. In order to speak nonstandard Negro dialect, one must know its phonological and grammatical systems. In other words, one must know precisely what to do with certain phonological and grammatical features of standard English. Not many people are aware of this, consequently,

few people outside the black subculture can speak the nonstandard Negro dialect *correctly*.

On the other hand, many, if not most, parents—particularly those from the much maligned Black middle class—reject the language of their group, saying that the poor Black child needs to learn the standardized dialects as well as to learn to develop and expand his own:

> One parent said to me, "One thing I don't like about the schools. You don't teach our children to talk good English."

> Another, while emphasizing the need for a child to learn correct English, said, "I always be telling my son not to say *ain't*."

The feeling of this group of parents (and teachers) is that the Black child will be disadvantaged enough by racism, and need not be further penalized by being denied the basic tools his competitors and opponents receive.

A final view (1968) of the relationship between dialects is that of Juanita Williamson, a Black linguist who, having studied the speech patterns of a group of Black Tennessee youth, contends that their dialect is not Black, but Southern:

> The phonological system of the students' speech is the same as that found in the Southern area. The phonemic system is the same as that of standard Southern speech. Almost all of the vowel phonemes have diphthongal allophones. This is one of the characteristics of Southern speech. A few allophones of the vowel phonemes occur chiefly in substandard speech. The incidence of the phonemes in their speech is generally the same as that found in standard Southern speech. In some instances, however, the incidence is like that found in substandard Southern speech or substandard American speech in general.

> The grammatical patterns found in the speech of the level III students (above average academic achievement) are generally those found in standard English. A number of the patterns found in the speech of level I and II students (below average and average academic achievement) occur chiefly in substandard English. Two forms used by them, the singular possessive noun form which is identical with the base form of the noun and the plural possessive pronoun for *they*, are not mentioned in any study of substandard speech consulted. The zero copula which is found in their speech may occur in the Southern mountain area.

In spite of this variety of opinion on the subject of Black dialect itself, and the equal variety of opinion (mostly negative) upon the question of its use in the schools, we gained support for our programs mostly because the parents of our pupils knew us and had confidence in our sincerity and our interest in their children. Those who were disturbed could easily reach us to find out just what we were doing. Many accepted our approach because they understood that we did use and teach standard patterns, too.

In recruiting teachers and classes to use the materials, we were frank in our discussions with Black faculty and parents as to why we developed the programs and why we attempted to introduce the programs into the schools. We described our thinking, the changes we went through, and why we were sold on what we had done. As the programs expand slowly in the public schools of Chicago, those teachers who use the materials also (for the most part) will gain the trust of the parents of their pupils.

EVALUATION

In evaluating the programs to teachers and parents, we pointed out that our primary goals were to teach the child how to read and to introduce standard English as an additional dialect. We weren't concerned about the length of time it took the child to do either, but more that the experience made sense to him and maintained his sense of achievement. Our program consisted of a series of eight books which increase in complexity, but we did not have any "rating" of these books according to standard basal reader grade levels. The following information is only suggestive of the relative success of the program, and is certainly not offered as convincing "proof" that our program is superior.

Of 80 children, divided among four classes which had started the program eighteen months previously, the following breakdown shows into what level these children moved after having completed our program:

> 7 were in primers
> 28 were in 1st-grade readers (either 1^1 or 1^2)
> 30 were in 2^1 level readers
> 15 were in 2^2 level readers

A controlled comparison involved three classes of children who measured "Not read" on the Metropolitan Reading Readiness Test. One of these classes of children (21 pupils) was placed in our program. The other two classes (18 pupils, and 20 pupils) went into a "standard" reading readiness program and on into preprimers and basals. At the end of two years, the classes compare as follows:

Experimental Group	Control 1 (18)	Control 2 (20)
2—preprimer	1—reading readiness	3—preprimer
3—primer	4—preprimer	5—primer
3—basal 1	2—primer	12—basal 1
8—basal 2^1	5—basal 1	
5—basal 2^2	6—basal 2^1	

In addition, the teachers who used our program were particularly pleased with the kind and amount of original writing done by the children.

More subjective is the evaluation of the success of the oral language program. We define mastery of School Talk as (1) the child's recognition of the standardized patterns as such and (2) the child's use of the standardized forms when asked to do so. Every lesson includes this kind of "testing"; and it is evident to the teacher who can and who can't. Most of our "evidence" of the value of the lessons on School Talk is anecdotal. For example, a second grade class was preparing to go on a field trip. One of the girls told one of the boys, "Now be sure to use School Talk when we ask questions." The third grade teacher of a girl who had been with us her first two years of school remarked how unusually well this child spoke, and how she talked with pride of her former School Talk lessons.

The number of teachers in the Chicago public schools who want to use the materials is growing slowly. At least fifty teachers are using the program now. A large number of them are enthusiastic about the materials. They say that they are more comfortable in using the children's language and ideas now, and are more confident of the children's ability to learn and to achieve. They are more sensitive to the children's language and listen to them more. They give the children many more opportunities to write their own stories for reading materials and feel freer to accept the writing without correcting "mistakes." Those who feel strongly that the children must learn standard English are pleased with the approach of going from the child's pattern to the standardized pattern. Finally, they are very pleased with the children's reactions to the content of the stories, the vocabulary, and the reflection of themselves in the stories.

We are pleased at the results. We know full well that these programs are not *the* answer to the language problems of the schools, but we feel that they definitely suggest a way.

REFERENCES

Davis, Olga J., Gladney, Mildred R., and Leaverton, Lloyd *The Psycholinguistics Reading Series.* Chicago: Board of Education, 1969.

Gladney, Mildred R. and Leaverton, Lloyd "A Model for Teaching Standard English to Non-Standard English Speakers," *Elementary English,* 1968, *45,* 758–763.

Johnson, Kenneth R. "False Assumptions Teachers Make about Nonstandard Negro Dialect." Paper presented at the TESOL Convention, San Francisco, March, 1970.

Leaverton, Lloyd, Gladney, Mildred R., Hoffman, Melvin J., Patterson, Zoreda R., and Davis, Olga J. *Psycholinguistics Oral Language Program: A Bi-Dialectal Approach.* Chicago: Board of Education, 1969.

Rodgers, Carolyn M. "The Literature of Black," *Black World 1970, 19* (9), 5–11.

Williamson, Juanita "The Speech of Negro High School Students in Memphis, Tennessee." Final Report, June 30, 1968, Project 5–0592–2–12–1, USDHEW, Office of Education, Bureau of Research.

Williamson, Juanita "A Look at Black English," *The Crisis,* 1971, *78* (6), 169–173, 185.

FOR FURTHER READING

Baratz, Joan C. and Shuy, Roger W. (Eds.) *Teaching Black Children to Read*. Washington, D.C.: Center for Applied Linguistics, 1969.

A collection of articles on the special problems and techniques involved in teaching reading to children whose linguistic system is measurably different from middle-class children of other races.

Fasold, Ralph W. and Shuy, Roger W. (Eds.) *Teaching Standard English in the Inner-City*. Washington, D.C.: Center for Applied Linguistics, 1970.

A collection of articles on the special problems involved in teaching standard speech to nonstandard speakers, including sections on the linguistic features to be taught, methods of determining degrees of cruciality of the stigmatized features, and suggestions for revising teacher training programs.

Labov, William *The Study of Non-Standard English*. Washington, D.C.: Center for Applied Linguistics, 1969. Available through National Council of Teachers of English, Urbana, Illinois.

Presents a concise, readable report of research methods and results, and of some basic features of nonstandard English.

FOUR · THE NATURE OF

THE WRITING SYSTEM

An underlying theme of the papers presented in the preceding sections is that language is a system. To acquire and use language, a child *must* understand the rules which govern that system. The way a child speaks and interprets language expresses how well he understands these rules.

In making the point that language is rule-governed, the foregoing papers have focused primarily on *spoken* language. However, reading involves the processing of written expressions of language and also is governed by rules.

Methods of reading instruction are inherently based upon theoretical views about the nature of the rules that govern the written code. Some reading programs are developed out of the belief that there are systematic relationships between the graphic symbols of writing and the vocal symbols of speech. These programs place a heavy emphasis on phonics, or letter/sound relationships. Other reading programs, however, strongly emphasize whole-word analysis, or "look-say" methods, and generally have their basis in the belief that few useful relationships exist between graphic symbol and spoken sound.

In recent years, linguists, and other interested researchers who study our written code, have illuminated the basically systematic nature of English spelling. As is the case in other areas of language study, theories held by researchers have influenced the manner in which the relationships between spoken and written expressions of the language are described.

In the two papers that follow, the authors discuss fundamental insights of the systematic nature of the rules which govern our writing system and apply this information to reading. Both authors have extensive backgrounds in teaching and in language research. Professor Paul David Allen, of the University of Missouri at Kansas City, is a former classroom teacher whose doctoral research at Wayne State University involved a study of reading miscues (these are discussed in depth in Section VI). He has a deep interest in the education of children and teachers. Dr. Sarah Gudschinsky, an educator and linguist, is Literacy Coordinator of the Summer Institute of Linguistics, based in Santa Ana, California. The Institute is dedicated to the promotion of literacy throughout the world.

Allen and Gudschinsky focus on the theme that a writing system only partially represents speech. To them, writing is also a specialized medium for the transmission of information through visual means, and has its own stylistic characteristics which distinguish it from spoken forms of communication. Viewed in this way, to regard a writing system solely as a set of relationships between alphabet letters and speech sounds is a misconception. Writing, say both authors, is much more than simply "talk written down," and, in his paper, Allen dispels a number of misconceptions about the writing system which have long been a part of the lore about writing.

Gudschinsky's paper presents an analysis of writing systems which emanates from a theory of language called Tagmemics. This theory views language as an interrelated, three-leveled hierarchy of phonology (sound), lexicon (word), and grammar. Gudschinsky discusses the implications of the Tagmemic view of the writing system for reading instruction. Her scholarly presentation demands careful reading in order to fully appreciate the wealth of linguistic information that she presents. As does Allen, Gudschinsky asserts that reading should be taught in relation to natural speech. Both authors also believe that the syntax of most beginning reading texts overlooks the fact that young readers bring to the reading situation a reservoir of knowledge about language. (Frank Smith succinctly points this out in Section II.)

WHAT TEACHERS OF READING

SHOULD KNOW ABOUT

THE WRITING SYSTEM

Paul David Allen

Writing is often referred to as "talk written down." This rather simplistic explanation of the writing system is but one of several misconceptions that many of us hold. The purpose of this paper will be to examine some of these misconceptions in the light of more recent evidence provided by linguists and educators in this field, and to present what is generally believed to be known today about the writing system of English. We shall also look at some of the implications this knowledge has for teachers of reading.

Some of the misconceptions to be examined are:

1. Writing is just talk written down.

2. The conventions of the English writing system embody some universally valid canons of logic.

3. The spelling system of English
   a. is riddled with inconsistencies;

   b. in order to be an optimal system for the lexical representation of English words, should have complete letter-to-sound or grapheme-phoneme correspondence;

   c. contains only letter/sound relations as the most important information available to the reader.

IS WRITING JUST TALK WRITTEN DOWN?

Whether or not writing is talk written down is dictated by circumstances, the purposes for the writing, and the reader for whom the writing is intended. A personal letter from a boy in Vietnam to his girl stateside will be quite different from the business letter the office of

87

admissions will send to an aspiring graduate student. If that graduate student makes it, his spontaneous written exams will differ considerably from his term papers. My wife's grocery list has meaning only for me (most of the time) while my hastily jotted notes can only be understood by her (part of the time).

Many of us have had the experience of seeing a typescript of an informal talk we have given, transcribed from a tape recording made by some obliging student. I have; and my first reaction is always, "I couldn't have said that, or at least not in that way." We all know that informal speech written down looks terrible, or at least mine does. There are those fortunate individuals who, as a seven-year-old acquaintance of mine says, "talk like a book," but most of us do not, or, for that matter, would not care to.

When we write, however, we sometimes do want to talk more like a book. Written English is often more precise than speech. Written English is sometimes more restrained and compact. Written English is often carefully edited. Words and phrases are carefully chosen, metaphors are carefully selected. We write and rewrite. Past (1970) has stated that Hemingway rewrote the final page of A Farewell to Arms thirty-nine times and when asked what technical problem had stumped him, Hemingway replied, "Getting the words right."

Perhaps Papa Hemingway's reply is deliciously simple to the young student of writing, but it is possible that much more was involved than "just getting the words right." Construction, or syntax, or style was as great a consideration as the right words. Still another reason why writing is different from speech is that the writer employs many forms of English that are different from speech. It is doubtful, for instance, that any of us has uttered a sentence in the passive. Yet, we use the passive frequently in our writing, to the extent that much of scholarly writing, including that graduate student's writing mentioned above, can often be referred to as the "massive passive."

The writing of this paper for the purposes of a speech offered the writer several options. He could make an outline, some brief notes, and speak from "the top of his head." There, he might run the risk of receiving the inevitable typescript with all of those mazes, pauses, and regressions. Or, he could choose to make his paper very formal and precise at the risk of losing some of his audience to other mental pursuits. He chose, however, to make it somewhat informal. In preparing the presentation for publication it was necessary to rewrite it, to tighten it, and in some respects to strip it of many of the personal attributes the paper originally contained. It's unfortunate, in a way, because the author's words are important to him; but, in the long run, he must consider that the specific purpose of the paper is to inform, rather than to entertain.

However, there was a much more legitimate reason for choosing the informal format. The reason is that the paper was read and the role of the audience was basically that of a listener rather than that of a reader, and therein lies a matter of major importance. The listening process is quite a different matter from the reading process. In reading, confusing sentences may be reread, unfamiliar words can be looked up in a dictionary, and the whole procedure can be interrupted if the reader wishes to step out for a cup of coffee.

Listening requires a different set of skills. Attention is prerequisite to understanding what is being said; and, indeed, immediate reactions to what is being said may have much to do with the way in which the speaker proceeds. If there are areas of the speech that need to be clarified, there will probably be an opportunity to have them clarified later. Although a listener may leave for a cup of coffee, when he returns, he will have missed a great deal of what was said. After all, one of the purposes of conferences is to provide opportunities for personal interaction and the exchange of ideas. If this were not the case, it would be much easier and inexpensive to bind the conference proceedings in a tidy volume and mail them to all of the registered participants.

If indeed writing is not always talk written down, of what importance is this to the teacher of reading?

First, we need to be aware of the various modes of writing and the reading strategies needed to accommodate these modes. For example, Wardhaugh (1969) points out that "the language of poetry is deviant, in the sense that it varies from a norm of some kind. . . . and to understand the language of poetry, it is necessary to know how that language varies from normal language [p. 78]." Goodman (1969) indicates that "literary prose employs structures and language devices differently from common language [p. 23]." The same could be said of the various kinds of instructional and informative materials children will come in contact with as they read in order to learn about their world. Obviously, the written language of a science text will differ from the written language of a social studies text. Similarly, a trade book on insects will probably be organized somewhat differently from a chapter on insects in a science text. The recipe or science experiment requires a set of reading strategies quite different from those needed for interpreting a newspaper editorial. Finally, the language of a "classic" in children's literature will differ considerably from that in a contemporary offering. If we believe, as Goodman (1969) states, that the "development of reading competence is best achieved when the learner's focus is on the content of materials and not reading itself [p. 22]" then we need to know considerably more about the nature of this content, particularly in regards to the ways it varies from normal or common language.

Although some arguments have been presented as to why writing isn't always talk written down, do we need to ask the question, "Should, at some point, writing closely resemble talk written down?" The point in mind here is at the beginning reading stages. Surely, few of us would say that the language found in most primers is talk written down, or for that matter that the language found in most experience charts—the teacher-written record of a child's orally dictated story—is talk written down. Educators and linguists generally agree that whatever is used for beginning reading instruction should be real language, but how closely this language should parallel or mirror the language of the child is a matter to be carefully investigated.

For example, the concern for controlled vocabulary, sentence length, the number of running words on a page, and so forth, will have some effect on the fact of whether the language used in beginning readers is real language or not. Such are the concerns of an author of a basal pre-primer. But also as great are the concerns of a teacher who, with the best intentions, will say to a child who has just given her a sentence for an experience chart, "Can't you say that in another way?" or worse perhaps, "Can't you say that in a better way?" The revised sentence is no longer the child's, and in some ways the whole value or purpose of the experience chart may have been lost.

THE CONVENTIONS OF THE WRITING SYSTEM

The second misconception, the notion that the conventions of writing embody some universally valid canons of logic, was borrowed from Bloomfield's (1933) description of the prescriptive linguist's attitude toward the structure of Latin. The phrase overstates the writer's point, but it is a point to be aware of. Simply stated, the writing system of English represents many arbitrary decisions made during its development by scribes, printers, and typesetters. According to Huey's 1908 interesting discussion of the evolution of the printed page, such decisions concerned direction, word spacing, and other conventions such as paragraph separation, division of words at the end of the line, punctuation, and quotation marks. For example, we know that ancient men have written and read in all conceivable directions. Early Greeks read from right to left, later from right to left in the first line and then from left to right in the second line and so forth. Even the characters faced in the direction in which the reading was done. Later the reading went from left to right and then right to left in the second line and so forth. Finally the system used today evolved.

Huey also states (1908) that the practice in "Greek and Latin literary texts was usually to write continuously without spaces or other divisions between the words [p. 237]," and "when the separation of the words gradually appeared, the prepositions were still attached to their related word, and there was always a tendency to detach a final letter and to attach it to the following word [p. 233]." By the eleventh century, a system of separately written words was established.

These and other developments that Huey (1908) and Gelb (1963) discuss at length are more than a matter of historical interest. Surely, teachers aware of these developments will approach some aspects of beginning reading much differently. Surely, the manner in which they treat aspects of directionality, word introduction, word identification, and other conventions in writing will be tempered by the awareness of these developments. For instance, the writer has noticed that his thirteen-month-old son, who recently started feeding himself, moves across the three-sectioned feeding dish from right to left, following the pattern established by his mother who moved in a left-to-right pattern facing him. Reversing the dish or the order of the food (meat, vegetables, fruit) had little effect on his learned pattern of right to left. When we read to our son from one of his little cloth books, he is just as likely to start looking at the pictures on the right hand page as those on the left hand page. These left to right patterns will have to be learned by him, hopefully, by being read to over a period of years. One of our subjects in the reading miscue research at Wayne State University insisted on holding his book sideways when he read, and during one session he was even observed reading upside down. It was later discovered that the boy's father read aloud to the children in the family while they sat around him in a semi-circle, and our subject's place was always to the side, so he was facing the book from the side, and was used to following along in that position. This learned pattern was carried over to the school situation. Huey (1908) refers to the reading habit as an "unnatural one, intensely artificial in many respects [p. 8]." If this is the case, we need to understand what "habits" need to be learned.

Take the concept "word," for example. The writer has often seen first graders count the letters of a word when asked how many words the teacher is pointing to. This was not unlike Bill Cosby's kindergarten experience when after learning that one plus one equals two, he asked "What's a two?" We need to look seriously at the way we introduce the child to print, to the available information on the page, and the best way for him to process that information to get meaning. We need to ask if our concentration on words, or smaller parts of words in beginning reading, or at any stage of reading for that matter, is the best way for us to proceed. Kolers (1969) suggests that instruction in reading "tends to preserve the historical sequence of literary development of a system for phonetic transcription. There is no reason in principle that requires that the sequence of instruction follow the analytical sequence of development and discovery from letters and their sounds, then to phrases, and finally to meaning [p. 15]." In fact, he feels that "this developmental sequence of phonetic transcription actually violates the historical sequence of linguistic representation [p. 15]."

Huey also raises an interesting point concerning the fact that most experimentation with print ceased with the invention of the printing press, and that the printed page has changed little in the last 500 years. Few of us concerned with the teaching of reading have concerned ourselves with experimentation with the printed page, changing it so that the reader, in Huey's (1908) words, could read "with one-fourth of the eyework required by the page of the present [p. 11]," or trying other creative approaches that might make learning to read and reading itself a much easier task. The mind boggles as to what might have been or what could be.

THE SPELLING SYSTEM OF ENGLISH

The spelling system of English has been under attack for years by such distinguished opponents as George Bernard Shaw and Sir James Pitman. To make his point, Shaw used the now famous spelling *ghoti* to spell *fish*.[1] Actually, it was a poor choice since it is impossible for this arrangement of letters to represent the sounds in *fish* in our orthography. More about this later. The efforts of Sir James Pitman can presently be seen in the initial teaching alphabet (i.t.a.) he constructed. The i.t.a. ostensibly matches each speech sound with its own unique graphic symbol. It is now receiving some measure of acceptance in elementary schools across the country as a beginning reading approach.

However, linguists today are telling us that traditional orthography (t.o.) is not all that bad. According to Chomsky and Halle (1968) in their book *The Sound Pattern of English*, ". . . English orthography, despite its often cited inconsistencies, comes remarkably close to being an optimal orthographic system for English [p. 49]."

It would seem that a major hang-up with us regarding English orthography in relation to reading is an insistence on grapheme-phoneme correspondence. Adherence to this insistence has naturally led to the often cited inconsistencies. Wardhaugh has traced the problems linguists have had over the years in their procedures for phonemicization. Many linguists generally have not been concerned with grammatical and lexical information in these procedures, and have insisted that statements about the phonemic system of a language should make reference only to phonemic information. Such a view, according to Wardhaugh (1969), has "been dominant in American linguistics until very recently and has been behind nearly all work conducted so far into grapheme-phoneme correspondences [p. 102]."

Much of the early *influence* linguistics had on reading instruction was based on grapheme-phoneme correspondence and led to several reading series with "linguistic labels." An evaluation of such series is not the purpose of this paper; yet, it can be said that one effect these series have had on reading instruction has been to focus on a more legitimate method of teaching phonics. Obviously, many people in reading feel that this is not enough and that linguistics has much more to offer the field of reading than just the concept of grapheme-phoneme correspondence.

Actually, linguists have begun to look at phonemic theory in other ways. Weir and Venezky, in fact, entitled a paper (1968) on the subject,

[1] Editors' note: In this example, Shaw maintained that *ghoti* was an equally logical spelling of *fish*, since *gh* represents an /f/ in *rough*, *o* represents an /i/ in *women*, and *ti* represents a /sh/ in *nation*.

"English Orthography—More Reason Than Rhyme." This paper cleverly shifts the emphasis from spelling-to-sound to other concerns. Venezky sums up their position in this manner:

> Whatever may have been the relationship between writing and sound when the first Old English writings were inscribed in Latin script and whatever may have been the reason for the subsequent development of this system, be they due to random choice or to an all pervading National Orthographic Character, the simple fact is that the present orthography is not merely a letter-to-sound system riddled with imperfections, but, instead a more complex and more regular relationship wherein phoneme and morpheme share leading roles [p. 77].

What emerges from Venezky's work in this area, and also in Chomsky and Halle's work in *The Sound Pattern of English,* is that a native speaker of English brings certain phonological habits or rules to the task of pronouncing words in English and that where these rules are applicable, phonetic variation is not indicated in the orthography. Consequently, in the areas of stress placement, and regular vowel and consonant alternations, the orthography remains constant. We know that *sane* becomes *sanity,* that *crime* becomes *criminal,* and that *deduce* becomes *deduction.* In each of these examples, the same orthographic symbol is used to represent both vowel sounds. This is also true in some consonant alternation patterns such as *damn/damnation,* and *design/designate;* where the *n,* and *g* are "silent" in the base form, but are pronounced in the derived form. Stress placement and vowel reduction are generally not reflected in the orthography either.

If we examine the spelling system from a morphophonemic point of view, other factors concerning spelling-to-sound relationships emerge. Several factors may determine the correspondence of a spelling unit. Position alone may determine choice of spelling. For example, initial *gh* always corresponds to /g/ as in *ghastly* and *ghetto,* and never to /f/, as in the previously mentioned *ghoti.* Stress may also play a prominent role in determining spelling-to-sound correspondence. The *x* in *ex'pert* and *expert'* are different; x = /ks/, in the first, and x = /gz/ in the second. Generally speaking, the retention of the medial /h/ depends upon the position of the main word stress, as in *prohi'bit* and *prohibi'tion,* *ve'hicle, vehi'cular.*

There are also morphemic features to be considered in spelling-to-sound correspondences. Morpheme boundaries need to be known in order to predict certain correspondences. The *th*'s in the sentence *Your father is a fathead* have quite different correspondences. The *th* in *father* corresponds to /ð/ because it lies within a single graphemic allomorph, while the *th* in *fathead* is treated as separate letters because two morphemes are involved and morpheme boundaries are crossed. This is also true of the spelling *ph* as in *phone* or *Philadelphia* as opposed to *upheaval*. Morpheme boundaries are also involved in such words as *finger, anger, anchor*, where the spelling *n* precedes spellings which correspond to /g/ or /k/.

This leads to another consideration, that of form class. Consider the following words: *singer, swinger, longer, longest*. The spelling *ng* plus -*er* comparative or -*est* superlative is pronounced differently in most dialects of English than the spelling *ng* plus -*er* agent. Another example of form class identity involves the pronunciation of initial *th*. Functors such as *the, that, them* have the voiced interdental spirant /ð/ while contentives such as *thicket, theory, thermal* have the voiceless spirant /θ/.

One other often cited example of the morphophonemic basis of the orthography should be mentioned here. Consider the inflections for the plural marking of nouns and the third person and past markings of verbs.

PLURAL	THIRD PERSON SINGULAR	PAST TENSE
figs	he drags	he looked
pots	he drips	he closed
judges	he judges	he sounded

The plural of nouns and the third person singular of verbs are marked by *s*, but the plural morpheme and the third person singular morpheme have three different allomorphs: {s}, {z}, and {əz}. The past tense morpheme also has three allomorphs: {t}, {d}, and {əd}. The important point here is that any native speaker of English intuitively makes the allomorphic distinction.

One of the implications to be gained from an understanding of the spelling system is the fact that many of the examples discussed in this section represent patterns which result from English phonological habits. We need to differentiate between these patterns and those patterns based upon the orthography. After this is accomplished, the following steps may be needed:

1. Upon identifying the set of language habits a beginning reader brings to the task, we then can help him develop strategies that will make optimum use of these habits.

2. We can select out those patterns based upon the orthography that possibly need to be taught. Obviously, new information is needed by the beginning reader who encounters initial c in *circus* or *centipede* as opposed to initial c in *cotton* and *cat*. The way this is to be done is a pedagogical concern—for example, whether to use an inductive or a deductive approach.

3. We know that children form some spelling-to-sound generalizations while they are learning to read and continue to do so throughout their lifetime as the nature of their reading changes to meet their ever changing needs and interests. What we don't know is the nature of these generalizations, how they come about, and how they differ from one individual to another. We do know that children have learned their language by the time they enter school and that this entailed forming rather sophisticated generalizations on their part. This suggests a more productive kind of teaching, in the manner in which Emig (1967) defines *productive* as "helping the student extend the use of his native language in the most effective way [p. 607]."

4. An understanding of the spelling system of English should point out to us the rather shaky ground we trod on when we give children a strategy or generalization that just isn't reliable, such as looking for the little words in the big one, for example. However, the writer is not so sure that we should now formulate rules to give children based on what we know of morpheme boundaries.

5. It seems that the spelling system begins to appear more systematic only when we apply to it other criteria, such as grammatical and lexical information along with spelling-to-sound correspondences. In the broader view, is not this the whole business of teaching a child to read: to use all of the information available to him, in the most economical, productive manner, in order to gain meaning from the printed page?

This fact of a broader view of reading, in which the spelling system is but one component, is most important. For instance, we know that there are times when knowing how to pronounce the word isn't necessary at all. In her recent study, Burke (1969) found that her subjects seldom were able to pronounce correctly the word *ewe* in a story where the concept *ewe* was crucial to the understanding of the story. Yet, more of her subjects were able to say what a *ewe* was when questioned at the end of the story. Many of us probably have certain words that we often come across in our professional reading materials that we know the meaning of, yet rarely take the time to try to pronounce. *Paradigm* was such a word for the writer for several years. He was simply able to ascribe meaning to the word. He has no trouble with the pronunciation of *dyslexia.* It is possible for us to spend too much time and effort on the trees and miss the forest completely.

SUMMARY

In summary, it is necessary that we think of the writing system as but one component of a reading situation. The other two components are the writer and the reader. It would seem that the quality of reading, or the effectiveness of the reading, or the level of comprehension achieved by the reader will depend greatly on the interrelationship of these three components. Consider the following situations:

A teenager and an adult reading the Beatle song, *Morning Star*

A new-home owner and a lawyer reading the deed to the property

A German and an American reading *The Tin Drum*

A "hawk" and a "dove" reading a Nixon speech on Cambodia

The only constant in all of these situations is the writing system. We can only surmise about what information has passed from writer to reader. We can only guess at the emotions that have been stirred; and we can only conjecture about what influence the writer has had on the reader's opinions and future actions. Certainly the writing conventions, choice of words, and the grammatical structure will have some effect on the reader's understanding of what the writer is saying, but, in the final analysis, it will be necessary to consider the interrelationship of all three components.

Obviously, then, the printed page is only one of our concerns. Or rather, despite arguments to the contrary, the writer feels that print represents *more* than surface structure. Although the topic of deep structure has purposely been avoided in this paper, perhaps we ought to consider it for a moment. Wardhaugh (1969) states that ". . . it is at the level of deep structure that sentences actually must be interpreted, not at the level of surface structure [p. 67]"; and a little further on he states that, "sentences are perceived at the level of surface structure, but they are comprehended only at the level of deep structure [p. 68]." Surely, some of the author's research in oral reading miscues indicates that children are doing more than operating on the surface structure alone. Consider the following miscues:

    There's a lot
1. *There are lots* of things babies use

    What do you want?
2. *What can I do for you?*

      its   protects
3. Unless *it's* a mother *goat protecting* her young

    we'll   have
4. And *we'd* each *had* one helping of potato salad

The above miscues have high graphic similarity to the expected response. It would be misleading, however, to examine only these relationships. It is also important to note that the miscue must be examined in a broader context than just the word-to-word relationship. A word approach to the reading process could not account for the use of *we'll* and the subsequent choice of *have*. The reader must be operating at a level other than the surface structure. Thus, in closing, it would be appropriate to quote the title of Paul Kolers' (1969) article, "Reading is only Incidentally Visual."

REFERENCES

Allen, Paul D. *A Psycholinguistic Analysis of the Substitution Miscues of Selected Oral Readers in Grades Two, Four, and Six and the Relationship of these Miscues to the Reading Process: A Descriptive Study.* Unpublished doctoral dissertation, Wayne State University, 1969.

Bloomfield, Leonard   *Language,* New York: Henry Holt and Company, 1933.

Burke, Carolyn L.   *A Psycholinguistic Description of Grammatical Restructuring in the Oral Reading of a Selected Group of Middle School Children.* Unpublished doctoral dissertation, Wayne State University, 1969.

Chomsky, Noam, and Halle, Morris   *The Sound Pattern of English.* New York: Harper & Row, 1968.

Emig, Janet A.   "Language Learning and the Teaching Process," *Elementary English,* 1967, *44,* 602–608.

Fox, C. C.   "Picnic for Elmer," in Helen Robinson, et. al. (Eds.), *Open Highways.* Box 4, Curriculum Foundation Series. Chicago: Scott, Foresman and Company, 1965.

Gelb, I. J.   *A Study of Writing.* (2nd ed.) Chicago: University of Chicago Press, 1963.

Goodman, Kenneth   *Reading.* Unpublished Report to the N. C. T. E. Commission on the English Curriculum, 1969.

Hayes, W. D.   "My Brother is a Genius," in E. A. Betts and Carolyn Welch (Eds.), *Adventures Now and Then,* Book 6. (3rd ed.) Betts Basic Readers. New York: American Book, 1963.

Huey, E. B.   *The Psychology and Pedagogy of Reading.* New York: Macmillan, 1908. (Republished: Cambridge, Mass.: M.I.T. Press, 1968.)

Kolers, Paul A.   "Reading is Only Incidentally Visual," in K. Goodman and J. Fleming (Eds.), *Psycholinguistics and the Teaching of Reading.* Newark, Del.: International Reading Association, 1969.

Past, Ray   *Language As a Lively Art.* Dubuque, Iowa: William C. Brown Co., 1970.

Venezky, Richard L.   "English Orthography: Its Graphical Structure and Its Relation to Sound," *Reading Research Quarterly,* 1967, *2* (3), 75–105.

Wardhaugh, Ronald   *Reading: A Linguistic Perspective.* New York: Harcourt Brace Jovanovich, Inc., 1969.

Weir, Ruth H. and Venezky, Richard L.   "English Orthography—More Reason than Rhyme," in K. Goodman (Ed.), *The Psycholinguistic Nature of the Reading Process.* Detroit: Wayne State University Press, 1968.

THE NATURE OF

THE WRITING SYSTEM:

PEDAGOGICAL IMPLICATIONS

Sarah C. Gudschinsky

It is the purpose of this paper to sketch briefly the scope and variety of the relationships between language structure and the writing system, and to indicate some of the practical implications of these relationships for the teaching of beginning reading. No unified study has ever been made of all these aspects of the writing system, so that this material must be taken as programmatic—perhaps, as a series of working hypotheses for further research—rather than as a summary of completed work.

A writing system is a means of visual communication. It is analogous to, but not identical with, the system of oral communication on which it is based. Recent interest in the attempts to relate the underlying linguistic structure of the writing system to the teaching of reading has led to the use of the term *linguistic method*. Unfortunately, this term is often misused by those who are looking for a panacea. Even the genuine contributions of competent linguists have been narrowly conceived and incomplete. Fries (1962), Bloomfield and Barnhart (1961), and Hall (1961) have been primarily concerned with orthography as a representation of phonemes and have taken the orthographic word as the basic unit of reading instruction. Consequently, the reading programs developed from their linguistic materials focus almost exclusively on modified phonics methods or spelling methods. LeFevre (1964), on the other hand, in using the sentence as the primary meaningful unit is in danger of losing sight of the importance of the smaller units for the accurate decoding of written material. The reading models of Venezky and Calfee (1970), Carroll (1970), and Goodman (1968, 1969) stress the importance of grammatical as well as phonological factors in reading, but they have not yet been related to language structure and the writing system in any detailed way. Even Venezky's careful work on English orthography (1967) is limited to the relationships at the level of phoneme and morpheme.

The use of linguistic terminology in the following sections is based on the Tagmemic model of language structure (see Pike, 1966, 1967). In this model, phonology (sounds), lexicon (word forms), and grammar (syntactic arrangements) are seen as separate but interlocking hierarchies of language, while within each hierarchy are units which themselves are hierarchically arranged. For example, the grammar contains hierarchical units of word, phrase, clause, sentence, paragraph, and discourse levels.[1]

There are at least three aspects of the writing system that have important implications for the teaching of beginning reading:

1. It represents various levels of all three of the linguistic hierarchies incompletely, but in complex interrelationships.

2. It is artificially discrete and linear in its representation of units which in speech are fused, simultaneous, slurred, and embedded in larger structures.

3. It represents a wide range of regional and social dialects. These dialects include formal written styles that are rarely used in speech, and a vocabulary that is used with a uniformity which obscures its variations and is enormously larger than that used by any single individual.

The balance of this paper discusses each of these aspects, providing a brief sketch of the nature of the writing system, followed by a listing of the practical implications for the teaching of reading.

THE ORTHOGRAPHY REPRESENTS PHONOLOGY, LEXICON, AND GRAMMAR

An alphabetic writing system is traditionally assumed to be a more or less regular graphic representation of the phonemes of a language, with perhaps some special spellings to represent morphophonemic data. Actually, any orthography, and especially the English system, is much more than that. At every level, the lexical and grammatical hierarchies are represented, as well as the phonology. The interrelationships will be discussed here at four levels: (a) the level of the syllables, dissyllabic phonological units, and morphemes which may be the matrices of the basic spelling patterns; (b) the word level, including a consideration of

[1] Editors' note: See Carolyn Burke's paper in Section I, pp. 24–30 for an additional discussion of the interdependence of language elements.

word space, hyphen, apostrophe, and word level capitalization; (c) the sentence level, including a consideration of capitalization and punctuation; and (d) the paragraph and discourse levels marked by special spacing, titles, etc.

Syllable and Morpheme Level   It should be obvious that the graphic elements of English orthography—the alphabet letters and other graphic symbols such as punctuation marks—do not follow one another like beads on a string, but are interwoven within a matrix of surrounding language substance which may be a syllable, a dissyllabic sequence (couplet), or a morpheme or morpheme sequence. (See Venezky, 1967, for a study of some of these relationships.) The vowel contrasts in *lade* and *lad,* for example, are signaled by the presence of *e* in *lade* and its absence in *lad.* The same vowel contrast is signaled in *lady* and *laddie* by the "doubling" of consonant letters within a dissyllabic matrix. But, the contrasts in *sanest, sanity,* and *mannish* are intimately related to the morphemic structure of the words, and the specific suffixes involved. There are some sets of contrastive spellings of the same phonemes which provide for sets of homonyms that would be spelled alike in a strictly phonemic orthography (e.g., *pair, pear,* and *pare*).

Word Level   Similarly, word level orthographic symbols—word space itself, hyphen and apostrophe, and capitalization of specific words— represent grammar and lexicon as well as phonology. Word space is used to mark grammatical boundaries that have no necessary phonological correlates; for example, *the* and *to* in phrases such as *the great big dog* (pronounced *th' great big dog*) or *I want to go* (pronounced *I wanna go*). Among the uses of the hyphen are clues to pronunciation as in the contrast between *co-op* and *coop;* lexical contrast as in the difference between *refuse* and *re-fuse;* and the joining of a clause to function as a single "word" within another clause, as in *his I-don't-care-what-happens-to-you attitude.* An apostrophe, on the other hand, may mark either a grammatical boundary without a phonological correlate as in *mother's,* or a grammatical boundary obscured by a spelling based on the phonology, as in *I'm* or *don't.* The capital letters used on proper names or on pronouns referring to the Deity provide special lexical signals that are not directly related to either the phonology or the grammar.

Sentence Level   At sentence level, the capital letters and punctuation marks again represent phonological, grammatical, and lexical information. Probably the most basic use of these symbols is grammatical. Phonological hesitation phenomena may be marked by a dash, however; and hesitation or uncertainty may be indicated with a question mark where there is no grammatical question. Also at this level, there are special uses of such graphic symbols as parentheses, semicolons, and colons, as conventions of formal written styles.

Paragraph and Discourse Levels   The relationship of the linguistic levels above the sentence to the writing system is usually ignored completely. (In fact, some linguistic models make no provision for even the linguistic study of paragraph and discourse structure.) The use of spacing (including indentation at the beginning of paragraphs), and special type styles for titles and subheads, clearly marks these larger divisions orthographically. At these levels, it is probably the lexical structure that is visually symbolized. There are, however, grammatical characteristics of paragraph structure which are among the clues that the reader needs in order to read with comprehension. There are also some units at these levels that are closely related to high level phonological structure; for example, conversational paragraphs, stanzas and lines of poetry, etc.

IMPLICATIONS FOR THE TEACHING OF READING

At every level, the complex mapping of phonological, grammatical, and lexical data onto the writing system has implications for the teaching of reading.

At the lowest level lies the problem of recoding graphic symbols to equivalent elements of speech.[2] Since the relationship is much more complex than a simple "symbol equals phoneme," the pupil must be taught a variety of strategies:

1. He needs strategies from the beginning of reading instruction for choosing the most appropriate matrix for recoding a single syllable, a couplet, a morpheme, or a morpheme cluster. These strategies include

[2] Editors' note: By *recoding* in reading is meant the process of changing graphic information into another code such as aural information rather than decoding directly for meaning.

the various kinds of word analysis skills as well as the use of contrasting matrices and contrasting spelling patterns from the outset of reading instruction.

2. He needs to learn to recode the regular spelling patterns in these matrices. (Many of the more irregular spellings occur in function words or affixes, and are discussed in the following section in connection with the artificial discreteness of orthographic words.)

3. Where different spelling patterns signal lexical rather than phonological contrast, as in the case of homonyms, he needs to learn to use these patterns for direct decoding of the words. He also needs some direct decoding strategies for content words which are irregularly spelled, such as the "-ough" words *rough* and *dough*. It is a part of his reading strategy to know that some spelling patterns of this sort do not have any one dependable correlation with pronunciation.

4. He needs flexibility in trying other strategies when his first attempt is unsuccessful. The materials should be so designed that he can expect to measure his success in recoding and decoding by his comprehension. Materials that do not make sense when they have been correctly decoded will seriously hinder the learning process.

5. All of the above further implies that the sequencing of reading materials cannot be from the simple to the complex, nor from the regular to the irregular, nor from the most frequent to the least frequent. Rather, the small number of patterns in the initial lessons must include a sampling of the kinds of complexities and contrasts for which the pupil needs recoding strategies. These may be chosen for their usefulness in making natural and interesting content—avoiding both the deadly monotony of a limited "look-say" vocabulary and the tongue twister effect of one-pattern-at-a-time methods—while sufficient control over the material to make the lessons teachable is retained. (See Gudschinsky, 1959, on the fallacy of saving difficulties until late in the instructional sequence.)

The use of sentence level punctuation and capital letters to signal both grammatical and phonological information implies that we must abandon our simplistic notions of a direct equation of punctuation with intonation; or the direct equation of punctuation with grammar. Rather, the educator must be aware of the function of each punctuation mark in each different kind of environment, and must help the pupil to learn the use of these marks as an aid to the decoding of a complete passage.

One of the most serious fallacies in the teaching of reading is the supposition that the sentence is the largest unit that must be taken into account. This notion on the part of authors of children's textbooks sometimes results in very unnatural nonparagraphs and nonstories. The fact that there is paragraph and discourse structure in language, and that it is represented in the writing system implies that the beginning reader should be taught to recognize these structural signals, and to use them in comprehending the author's message. The pupil needs to totally comprehend the manner in which paragraphs are divided in narrative prose or expository text on the one hand, and in conversational text on the other.

THE ORTHOGRAPHY IS ARTIFICIALLY DISCRETE

The most obvious and striking features of the writing system are the individual letters and the words, the letters because of their individual and separate shapes, and the words because they are set off from each other by space. The naive view of orthography is that each of these features has a natural counterpart in the sounds and words of speech, and that the process of learning to read is a matter of matching a visual symbol with its oral equivalent.

When the writing system is carefully compared with speech, however, it is immediately evident that the discrete linear nature of the graphic symbols is an artificial abstraction from phenomena which in speech are fused, slurred, simultaneous, and buried within larger structures. It is true, of course, that the naive speaker of a language manipulates and reacts to phonemes and morphemes as though they were discrete units —but he usually does this below the level of consciousness. Only a very sophisticated person can isolate these linguistic entities from his own stream of speech. (Gudschinsky, 1958)

Phonemes as such are never isolated in speech, and attempts to pronounce them in isolation result in unnatural allophones which do not occur in speech. This means that the naive speaker of a language does not have an inventory of conscious sounds which are ready to be equated with the graphic symbols. What he apparently does have is an awareness of contrastive differences within lexical or grammatical frames. He knows, for example, that *pin* and *bin* are different without being able to say exactly how they are different. There are some exceptions to this lack of awareness of phonemes in cases where there is cultural focus on them: for example, Pig Latin (*igPay atinLay*) produces a sharp focus on initial consonants, and rhyming games focus on the final consonant-vowel combination.

There are other problems in the equivalence of symbol to phoneme. In normal speech, the pronunciation of any morpheme may change in different linguistic environments: for example, the word *don't* ends with /t/ in *No, I don't*, and *you* begins with /y/ in *You are?* but the /t/ and /y/ fuse and become the phoneme /ch/ in the sequence *Don't you want to?* Similarly, the stressed vowel of *equator* becomes a neutral vowel when it loses its stress in *equatorial*. The writing system takes little account of these fusions and substitutions, providing only a single spelling for these morphemes in environments in which the pronunciation changes. It is left to the reader who is recoding the written material to supply the changes.

The orthographic, or written, word is not an exact match for any isolable entity in naive speech. (See Goodman, 1969 for a discussion of this topic.) As has already been noted, an orthographic word boundary marks a grammatical boundary that may or may not coincide with a phonological border. In this connection, it is useful to distinguish between "content words" (contentives) and "function words" (functors) (Fries, 1952). The content words belong to the large open classes such as nouns, verbs, adjectives, and adverbs. The functors belong to small closed classes, and mark grammatical relationships: for example, articles, prepositions, verb auxiliaries, etc. Functors are not easily isolated from the stream of speech. A child may say *up* meaning *Please pick me up*, but he is very unlikely to say *at* or *to* as isolated utterances. In normal speech, the functors are usually unstressed and closely bound to a neighboring contentive. Thus, the naive speaker not only does not normally isolate the functors, but when he hears them in isolation he may not recognize them because of the unnatural stressed pronunciation. On the other hand, orthographic words which consist of a contentive stem and the functional affixes which may be used with the contentive stem are more easily isolated: for example, the child may say *milk* meaning *I want some milk*, or *shoes* meaning *Look at the shoes*, or

Jump![3] It is not known, however, to what extent a first grade child is able to isolate the contentives that he uses constantly from the general stream of speech in which they are linked to articles, prepositions, etc.

IMPLICATIONS FOR THE TEACHING OF READING

The artificial discreteness of the orthography has implications for both prereading and the methodology of beginning reading instruction.

It should be obvious that in order to learn to equate orthographic units with speech units, the pupil must first be able to distinguish the units in his own speech. This is not a new idea; "ear training" has long been a part of reading readiness programs. What may be new is the implication that the exercises for phoneme and word recognition should be in the context of normal speech. There should be no artificial isolation of the nonisolable elements; no distortion of the phonemes by trying to pronounce them one by one; no distortion of the functors by pronouncing them apart from the contentives to which they are bound.

The artificial discreteness of the orthography implies that in the actual teaching of reading—even after prereading drills which focus on phonemes and morphemes—the spelling patterns and orthographic words should still be taught in natural contexts. This implication leads to three specific suggestions for teaching methods: (1) that the relatively nonisolable functors and the more isolable contentives be recognized by different strategies; (2) that the decoding strategy for functors be sight recognition as contrasting entities in a contextual matrix; and (3) that in the decoding strategies for contentives, the sound-symbol correlations be taught as contrastive patterns within the appropriate matrix: syllable, couplet, or morpheme.

One of the frequent fallacies of many reading methods is that contentives and functors are lumped together in "word recognition" skills. In the unnatural stress and focus given to functors, the beginning reader may fail to recognize them and so lose his comprehension of the grammatical structure. On the other hand, the pupil who learns sight recognition of words as his only strategy quickly reaches the saturation point in the number of new words that he can remember. Or, the development

[3] Editors' note: See Frank Smith's paper, p. 35, for a brief discussion of "one word" or *holophrastic* sentences.

of techniques for sounding out words may founder on the irregularly spelled functors where such techniques are not efficient. The solution is the use of two sets of strategies, dictated by the difference between functors and contentives with respect to their isolability in language.

Functors—but not contentives—should be recognized at sight in context, and should provide the grammatical framework within which the contentives can be figured out. *In context* means that they should never be isolated on flashcards or in a list of words, nor even picked out of a sentence to be read alone. They should always be read in, at least, the minimum meaningful context—a phrase or a clause. They can be taught by comparison and contrast in such a context. For example, the functor *the* can be localized by comparison of the phrases *the boy* and *the girl;* it can be recognized by contrast with *a* and *this* in the phrases *a boy,* *the boy,* and *this boy.* Each of these phrases in turn should be developed in still larger context in which the choice between them is relevant.

The sight recognition of functors has as a by-product a contribution to fluency and comprehension in reading. The beginner learns early to see meaningful chunks and to use the grammatical structure as the framework within which the content is understood.

Contentives can be recognized by strategies for equating symbols with speech equivalents. The use of syllables, couplets, and morphemes as matrices for the recoding of symbols was discussed in an earlier section, in connection with the interlocking of the phonological, grammatical, and lexical hierarchies in the writing system. Here, the focus is on the artificiality of the discreteness of those patterns, and the need for keeping them within a pronounceable context. Speech is not deciphered by listening for one phoneme at a time and then blending them. We recognize what we hear by the contrastive substitution of elements in a pronounceable matrix, in which each sound is conditioned by its neighbors in characteristic ways, so that the quality of the neighboring sounds is a part of the recognition process.

Strategies for recoding orthographic words should parallel this process. The pupil should be taught to recognize contrastive patterns within familiar frames. This is what underlies the contrastive recognition of *hat* and *bat* and *cat* and *cap* in many current methods, as in the sentence frames: That is a *hat;* That is a *bat;* That is a *cat;* That is a *cap.* What is lacking in most such methods is the notion of the variety of matrices that must be used.

THE ORTHOGRAPHY OBSCURES DIALECTAL AND INDIVIDUAL VARIATIONS

The writing system is not a direct representation of speech in that: (a) it represents a wide range of geographical and social dialects with a single set of spellings and other orthographic conventions, including special written styles that are rarely used orally; and (b) it represents a vocabulary which is enormously larger than that used by any single individual.

The writing system takes no account of the variety of pronunciations in the spoken language, nor of the degrees of slurring or elision that occur at different rates of speech and in different styles of speech. It includes many conventions for literary and technical styles that have no counterpart in speech—except perhaps in the oral reading of formal written material. An unabridged dictionary provides standard spellings for many thousands of words. But, every beginning reader speaks some specific regional and social dialect. He brings to the classroom a specific linguistic competence in the oral styles of his own environment. He is acquainted with written styles only if someone has read to him fairly extensively. He is in control of only a small part of the total vocabulary of the language, and he controls that vocabulary only within the universes of discourse that are related to his home culture and life style.

IMPLICATIONS FOR THE TEACHING OF READING

To learn what reading is and how to do it, the pupil must begin by equating the written language with his own speech.[4] The instructional materials, therefore, must be designed to match his linguistic competence and knowledge. This matching should include the literary genre used in his first stories, the universe of discourse or topics of those stories, the vocabulary, the grammatical constructions, and the phonemes and particular pronunciation of phonemes that are to be matched with the graphic symbols.

Part of this adaptation can be made in the printed materials provided for instruction in reading, although this may require variants of basic

[4] Editors' note: Roger Shuy's paper in Section III of this volume provides an elaborated discussion of this point of view about beginning reading. See also Mildred Gladney's paper in the same section.

materials for different regions, and for urban, suburban, and rural sub-cultures. In part, the adaptation depends on the linguistic sophistication of the teachers. They must be trained to recognize and adapt to differences of dialect and other variations in the linguistic background of the pupils.

The enormous vocabulary available in English, plus the fact that the orthography does not automatically provide a pronunciation for any particular word has important implications for teaching. It is impossible to teach the sight recognition of every word in English. Therefore, the primary goal of beginning reading instruction must be the perfecting of strategies for coping with words the pupil cannot remember having seen in print before. These strategies must include provision for recognizing words that are a part of his speaking or his listening vocabulary, and also for coping with words that are completely new to him. In general, these strategies should involve a sampling of the phonological, grammatical, and lexical information available to him in the text sufficient to answer the following successive questions:

1. Is this word in my familiar reading vocabulary? (i.e., Do I already recognize it at sight as corresponding to some element in my active reading vocabulary?) Does this word make sense in this context?

2. If this word is not in my sight vocabulary, is it in my active speaking vocabulary? (i.e. Can I recode it as something I might have said?) Does this guess make sense in this context?

3. If this word is not in my spoken vocabulary, can I recode it to something I have heard others say? Does this make sense in this context?

4. If I cannot find a correspondence for this word in my listening vocabulary, is it possible that it is completely new to me? If so, what might it mean? How might it be pronounced?

5. If I am not sure of my guess, how will I find this word in the dictionary? Or, how can I ask some adult what it means and how to say it?

A by-product of focussing on decoding strategies rather than sight recognition of contentives is liberation from the endless boring repetition of the same vocabulary. The decoding strategies can be practiced on vocabulary that is vivid and colorful, uniquely appropriate to the context, and repeated only where repetition is required by the lexical and grammatical structure. This freedom is tempered only by a delicately shifting balance between the familiar and the new. That balance should have enough that is new to keep the pupil stretching, learning, and growing—enough that is familiar to keep him encouraged and fresh for new struggle.

REFERENCES

Bloomfield, Leonard and Barnhart, Clarence L. *Let's Read, A Linguistic Approach*. Detroit: Wayne State University Press, 1961.

Carroll, John B. "The Nature of the Reading Process," in Harry Singer and Robert B. Ruddell (Eds.), *Theoretical Models and Processes of Reading*. Newark, Del.: International Reading Association, 1970.

Fries, Charles C. *The Structure of English: An Introduction to the Construction of English Sentences*. New York: Harcourt Brace Jovanovich, Inc., 1952.

Fries, Charles C. *Linguistics and Reading*. New York: Holt, Rinehart & Winston, Inc., 1962.

Goodman, Kenneth S. "The Psycholinguistic Nature of the Reading Process," in Kenneth S. Goodman (Ed.), *The Psycholinguistic Nature of the Reading Process*. Detroit: Wayne State University Press, 1968.

Goodman, Kenneth S. "Words and Morphemes in Reading," in Kenneth S. Goodman and James T. Fleming (Eds.), *Psycholinguistics and the Teaching of Reading*. Newark, Del.: International Reading Association, 1969.

Gudschinsky, Sarah C. "Native Reaction to Tones and Words in Mazatec," *Word*, 1958, *14*, 338–45.

Gudschinsky, Sarah C. "Recent Trends in Primer Construction," *Fundamental and Adult Education*, 1959, *11* (2), 3–32.

Gudschinsky, Sarah C. "Psycholinguistics and Reading: Diagnostic Observation," in William K. Durr (Ed.), *Reading Difficulties: Diagnosis, Correction, and Remediation*. Newark, Del.: International Reading Association, 1970.

Hall, Robert A. *Sound and Spelling in English.* Philadelphia: Chilton Books Co., 1961.

LeFevre, Carl A. *Linguistics and the Teaching of Reading.* New York: McGraw-Hill, 1964.

Pike, Kenneth L. "A Guide to Publications Related to Tagmemic Theory," in Thomas Sebeok (Ed.), *Current Trends in Linguistics.* Vol. 3. The Hague: Mouton, 1966.

Pike, Kenneth L. *Language in Relation to a Unified Theory of the Structure of Human Behavior.* (2nd ed.) The Hague: Mouton, 1967.

Venezky, Richard L. "English Orthography: Its Graphical Structure and Its Relation to Sound," *Reading Research Quarterly,* 1967, *2* (3), 75–105.

Venezky, Richard L. and Calfee, Robert C. "The Reading Competency Model," in Harry Singer and Robert B. Ruddell (Eds.), *Theoretical Models and Processes of Reading.* Newark, Del.: International Reading Association, 1970.

FOR FURTHER READING

Chomsky, Carol "Reading, Writing, and Phonology," *Harvard Educational Review*, 1970, *40* (May), 287–309.

A discussion of the relation of standard English orthography to the sound structure of the language from a generative-transformational point of view. The implications of this view of the orthography for reading and spelling are provided.

Gelb, I. J.   *A Study of Writing*. (2nd ed.) Chicago: University of Chicago Press, 1963.

A basic reference for those who are interested in the history and evolution of writing systems.

Hanna, Paul R., Hodges, Richard E., and Hanna, Jean S.   *Spelling: Structure and Strategies*. Boston: Houghton Mifflin Co., 1971.

A professional text for teachers which presents a structuralist viewpoint of English spelling with implications for instruction.

Venezky, Richard L. "English Orthography: Its Graphical Structure and Its Relation to Sound," *Reading Research Quarterly*, 1967, *2* (Spring), 75–105.

A scholarly and readable report of research in which the spellings and pronunciations of 20,000 English words were analyzed for orthographic patterns in relation to reading.

FIVE · PERCEPTION

IN THE READING PROCESS

We learn about the world around us by receiving information of it from our senses. This sensory information is stored in our brains and later used to guide our behavior. Reading and speaking are forms of learned behavior. Both are based upon the intake and utilization of sensory information. But, reading, as Frank Smith noted in his essay, uses our visual perceptual processes in ways that speaking does not. The relationship between reading and visual perception has long been of interest to psychologists and reading researchers.

Professor Margaret Hubbard Jones is an experimental psychologist at the University of California at Los Angeles. Her paper discusses several different theories of perception and relates them to the learning process, especially to the way we learn to read. It also presents the results of research on this matter. Professor Jones characterizes perceptual processing as an exceedingly complex neurological and psychological operation. She says it is far more complicated than simply the intake of sensory stimuli, and discusses some basic differences in the way children and adults perceive the world around them. This discussion reiterates one of the basic points of this volume: children are not merely "miniature adults"; to understand the intellectual development of children (in this case, the development of perceptual knowledge related to reading), we must view them on their own terms. Jones also stresses the importance of experiencing contrastive information as a requisite to the growth of perceptual knowledge. Frank Smith and Sarah Gudschinsky stressed this in their papers, too. Finally, according to Jones, reading mastery involves the ability to use a minimum of cues to gain a maximum amount of visually perceptible information. This information guides the reader in his efforts to comprehend the printed message.

Professor Rebecca Barr is a reading researcher and Director of the Reading Clinic at the University of Chicago. Like Professor Jones, she points out that perceptual factors related to reading assume different roles in the development of reading maturity. Professor Barr deals more directly than Jones with the relationship of perceptual process studies to the matter of reading instruction. She emphasizes that teachers of reading should be conversant with the major generalizations about the nature of English orthography and with the perceptual processes that are involved in the translation of printed English into oral forms of language.

Although learning to read is dependent upon oral language abilities, Barr asserts that experimental evidence indicates (for English) that learning to read is both different and more difficult than learning to speak. When he begins to read, a child must place great demands upon his perceptual abilities. Thus, Barr suggests that beginning reading should maximize the young reader's opportunities to use his oral language strengths for acquiring those generalizations that are peculiar to the written expressions of language by making the syntax and vocabulary of initial reading materials more congruent with his own.

LEARNING TO PROCESS VISUALLY-

CODED SYMBOLIC INFORMATION

Margaret Hubbard Jones

Before we can discuss the role of perception in the reading process, we must come to some agreement about the meaning of the term *perception*. It is a word which has had so many different meanings, even in recent years, to psychologists and educators, that we must clear the air before we can address ourselves to reading: we must all be talking about the same psychological processes; and we must understand the implications of the model of perception which we espouse. In fact, the term *perception* has so many false connotations for so many people that it might be better to abandon it altogether.

PERCEPTION AS INFORMATION PROCESSING

In the face of recent research in neurophysiology, information processing, and developmental and comparative psychology of vision, what perception does not, and *cannot* mean is that anything remotely resembling a copy of the stimulus is somehow transmitted to the brain. At every level of the nervous system, even within the retina itself, there is an evaluation of incoming cues of several sorts, and at each level a kind of summing up that is passed along to the next level of the nervous system—an analysis of certain kinds of features of the changing external world which have proved useful in survival; not a copy or image, not a complete analysis of all possible features, perhaps not even the most efficient set of features for a modern task, like radar detection or reading. By "features," I mean abstract and rather simple perceptual characteristics, such as vertical vs. horizontal lines, open vs. closed arrays, complex vs. simple figures. It is a complex business, this balancing of light and shade that defines contours, this difference between vertical and oblique streaks, this matter of closed or broken forms, and much of it occurs very early in the visual neural system.

Additional complexities, which are perceptual even in the old-fashioned use of the term, are the recognition of similarity and familiarity. Indeed, without these one can hardly speak of perception; and today, long-term memory and conceptualization (which surely are high-level processes taking place in the cerebral cortex) are also called into play. Perception must, therefore, be considered exceedingly complex, both psychologically and neurologically. It refers to the processing of information, and includes a whole constellation of activities, starting with the input from a stimulus and ending only with the final judgment about it.

Of course, perceptions can be more, or less complex. It is simply not possible to prevent the central nervous system from constructing its own unique patterns from sensory input; and the roles of the organism and of the external environment may be larger or smaller (with very restricted sensory input, cerebral organization breaks down—Schultz, 1965).

Because perception involves both sensory inputs from the environment and the organism's processing of these inputs, it becomes impossible to draw a line between perception and cognition; they fade into each other. In both perception and cognition, short-term memory, categorization, and judgments are involved. Pure, unorganized sensory input is a myth. We can, therefore, expect the perceptual contribution to the reading process to be a complex and pervasive one (see Neisser, 1967, for a similar view).

PERCEPTUAL DEVELOPMENT

It is quite obvious from this view that information processing must begin, in the young child, as a much simpler process than it eventually becomes in the adult, although recent research on the visual discriminations of infants shows that their world is not full of undifferentiated blobs (Fantz, 1964; Hershenson, 1964; Kagan, Henker, Hen-tov, Levine & Lewis, 1966). The infant's visual world must, of course, have some clearly differentiated features; otherwise, he could not learn to see identifiable units called objects; and he learns very rapidly to construct useful perceptual units (Bower, 1965).

The earliest problem in information-processing is the segregation of the gross unit to be attended to—the "chunk" of the environment selected for further processing. The old 'laws of perception'—proximity, common fate, similarity—serve reasonably well to describe the general kinds of factors that are involved in learning to segregate these gross units. There is a diversity of evidence that perceptual learning goes on for many years, even in commonly experienced situations and certainly through the elementary school years. For example, right-left orientation is not mature until about 12 years (Benton, 1959). Both preschoolers and adults can identify certain patterns when rotated; children in early school years have more difficulty. But adults identify the rotation, whereas the preschoolers simply don't discriminate—they are using a simpler set of features for analysis of the pattern than either adults or older children (Ghent, 1960; Ghent & Bernstein, 1961; Gibson, Gibson, Pick, & Osser, 1962).

Unlike adults, children in early school years tend to see global patterns, large wholes, and outlines (see Wohlwill, 1960). Some transformations are very difficult for them to distinguish, particularly rotations and reversals, and these are, unfortunately, often critical for letter identification, e.g. b and d; n and u. They also find gaps in outlines difficult; yet, this again is essential for letter identification, e.g. o and c; e and c; a and c. Similarly, too great complexity (too much information, in the technical sense) makes discrimination of letters difficult, and accounts for the confusion of m and n, or f and t, or c and g (see Gibson, Osser, Shiff, & Smith, 1963; Dunn-Rankin & Leton, 1968; Hodge, 1962). Some of these distinctions are not critical for objects—a teddy bear doesn't become a different toy just because it's upside down—so the rules for the game of reading are new. Symbols require different rules from objects, designs, or representational drawings, and these rules must be learned.

Other distinctions are a question of general perceptual development in attending to such details as prove essential. Since one cannot attend to all details, it is a matter of learning what details to attend to in any new situation. Beginning bird watchers know what I mean. Gradually, children come to know what kind of detail counts: not the smudge above the line; or the difference in slant between lower-case and italics; or the vast difference in shape between capital G and lower-case g, or capital E and small e; but the little tail of the capital Q, or the direction of that insignificant squiggle at the *bottom* of the q and the g (and what child looks at the bottom—they look at the top part of a figure and the line is the dominant element) (Ghent, 1961).

Certain confusions among letters "come naturally," and cannot be avoided without redesigning the alphabet (note that none of the proposed new alphabets take into consideration any of the perceptual difficulties of children, nor even the typical confusions of adults!). Most children eventually learn to use the features of letters which enable them to discriminate between the different letters. These features are such abstractions as vertical line, curved or straight, open or closed, ascending or descending stroke, and much or little information (e.g., *m* vs. *o*). Adults also confuse letters (see Morton, 1964; Foote & Havens, 1965). They depend more heavily on context to tell them what *should* be there; hence proofreaders' errors (see Smith, 1969).

PERCEPTUAL LEARNING AND READING

Perceptual learning is a process quite different from what is ordinarily thought of as learning. Ordinary learning, as in learning a poem, the multiplication tables, a history assignment, or writing a story, is a reorganization of items already in verbal storage, and occurs rather quickly. Perceptual learning, on the other hand, is a very laborious process of carving new units out of experience, making them highly familiar, relating them to each other, and building classes and hierarchies. It involves tremendous amounts of sheer practice, rather than encouragement, verbalization, or reinforcement (see E. Gibson, 1969; Dowling, 1970).

In reading, perceptual learning is a continuing process which may last into the late teens. There is a continual progression in building larger and larger perceptual units which does not cease until the individual has reached the limit of his capacity. The magnitude of overlearning necessary for adult-level performance in perceptual skills in reading is clearly evident in a series of researches on pattern recognition. For any sort of ordinary visual patterns, recognition time becomes longer as the number of alternatives in the recognition set increases, but not in the case of recognizing letters of the alphabet (see Neisser, 1967 for a summary) for adults. The visual symbols used in reading are so highly overlearned that normal perceptual rules do not hold. There is no evidence that bears on the question of whether this recognition process can be speeded up by appropriate training techniques because little analytical work has been done with children. It seems reasonable to suppose that perceptual training situations containing fewer false cues could be devised, but care must be exercised that ultimate progress is not slowed down by fixation on a simpler stage of development (see Senf, Rollings, & Madsen, 1967). This sort of research would have to be done on a large scale and would require careful evaluation of reading performance over a number of years. It is not to be expected that the usual 10 or 15, or even 100 or 1000 practice trials will do the job. We are talking about another order of magnitude entirely—hundreds of thousands. And some clever soul will have to invent an appropriate game, which is as exciting to little kids as the UCLA-USC football classic is to big kids, in order to get children to practice as much as that.

Another interesting bit of evidence regarding basic differences between child and adult readers comes from a study of high-speed visual scanning (Bracey, no date). It shows that fourth graders apparently cannot process information as effectively in the early perceptual stage as adults. Presumably, younger readers would show even greater differences. Also a word-comparison task, which is a semantic task for adults, is basically a perceptual task for six-year-olds (Orpet & Meyers, 1966).

The construction of suitable perceptual units for processing the visual symbols of reading material is a private affair about which little is known. People cannot tell you what kinds of units they use in comprehending either written or spoken language. Many people assume that words are the natural units, but linguists have not even satisfactorily defined the term "word" (Greenberg, 1957, p. 27). It is a printer's convention, defined only by the blank spaces between strings of letters (see Jones, 1968). Evidence of several sorts leads us to believe that people do not process verbal information in terms of single words as demonstrated in a number of different kinds of studies: eye-voice span in reading (Levin & Turner, 1966), number of fixations per line of print (Tinker, 1958), stress patterns in spoken language (Carterette & Jones, 1968), occurrence of hesitations in speech (Jones, 1967), sheer speed of reading, and the decrement in comprehension which accompanies a discontinuity in print which does not correspond to a natural unit (Graf & Torrey, 1966). Young children do not know what a word is (Huttenlocher, 1964; Holden & MacGinitie, 1969; Baldwin & Baum, 1963), even in spoken language. Even with extremely familiar concrete count nouns, it is only a very young or stupid child who, when asked what he wanted, would reply "ball" instead of "the ball," *the ball* being a tightly-knit unit acquired early in the language-learning process.

The beginning reader is in a quandary, since his natural auditory language units do not appear in the visual code. Moreover, the visual code, for English, does not bear a simple one-to-one correspondence to the auditory code. The sound-to-spelling correspondences consist of more complex patterns than single phonemes and single letters: the characteristic pattern for indicating a long vowel as opposed to a short one (e.g., *cape* vs. *cap*) is a more complex visual pattern. The additional English language requirement that stress often changes the phoneme in a given location, and also the rate at which it is uttered, causes further lack of correspondence between the visual and auditory perceptions. Good third grade readers show some ability at mastering spelling-to-sound correspondences, but usually mastery does not occur until sometime in high school (Calfee, Venezky, & Chapman, 1969).

RELATIONSHIPS BETWEEN VISUAL AND AUDITORY ASPECTS OF LANGUAGE

Perhaps this is the place to point out the intimate relationship between the auditory and the visual aspects of language. As we all know, comprehension of the native language is based upon auditory perceptual learning, its units defined largely by intonation patterns. Comprehension of language requires that the parts of a linguistic unit be stored in short-term memory until that unit is complete. At this time, a single semantic unit is formed from the parts; and this semantic unit is stored in long-term memory. A young child has a very small short-term memory store. By first grade its capacity is only about three items, and that capacity grows slowly. Even the average adult has a short-term memory capacity of only about four or five items. This is a severe limitation in comprehension of language, for clauses are often much longer than this. How, then, are we able to circumvent these very rigid limits to information processing? By the formation of larger and larger perceptual units.

We do not perceive language word-by-word; if we did, we could never learn to comprehend complex sentences. The very young child comprehends only short and simple sound strings. Gradually, he builds up phrase units. By first grade, phonemic "words"—strings of sound without pauses—are rather large (Carterette & Jones, 1965). The size of unit increases very gradually with massive experience, until a highly verbal adult can comprehend very long clauses, but only by virtue of perceiving as units long strings of sounds, and storing these as single units in a very limited short-term memory store. These perceptual units are laboriously formed, guided by intonation patterns (temporal rhythms —one of the few effective strategies for learning nonsense materials), and cannot appear without massive experience. Verbal instruction will not help someone learn to do it, but strong perceptual cues might help.

A child about to begin to read has a moderately good command of the simple, basic grammatical structures of his native language, a good understanding of its intonation patterns, and an ability to comprehend simple clauses in auditory form. He comprehends these clauses by forming a semantic judgment based upon the contents of an auditory short-term memory store, which must somehow be related to whatever is relevant in the long-term memory store—word meanings, relationships, associations, etc. When he begins to learn to read, he is faced with a strictly visual set of symbols which are arranged not temporally, but spatially. These symbols contain no indication of rhythms, or at best only some unfamiliar ones, and are both easily confused and variable. Then, he must learn to discriminate the visual patterns which are the symbols, and to build up the larger perceptual units which are essential to useful reading. In between, he must learn to break the code—that is, he must learn to relate the visual perceptual units to his auditory language units, because only in this way can he comprehend the message.

Auditory language units are crucial to the reading process: auditory components are present in skilled adult readers (Holmes & Singer, 1961; Harrington & Durrell, 1955); mature readers use "silent speech" when confronted with difficult material (Edfeldt, 1960, p. 163); auditory similarity causes confusion in short-term memory (Conrad, 1964); auditory tests, for first graders, predict reading achievement (Feldman, 1970); and auditory patterning ability is related to reading comprehension above and beyond its relation to mental age (Sterritt & Rudnick, 1966). There seems to be a sort of tune that goes along with the lyric in reading, perhaps giving cues to the phrasing and temporal ordering which are essential for meaning. This coordination of input from the two senses appears to be a special kind of skill in itself, a skill in which people differ; and, it looks as though children who are deficient in this cross-modal integration are often poor readers (though more needs to be known about this kind of visual integration) (Madsen, Rollins, & Senf, 1970; Senf & Feshbach, 1970; Senf, 1969; Katz & Deutsch, 1963).

PERCEPTUAL DIFFERENCES BETWEEN BEGINNING AND SKILLED READERS

The building up of larger and larger visual perceptual units is essential for rapid reading and for any comprehension of complex clauses. Third graders, for example, have not built as many of these units as adults. A relatively simple visual recognition task is harder for them than a simple auditory task. Adults, on the other hand, perform both tasks equally well. (Carterette & Jones, 1967; see also Senf & Feshbach, 1970). When children first begin reading, they process letters or simple words. They use only certain letter features for purposes of discrimination, and their word cues are probably derived from first and last letters, and word length and shape (Gibson, Bishop, Shiff, & Smith, 1964). This is not really reading; it is decoding[1] and there is very little semantic content at this stage. A semantic message is possible only when some larger linguistic unit is stored in short-term memory long enough to be processed; to accomplish that requires sufficient perceptual speed to enter the last part in short-term memory before the first part has faded.

Perceptual speed comes with age and practice, but it also requires a changing perceptual strategy. Children make many fixations per line of print, skilled adults few. Children's eye-voice span is smaller than that of adults. Children typically require more cues—more complete information—than adults in any perceptual situation; and reading is no exception. Adults may need only the features of an initial vertical line and a very short word to perceive *the* in the proper context, but a beginner will probably need some general features of each letter. Also, mature readers have learned to depend heavily on context. Children are less successful than adults at restoring words missing from a text, an ability used in the "Cloze" test (Bormuth, 1963; Weaver & Kingston, 1963; Taylor, 1957; Peisach, 1965) which predicts reading comprehension in elementary school children. Research is prevalent that indicates the extent to which context is tremendously influential in many kinds of

[1] Editors' note: *Decoding,* as used by Jones, is roughly synonymous with *recoding* as used by Goodman and Gudschinsky in their respective papers. (See also Glossary.)

verbal recognition tasks, both visual and auditory (for a review, see Carterette & Jones, 1965; also Morton, 1964). Goodman (1965) has reported that even first, second, and third graders can read many words in context that they cannot read in isolation. This is as it should be if they are beginning to enlarge their visual perceptual units so that these match more closely the natural auditory units. Finally, children are less able to use knowledge of the constraints of language in processing nonsense "word" strings which variously approximate real English words (Bruce & Pugh, 1966).[2]

Thus, there are vast differences between the perceptual skills of beginning and mature readers; and the many separate skills change in relative importance as learning progresses. A rank beginner must learn to discriminate, rapidly and unerringly, each letter from every other. As soon as he is able to do this, he must begin to ignore letters as such, and use certain features of them as cues to larger units. Once he can rapidly and accurately read words, he must cease to do so, and learn to see whole phrases and, ultimately, clauses. Amble (1966) has shown that intensive training in reading phrases has a lasting effect on reading achievement for children at a certain stage of reading skill. There is indirect evidence that the length of clause (a minimal semantic unit) is the critical measure for language maturity (Hunt, 1965). Also, although it is a complicated argument, there is evidence that highly verbal high-schoolers grasp compound sentences as single units (Nihira, Guilford, Hoepfner, & Merrifield, 1964, p. 37).

However, let us remind ourselves once again that reading is not all visual. One merely uses a visual code for an essentially auditory language. Therefore, it is unlikely that a child who has poor comprehension for his own dialect can ever become a good reader. However, there are people who comprehend spoken language well, but who do not read well. Their difficulties, aside from those emotionally based ones, must stem in large measure from visual perceptual inadequacies or from poor correlation across sensory modes. To solve these problems we need basic research which is developmentally oriented (the perennial college sophomore used as a subject of experimental studies tells us little) and theoretically sophisticated. Only on such a basis can we discover how to help a reader shed old perceptual habits and gain new ones; until he

[2] Editors' note: See *redundancy* and *sequential constraint* in Glossary.

does, he cannot progress to any significant degree. Eventually, reading time must be largely freed from strictly sensory processing to enable the reader to relate, evaluate, and think while reading. This can happen only when very minimal cues to very large perceptual units will serve to guide comprehension of the message.

REFERENCES

Amble, B. R. "Phrase Reading Training and Reading Achievement of School Children," *Reading Teacher*, 1966, *20*, 210–218.

Baldwin, A. L. and Baum, E. "The Interruptability of Words in the Speech of Children." Final Report, H. Levin et al. (Eds.). In *A Basic Research Program on Reading*, a mimeographed report, U.S. Office of Education Cooperative Research Project No. 639. Ithaca, N.Y.: Cornell Univ., 1963.

Benton, A. L. *Right-Left Discrimination and Finger Localization*. New York: Hoeber, 1959.

Bormuth, J. "Cloze As a Measure of Readability," in J. A. Figurel (Ed.), "Reading As an Intellectual Activity," Conference Proceedings of the International Reading Association; VIII, 1963, New York: Scholastic Magazines, pp. 131–134.

Bower, T. G. R. "The Determinants of Perceptual Unity in Infancy," *Psychonomic Sci.*, 1965, *3*, 323–324.

Bracey, G. W. *Stimulus Encoding and High Speed Memory Scanning in Children and Adults*. Princeton: Educational Testing Service, no date.

Bruce, D. J., and Pugh, H. M. "Immediate Verbal Memory and Linguistic Sophistication of Six-Year-Old Children," *Language and Speech*, 1966, *9*, 69–83.

Calfee, R. C., Venezky, R. L., and Chapman, R. S. "Pronunciation of Synthetic Words with Predictable and Unpredictable Letter-Sound Correspondences." Technical Report No. 71, February 1969, Wisconsin Research and Development Center for Cognitive Learning.

Carterette, E. C., and Jones, M. H. "Contextual Constraints in the Language of the Child." Final report, U.S. Office of Education Cooperative Research Project No. 1877. Los Angeles: Univ. of Calif., 1965.

Carterette, E. C., and Jones, M. H. "Visual and Auditory Information Processing in Children and Adults," *Science,* 1967, *156,* 986–988.

Carterette, E. C., and Jones, M. H. "Phoneme and Letter Patterns in Children's Language," in K. S. Goodman (Ed.), *The Psycholinguistic Nature of the Reading Process.* Detroit: Wayne State University Press, 1968.

Conrad, R. "Acoustic Confusions in Immediate Memory," *British Journal of Psychol.,* 1964, *55,* 75–83.

Dowling, W. J. Personal communication to the author. 1970.

Dunn-Rankin, P., and Leton, D. A. "The Similarity of Lower-Case Letters of the English Alphabet. Paper, WPA, 1968.

Edfeldt, A. W. *Silent Speech and Silent Reading.* Chicago: University of Chicago Press, 1960.

Fantz, R. L. "Visual Experience in Infants: Decreased Attention to Familiar Patterns Relative to Novel Ones," *Science,* 1964, *146,* 668–670.

Feldman, B. *Prediction of First Grade Reading Achievement from Selected Structure-of-Intellect Factors.* Doctoral dissertation, University of Southern California, 1970.

Foote, W. E., and Havens, L. L. "Stimulus Frequency: Determinant of Perception or Response," *Psychonomic Sci.,* 1965, *2,* 153–154.

Ghent, L. "Recognition by Children of Realistic Figures Presented in Various Orientations," *Canad. Journal Psych.,* 1960, *14,* 249–256.

Ghent, L. "Form and Its Orientation: A Child's Eye View," *Amer. J. Psychol.,* 1961, *74,* 177–190.

Ghent, L., and Bernstein, L. "Influence of the Orientation of Geometric Forms on Their Recognition by Children," *Perceptual and Motor Skills,* 1961, *12,* pp. 95–101.

Gibson, E. *Principles of Perceptual Learning and Development.* New York: Appleton-Century-Crofts, 1969.

Gibson, E. J., Bishop, C. H., Shiff, W., and Smith, J. "Comparison of Meaningfulness and Pronunciability As Grouping Principles in the Perception and Retention of Verbal Materials," *Jour. Exper. Psychol.*, 1964, 67, 173–182.

Gibson, E. J., Gibson, J. J., Pick, A., and Osser, H. "A Developmental Study of the Discrimination of Letter-Like Forms," *J. Comp. Physiol. Psychol.*, 1962, *55*, 896–906.

Gibson, E., Osser, H., Shiff, W., and Smith, J. "An Analysis of Critical Features of Letters, Tested by a Confusion Matrix." Final report, H. Levin et al. (Eds.). In *A Basic Research Program on Reading*, a mimeographed report, U.S. Office of Education Cooperative Research Project No. 639. Ithaca, N.Y.: Cornell Univ., 1963.

Goodman, K. S. "A Linguistic Study of Cues and Miscues in Reading," *Elementary English*, 1965, 639–643.

Graf, R., and Torrey, J. W. "Perception of Phrase Structure in Written Language." From pp. 83–4 of the proceedings of the 74*th* Annual Convention Amer. Psychol. Assoc., 1966.

Greenberg, J. H. *Essays in Linguistics.* Chicago: University of Chicago Press, 1957.

Harrington, M. J., and Durrell, D. "Mental Maturity Measures Versus Perceptual Abilities in Primary Reading," *J. Educ. Psychol.*, 1955, *46*, 375–380.

Hershenson, M. "Visual Discrimination in the Human Newborn," *J. Comp. Physiol. Psych.*, 1964, *58*, 270–276.

Hodge, D. C. "Legibility of a Uniform-Strokewidth Alphabet: I. Relative Legibility of Upper and Lower Case Letters," *J. Engr. Psych.*, 1962, *1*, 34–46.

Holden, M. H., and MacGinitie, W. H. "Children's Conception of Word Boundaries As a Function of Different Linguistic Contexts." Paper AERA (Abstracts p. 72), 1969.

Holmes, J. A., and Singer, H. "The Substrata-Factor Theory: Substrata Factor Differences Underlying Reading Ability in Known Groups at the High School Level." Final Report covering contracts No. 538, SAE-8176 and No. 538A, SAE-8660, U.S. DHEW, Office of Education, Berkeley, School of Education, University of California, 1961, p. 317.

Hunt, K. W. "Grammatical Structures Written at Three Grade Levels." Res. Report No. 3, National Council Teachers of English, Champaign, Ill., 1965.

Huttenlocher, J. "Children's Language: Word-Phrase Relationship," *Science*, 1964, *143*, 264–265.

Jones, M. H. "Hesitation Phoneme in the Informal Speech of Fifth Graders," *Proj. Literacy Reports*, No. 8, 1967, 37–46.

Jones, M. H. "Some Thoughts on Perceptual Units in Language Processing," in K. S. Goodman (Ed.), *The Psycholinguistic Nature of the Reading Process*. Detroit: Wayne State Univ. Press, 1968.

Kagan, J., Henker, B. A., Hen-tov, A., Levine, J., and Lewis, M. "Infant's Differential Reactions to Familiar and Distorted Faces," *Child Devel.*, 1966, *37*, 519–532.

Katz, P. A., and Deutsch, M. "Relation of Auditory-Visual Shifting to Reading Achievement," *Percept. Motor Skills*, 1963, *17*, 327–332.

Levin, H., and Turner, E. A. "Studies in Oral Reading: IX. Sentence Structure and the Eye-Voice Span," *Proj. Literacy Repts.*, 1966, No. 7, 79–87.

Madsen, M. C., Rollins, H. A., and Senf, G. M. "Variable Affecting Immediate Memory for Bisensory Stimuli: Eye-Ear Analogue Studies of Dichotic Listening," *J. Exper. Psych., Monogr. Supple.*, 1970.

Morton, J. "The Effect of Context on the Visual Duration Threshold for Words," *British J. Psych.*, 1964, *55*, 165–180.

Neisser, U. *Cognitive Psychology*. New York: Appleton-Century-Crofts, 1967.

Nihira, K., Guilford, J. P., Hoepfner, R., and Merrifield, P. R. "A Factor Analysis of the Semantic-Evaluation Abilities." Report No. 32, Psych. Lab., U.S.C., December, 1964.

Orpet, R. E., and Myers, C. E. "Six Structures-of-Intellect Hypotheses in Six Year-Old Children," *Jour. Educ. Psych.*, 1966, *57*, 341–346.

Peisach, E. C. "Children's Comprehension of Teacher and Peer Speech," *Child Devel.*, 1965, 36, 467–480.

Schultz, D. P. *Sensory Restriction: Effects on Behavior.* N.Y.: Academic Press, 1965.

Senf, G. M. "Development of Immediate Memory for Bisensory Stimuli in Normal Children with Learning Disorders," *Develop. Psych. Monograph*, 1969, *1*, No. 6, pt. 2, p. 28.

Senf, G. M., and Feshbach, S. "The Development of Bisensory Memory in Culturally Deprived, Dyslexic, and Normal Readers," *Journal of Educ. Psych.*, 1970, *61*, 461–470.

Senf, G. M., Rollins, H. A., and Madsen, M. C. "Recall Order of Dual Channel Input As a Function of Induced Recall Strategy and Stimulus Rate." From pp. 57–58 of the proceedings of the 75*th* Annual Convention, APA, 1967.

Smith, F. "The Featural Dependencies Across Letters in the Visual Identification of Words," *Jour. Ver. Lear. & Ver. Behav.*, 1969, *8*, 215–218.

Sterritt, G. M., and Rudnick, M. "Auditory and Visual Rhythm Perception in Relation to Reading Ability in Fourth Grade Boys," *Perceptual & Motor Skills*, 1966, *22*, 859–864.

Taylor, W. L. "Cloze Readability Scores As Indices of Individual Differences in Comprehension and Aptitude," *J. Appl. Psych.*, 1957, *41*, 19–26.

Tinker, M. A. "Recent Studies of Eye-Movements in Reading," *Psych. Bull.*, 1958, *55*, 215–231.

Weaver, W. W., and Kingston, A. J. "A Factor Analysis of the Cloze Procedure and Other Measures of Reading and Language Ability," *Jour. Communic.*, 1963, *13*, 251–261.

Wohlwill, J. F. "Developmental Studies of Perception," *Psych. Bull.*, 1960, *57*, 249–288.

PERCEPTUAL DEVELOPMENT

IN THE READING PROCESS

Rebecca C. Barr

In this paper, I will explore the influence of perception on reading and draw implications for the teaching of reading.

Several previous papers have suggested that reading skill acquisition might better occur under conditions similar to language learning;[1] that is, in an environment where a child tests hypotheses he has made concerning language regularity and receives confirmation or correction. Durkin (1966) has studied a sample of children who learned to read "spontaneously" at home, prior to school attendance. These children are unusual in that they learned to read in the same environment in which they learned to speak. She found that most of these preschool readers acquired their skill by printing word forms. Although some of these children learned letter names while getting help in spelling, most did not learn the sounds that correspond to letters in the beginning stages of reading.

Most children do not learn to read at home prior to school instruction, even where there are numerous printed symbols available and when opportunities to look at printed words while hearing a story are present. Why is reading skill seldom acquired as easily as oral language in the home environment? Perhaps, there is something more complex in reading than in oral language acquisition that requires a more careful structuring of the stimulus perceived in order for generalizations to be made. Perhaps, many children are not perceptually ready to cope with reading until approximately five or six when most of their time is spent in school rather than at home. Or perhaps, there is sufficient mythology surrounding the teaching of reading that mothers do not attempt it.

In the remainder of this paper I will present evidence that (1) reading differs in important ways from language acquisition, (2) reading English

[1] Editors' note: See, for example, the papers by Frank Smith and Dolores Mather in Section II.

131

is more difficult than reading some other languages, and (3) the role of perception changes as a child gains skill in reading. Next, I will discuss research findings concerning perceptual development and reading acquisition within each of these areas and, finally, I will discuss ways in which a teacher may aid perceptual development in the reading process.

LANGUAGE LEARNING COMPARED WITH READING SKILL ACQUISITION

Most human beings learn to speak. In contrast, never learning to read is frequent; in fact, in some ethnic groups, and historically, in most cultures, illiteracy has been a general social condition. The oral traditions of man extend back thousands of years; but, man's learning to write and read is relatively recent.

Reading appears to be more difficult than speaking. Such difficulty may have to do with the nature of the stimulus and the number of examples from which a child can generalize; or, it may lie in the number of exceptions to the generalizations that need to be learned. Although perception is necessary in both hearing and vision, examples of oral language are more readily available in most environments than those of printed language. In order to read printed words, children need to focus on written symbols, remember them, and make comparisons that in turn allow them to generalize from those symbols to meaning. Speaking involves the identification of sound sequences, appropriately associating names with characteristics of things and processes, and learning the rules for interrelating these words correctly. Reading, by contrast, involves associating graphic sequences to an already developed language capability.

READING ENGLISH COMPARED WITH READING OTHER LANGUAGES

In addition to the evidence suggesting that reading acquisition may be different from and more difficult than oral language learning, there is also evidence to suggest that English orthography presents more problems in learning to read than does the orthography of other languages. In Europe, reading disability appears to be greatest among children with English as their native tongue, second among those speaking German, and least among native speakers of Romance languages. Japanese children show less than 1 percent occurrence of reading disability as opposed to approximately 10 or more percent in the United States.

Makita (1968), in comparing Japanese Kana script with English orthography, notes the following differences: (1) Kana symbols represent a syllable where consonant sounds are never—with the exception of the sound /n/—represented in isolation. In the Roman alphabet, certain consonant letters correspond to sounds that are abstracted from pronounceable units. (2) An English letter may represent different sounds, depending on its spelling context. The relationship between visually perceived letters and corresponding phonemes is consistent in Japanese Kana, but variable in English.

Most poor readers of Kana script acquire reading skill after the second grade. By fourth grade, few children have a reading disability. In contrast, there are many disabled readers in English-speaking countries. Makita argues that difficulty in acquiring reading skill lies in the nature of the relationship between the printed and oral language rather than in innate ability or teaching procedures.

Because of unique difficulties inherent in reading English, it is essential that the teacher know the generalizations relating printed words to language and the perceptual skills required for this translation. In a previous paper, Allen has described the work undertaken by Weir and Venezky (1965) to delineate functional generalizations in translating from spelling to sound. Venezky (1967) found information contained in single letter-sound associations to be insufficient. Cues for accurate translation, in effect, are also needed from the word and sentence level as well as from information contained in letter-sound associations, as Gudschinsky has also emphasized.

In his analysis Venezky has not identified a way to teach children to read, or a method that children should use, but rather, generalizations relating visual forms of language to spoken forms. These generalizations should be useful in planning basic reading programs. Nevertheless, as Allen has cautioned, more work needs to be done in identifying relationships between letters and sounds, and in specifying their connection to the learning and language habits of children.

PERCEPTUAL DEMANDS OF THE READING PROCESS

For a teacher to aid a child in identifying cues and seeing relationships, he needs to know something about the perceptual demands involved. There is evidence showing that the process of reading changes as the learner gains more experience in reading. Eye movement photography indicates that readers, in the initial stages of learning, exhibit more fixations per word than experienced readers, who can recognize the stimulus pattern from minimal cues. Thus, it is clear that beginning readers need more visual information than efficient ones, and that the perceptual demands are highest during the initial stages of reading, when the child is becoming familiar with word forms and learning the generalizations that permit translation from print to language.

Similarly, correlational data suggest that the process involved in the acquisition phase of reading differs from that of later phases. Estimates of visual and auditory perceptual skill, and of language facility, show similar degrees of relationship to reading skill measured during the acquisition phase. After a child has had approximately four normal years of reading experience, correlational data show language facility (vocabulary and listening comprehension) to be even more highly related to reading than it was previously. In contrast, an insignificant degree of relationship is found between perceptual skill and reading after approximately three years of reading experience. Evidence from descriptive eye movement photography studies and the more quantitative correlational studies support this finding. This evidence indicates that after the beginning reader has mastered the process of selection cues and forming generalizations about printed words, perceptual factors assume a different and less significant role in the reading process.

Studies of oral reading miscues conducted by Goodman (1969), Weber (1968), Clay (1968), and others have identified functional cues operating at several levels simultaneously. The reader obtains these cues at the graphemic level, and from his knowledge of word structure, syntax, and meaning. This knowledge of language guides his selection and organization of perceptions. Obviously, then, a child should be able to use his language strength during the initial stages of learning to read when the perceptual demands are heaviest; reading materials should use the vocabulary and syntax of the child; and the teacher should know the language characteristics of his students to select or construct appropriate materials for them.

PERCEPTUAL DEVELOPMENT, READING SKILL ACQUISITION, AND INSTRUCTIONAL IMPLICATIONS

When does the child acquire sufficient visual and auditory perceptual skill to cope with the demands of reading?

The majority of perceptual studies use adult subjects who have already acquired reading skill rather than studying children prior to and during the time they learn to read. Since perceptual demands are greatest during the acquisition phase of reading and because there is little research on the development of perceptual processes related to reading, more investigation of the interaction between perceptual development and reading acquisition is needed.

Jones has pointed out (in the paper preceding this one) that children come to school with general command in understanding and generating language. Nevertheless, it is questionable whether they can perceive some characteristics of words and sounds that may aid translation from visual forms to language. Some children of five, for example, do not recognize the word as a unit; they may have had no reason to form a concept of what a word is. In fact, it may be that the concept of "word" develops from experience in reading graphic forms.

At the same time, words seem to be immutable units: some children of four and five have difficulty fractionating words. Children of five make many errors in telling whether two words begin or end with the same sound. Some first graders have extreme difficulty abstracting the sounds of consonants and vowels from words. They discriminate consonants at the beginning of words more easily than at the end, with medial sounds the most difficult to discriminate. Children unable to discriminate among phonemes may have difficulty using letters as cues to word sounds. Many such children can learn to abstract phonemes from word contexts if they are given carefully sequenced printed and oral examples. Some children of six and older who can hear and reproduce phonemes have difficulty resynthesizing them into words. Consonants especially become distorted, miscuing the child to a different word.

Concerning visual perception in reading, the first task in accurately perceiving graphic form is identifying characteristics that make one letter distinct from another, as Gibson (1969) and her associates have noted in a series of studies pertaining to the child's growing awareness of graphic form. That skill in recognizing letters is important in acquiring reading skill is evident in the findings of predictive and training studies. Readiness measures with the strongest relationship to reading entail letter identification and discrimination. Similarly, the type of visual training appearing to have greatest impact on later reading skill acquisition involves exposure to letters and letter sequences.

The role of visual memory has also been examined by Gibson (1970) and others. Kindergarteners and beginning first graders can remember three to four letters on the average. These sequences increase in length by approximately one letter per year. For any reader, memory is greater for meaningful words than for pseudowords; as well as differences in remembering differently structured pseudowords. Several studies on the influence of language on visual coding (Gibson, 1962) measured accuracy in reading pseudowords presented with a tachistoscope, comparing those that conformed to rules of orthography with those that did not. Pronounceable forms were read with considerably greater accuracy than unpronounceable ones of similar length.

In a study in the Reading Clinic at the University of Chicago, readers and prereaders were compared on the way they remembered pseudowords differing in their degree of conformity to rules of orthography. Prereaders showed no consistent difference among pseudoword categories. In contrast, readers showed greater facility with letter sequences most similar to English words. It appears that children who have learned to read no longer have to process individual letters as nonreaders do. Rather, they have learned coding schemes reflecting their knowledge of letter-sound sequences prevalent in English. Prereaders possess no comparable coding scheme to aid visual memory.

Visual discrimination and memory activities in preparation for learning to read should be carried on within the context of reading, once a child is able to copy or match individual letters. English words are composed of letter patterns—some highly predictable. As children achieve a sense of what letter sequences in English are possible and probable, visual perception of letters and words can be accomplished with increasingly fewer visual cues. This knowledge of letter sequences also appears useful as a coding scheme in memory.

Studies of perceptual development make it clear that children vary greatly in the time when they are ready to cope with the perceptual demands of reading. Reading is a task that allows and facilitates the development of perceptual skill. For many children, reading instruction in first grade (or kindergarten) occurs considerably after perceptual readiness for reading. Other children need language stimulation or reading-related perceptual tasks during the primary school years before they can cope successfully with reading.

The degree of development in auditory or visual perception necessary for reading acquisition is difficult to specify. De Hirsch and her associates

(1966) found that a child was often able to compensate successfully for a deficiency in a prerequisite perceptual area. Children who showed deficiencies in several prerequisite areas were the ones who failed to acquire reading skill. In clinical cases, deficiencies in perceptual areas which seem to interfere most with reading acquisition are in the following areas: auditory discrimination, sound synthesis, visual memory, and —less frequently—visual discrimination. With such children, strengthening a deficient area is sometimes possible, though frequently it is necessary to help the child discover ways to circumvent the deficient area.

Children differ not only in their rate of perceptual development, but also in their ability to see patterns in words and to form generalizations. Some children need a great deal of repetition and many word examples from which to generalize. Others are extremely proficient in remembering words, making comparisons, selecting functional cues, and forming generalizations.

Lowenstein (1969) found that the type of help given by the teacher influenced the facility of children in identifying common patterns of letters. General instructions leading to search behavior by children permitted more effective learning than did instruction specifying what was to be noted.

SUMMARY AND IMPLICATIONS FOR TEACHERS

Perception involves the selection and organization of stimuli. It is a process in which concepts, learned at an earlier time, influence the selection and patterning of later perceptual experience. In this sense, reading is perceptual learning: the child selects and organizes graphic cues in terms of previously acquired language concepts (word structure, syntax, and meaning). Perception in relation to reading becomes efficient once a child has become familiar with the characteristics of the orthography and has identified cues relating printed symbols to language.

The teacher can help facilitate this process by (1) selecting or creating material that permits a child to draw on his language resources to aid perception; (2) being aware of the generalizations to be formed concerning the nature of English orthography, and the cues which permit accurate translation to sound or meaning; (3) being aware of perceptual skills used in reading, and being able to evaluate the development of individual children so that reading acquisition might begin at an appropriate time; and (4) aiding those children who have a difficult time generalizing to form concepts by carefully organizing stimulus words so that consistent patterns of letters and rules governing their relation to sound become apparent.

REFERENCES

Clay, Marie M. "A Syntactic Analysis of Reading Errors," *Journal of Verbal Learning and Verbal Behavior,* 1968, 7, 434–438.

de Hirsch, Katrina; Jansky, Jeanette J.; and Langford, W. S. *Predicting Reading Failure.* New York: Harper & Row, 1966.

Durkin, Dolores *Children Who Read Early.* New York: Teachers College Press, Columbia University, 1966.

Gibson, Eleanor J., Pick, A., Osser, H., and Hammond, M. "The Role of Grapheme-Phoneme Correspondence in the Perception of Words," *American Journal of Psychology,* 1962, *75,* 554–570.

Gibson, Eleanor J. *Principles of Perceptual Learning and Development.* New York: Appleton-Century-Crofts, 1969.

Gibson, Eleanor J. "The Ontogeny of Reading," *American Psychologist,* 1970, *25,* 136–143.

Goodman, Kenneth S. "Analysis of Oral Reading Miscues: Applied Psycholinguistics," *Reading Research Quarterly,* 1969, *5,* 9–30.

Lowenstein, A. M. "Effects of Instructions on the Abstraction of Spelling Patterns." Unpublished Master's thesis, Cornell University, 1969. Cited in Eleanor J. Gibson, *American Psychologist,* 1970, *25,* 136–143.

Makita, Kiyoshi "The Rarity of Reading Disability in Japanese Children," *American Journal of Orthopsychiatry,* 1968, *38,* 599–614.

Venezky, R. L. "English Orthography: Its Graphical Structure and Its Relation to Sound," *Reading Research Quarterly,* 1967, *2,* 75–105.

Weber, Rose-Marie "The Study of Oral Reading Errors: A Survey of the Literature," *Reading Research Quarterly,* 1968, *4,* 96–119.

Weir, R. H. and Venezky, R. L. "Rules to Aid in the Teaching of Reading." Final Report, U.S. Office of Education Cooperative Research Project No. 2584. Stanford, Calif.: Stanford University, 1965.

FOR FURTHER READING

Neisser, Ulric *Cognitive Psychology.* New York: Appleton-Century-Crofts, 1967.

An advanced text for those who wish to pursue the study of perception in some depth.

Smith, Frank *Understanding Reading: A Psycholinguistic Analysis of Reading and Learning to Read.* New York: Holt, Rinehart & Winston, 1971.

A most readable discussion of the fundamental aspects of the act of reading. Considerable attention is given to perception as an active process.

SIX · THE PROCESS OF READING

Jones and Barr have just discussed the extremely complex subject of visual perception in the reading process. In dealing with the question: what *cues* enable a child to relate printed text to his language, they have set the stage for the two papers which follow. Barr, in particular, has contrasted the processes of acquiring language with those of acquiring reading. She has also pointed out that reading requires the visual perception of printed symbols, and that units of visual perception vary as reading maturity develops. The work of both authors casts doubt upon the somewhat naive views of perception which have dictated the classical poles of reading methodology—the "look-say" and "phonics" approaches.

For several years, Professors Kenneth and Yetta Goodman have been engaged in a study of reading *mis*cues. Kenneth Goodman is Professor of Education at Wayne State University in Detroit, and is the Director of the Reading Miscue Research Center, supported by the U.S. Office of Education. Yetta Goodman is Associate Professor of Education at the Dearborn campus of the University of Michigan. She, with Carolyn Burke (whose paper appears in Section I), has been attempting to simplify the massive research techniques which her husband has developed for the analysis of children's reading into a form that can be used by the classroom teacher on a day-to-day basis.

In a very real sense, the Goodman papers are at the heart of this volume; for they demonstrate how the reading process can be analyzed using the vital linguistic, psychological, and language development information which has been described in preceding papers. Kenneth Goodman asserts that, until now, we have lacked the capability to develop a theory of the reading process, a theory which, he contends, must incorporate linguistic and psychological principles that are based upon the observed behavior of readers. While Goodman does not yet claim that we have a comparably sophisticated theory of reading instruction, he suggests in his paper the basis upon which such a theory can be constructed.

Yetta Goodman then shows how qualitative miscue analysis, the research technique used in the reading miscue studies, can help the teacher and the prospective teacher gain a better understanding of the reading process and analyze the strengths and weaknesses of individual readers. Such immediate application to the improvement of instruction in the elementary school curriculum is all too rare in educational research. In addition, miscue analysis and research are now questioning almost every aspect of traditional reading instruction in the schools: scope and sequence of skills; evaluation; remediation; and perhaps above all, the role of oral reading in the reading program.

THE READING PROCESS:

THEORY AND PRACTICE

Kenneth S. Goodman

Reading instruction is designed to help students use the reading process proficiently. But, reading instruction depends on theories of the reading process for its own theoretical and practical basis; and unfortunately, there are no such theories. All the present ones are too incoherent to be useful. The net result is that tests of reading achievement, methods of teaching reading, materials for reading instruction, and clinical and remedial practices have largely been based on common sense, trial and error, previous practice, and whim.

To be useful, a theory of the reading process must make it possible to explain the full range of reading behavior at all stages of proficiency. It must predict behavior under specific circumstances, in specific students, at specific points of development. It must provide viable answers to all questions relating to the reading process; and it must provide a framework for understanding the relative importance of those questions. In short, a theory of the reading process must make clear how the proficient reader operates and what it is we seek to teach when we teach reading. Such a theory cannot be translated into direct instructional practice. We need a *theory of reading instruction*. This theory must be based on a theory of the reading process which integrates learning theory, research on child development and language learning, and input from all other relevant disciplines.

This instructional theory can, in turn, spawn sound methods and materials which weave the wisdom gleaned by educators from years of teaching children to read into a theoretically sound, articulate, instructional program. There is no dichotomy between theory and practice. Theory must become practical; and practice must achieve theoretical validity.

In this paper, I intend to present the essence of a theory of the reading process and to suggest a few of the elements that a theory of reading instruction must deal with.

THE PSYCHOLINGUISTIC BASE

Whether we define reading in terms of its objectives, in terms of the behavior in which readers engage, or in terms of the inferable process, a reading theory must be built on a psycholinguistic base. The reader starts with a graphic display, printed or handwritten, and if he is successful, he ends with meaning, a reconstruction of the writer's message.

Language, in graphic form, is the code vehicle through which the message is transmitted. *To understand how reading works one must understand how language works.*

To reach his goal of meaning the reader must use language, interacting with the graphic display in such a way that he moves from the code to the message. This interaction involves language and thought. Further, since the graphic code itself contains no information which is itself the writer's message, it becomes apparent that the reader supplies a considerable amount of linguistic and conceptual input as he responds to the graphic display. *To understand reading one must understand how language is used.*

A reading theory built on this psycholinguistic base will place many traditional concerns in the study of the reading process in new contexts and suggest reevaluation of the relative importance of such traditional concerns. A key example is the overwhelming concern, in the past, with words and what has been variously labeled "word recognition," "word perception," "word attack." This focus grew out of a common sense view of language as a string of words, and of reading as the ability to cope with that string of words. But language is not a string of words. In any language use, the sum of the whole is in no sense the sum of the parts. And coping with the system or structure of language sequences is vital to successful reading.[1] Old insights about reading based on an overemphasis on words must be carefully reconsidered as the view of words is placed in proper perspective.

At the same time, new concerns are emerging whose significance was previously overlooked or only dimly seen. Grammar, as the system of language, emerges as one such colossal oversight. Whenever any language user attempts to derive meaning from language he must treat it as grammatical sequences, and be aware of grammatical interdepen-

[1] Editors' note: See, for example, the illustrations of how knowledge of the structure of language sequences is used by readers in Carolyn Burke's paper, pp. 24–30.

dencies. This is true when a reader deals with a simple sequence like *Tom saw Betty.* He must know that *Tom* is subject and *Betty* is object in order to comprehend. In a much more complex sequence, such as *See Flip run,* he must be aware that the subject *you* is not present in the surface structure; that *Flip run* is an embedding of an underlying structure *Flip runs* in another structure, *you see (Flip runs);* and that the clause functions as the object of the verb *see.* If he cannot process this information, he will not comprehend the message *See Flip run.* Both examples are three word sentences. The task of reading each sentence depends largely on the processing of grammatical information. Thus, when viewed from a psycholinguistic base, what has appeared to be a word recognition problem is a very different phenomenon.

CONCEPTS AND TERMINOLOGY

A word of caution is necessary. As a theory of the reading process is emerging and the process is revealed more clearly, terminology new to the reading field derived from linguistics and psycholinguistics is also emerging.

New terminology for old ideas is certainly not needed. However, new terms for new concepts are indispensable, and, in many cases, old terms must be redefined as misconceptions are clarified. Reading teachers, and teachers of reading teachers, must resist a tendency to equate new terms with old ones, and to overlook basic but subtle differences in concepts.

THEORY, MODELS, AND REALITY

Earlier, we pointed out a difference between directly interpreting behavior of readers and relating behavior to underlying theoretical views. If we confine our attempt to understand the reading process solely to observable phenomena, we will tend to see the behavior of readers as a kind of direct response to graphic stimuli with no intervening process. In fact, that view has in large measure prevailed. Reading has tended to be treated as a series of sound responses to letter stimuli, or word-name responses to graphic word shapes. The fallacy of this view has always been evident in the behavior of readers; but researchers and text writers have been reluctant to treat reading behavior as an observable indication of underlying competence. To understand the reading process, we must come to see reading behavior as the end product of that process. We must also see reading behavior as a means to understanding the process.

When Galileo dropped his weights from the tower of Pisa or stared through his first crude telescope at Jupiter and saw its moons disappear behind it, he could not serve the ends of his investigation by stopping at a superficial description. It was necessary for him to link these observations to theoretical explanations. Recently, the apparently erratic behavior of our unmanned and manned satellites as they orbited the moon indicated that there was something wrong with the calculations of how they should respond to the moon's gravitational pull. A description of the deviational behavior was not enough. Nor could we blame the phenomena on genetic weaknesses of the vehicles. From the deviations, it was necessary to infer possible flaws in gravitational theory, to reconstruct a theory which could explain that behavior, and then to test the theory against the predicted behavior of new satellites.

Theories make it possible to organize observational data and generate hypotheses. In turn, theories are tested against reality, which confirms them or suggests modification. By means of theoretical models one may relate behavior to the process of which it is the product. Frequently, of course, once a theoretical model is articulated, previously available data take on new significance to the point where we wonder how we could ever have overlooked them.

Theoretical models are necessary whenever a process, whether physical, or psychological, or psycholinguistic, is not directly observable. A model never becomes identical with a process; that would mean that the process was observable. But models are useful to the extent that they can predict the end products of a process. There is now sufficient evidence to construct a model of the reading process. We can infer from the behavior of readers, utilizing linguistic data, and psycholinguistic data about the use of language, what competence underlies the reading behavior and how the reading process works.

One source of knowledge for making such inferences is research in reading miscues, such as our own. By comparing observed oral reading responses with expected responses, we can see how the reader uses available linguistic information and what resources of his own he utilizes. Furthermore, we can see the points at which the process breaks down and the strengths and weaknesses of the reader.

CHARACTERISTICS OF THE READING PROCESS

A strange contradiction exists between actual reading behavior and the widely held common sense view of it. In reading orally materials they haven't seen before, readers do not read in the precisely correct way that they are expected to read. Since, in the common sense view, proficient readers are supposed to read accurately—that is, without errors—when they don't do this, the errors are ignored, explained away, or taken as evidence that they really aren't so proficient after all.

Our research indicates that *all* readers produce the unexpected responses which we call *miscues*. These miscues occur because the reader is not simply responding to print with accurate word identifications. He is processing information in order to reconstruct the message the writer has sought to convey.

In the sense that the reader uses each graphic cue available to him, reading is not an exact process at all. Instead, the reader engages in a form of information processing in which he uses his knowledge of how language works. As he strives to comprehend, he is highly selective in choosing graphic cues and in predicting language structures.

Figure 1 will help to illustrate the essential tasks the reader faces as he moves from a graphic display to meaning. This figure employs the transformational-generative view of language, not because of any commitment to that view, but because it appears to explain the actual behavior of readers.

Figure 1

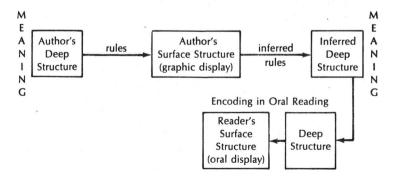

Meaning cannot be derived directly from the printed page. The graphic display on the page can however be considered a written surface representation of language. A writer starts with meaning. He then assigns a deep underlying grammatical structure. Using the transformational rules, he then generates a written surface structure. Finally, he utilizes the rules of English orthography (spelling, punctuation) to produce the graphic display. The reader must infer from that graphic display the rules that have produced it and its underlying deep structure. Only then can he reconstruct the writer's message, that is, comprehend the meaning.

If he is reading orally, the reader must then encode the message as oral output producing an oral surface structure. There is no direct connection in this representation between the graphic display and the oral reader's output. In fact, to achieve comprehension, there is no necessary reason to involve oral language in the reading process at all. It is possible, even probable, that some association between oral and written language occurs as the reader moves toward meaning, but that association is not in any sense essential to comprehension. For the proficient reader, two forms of language exist—one written and one spoken. They have the same deep structure, but *after* applying his transformational rules, he may apply either phonological rules or orthographic ones.

Miscues may occur in reading at any point in the process. They will always involve the reader's use of written language; but they will not always interfere with comprehension. Here are some situations which may lead to miscues:

1. Misperception At any time, what the reader thinks he sees is partly what he sees and partly what he expects to see. A misperception may result from inadequate selection of visual cues, predictions at variance to the text, or misprocessing of the selected visual cues.

2. Inability To Process The reader may be unable to deal with the graphic display in any sense that yields language information which he can process. This would be most characteristic of beginning readers lacking in proficiency; but, it is also true in other cases. Reading a text in obscure handwriting or partially obliterated print is an example.

3. Inference Of Different Deep Structures Readers process language information from the surface structure in such a way that they may predict the deep structure long before they have used all the cues which the surface structure provides. Variant deep structures may be inferred from one text for several reasons:

    a. The reader's language rules may vary somewhat from the writer's. His dialect may be different, hence he may miss or misuse some cues.

    b. There may be a point in the surface structure where an analysis of the surface structure could go either of two ways, each analysis predicting a different deep structure. Thus, the reader can predict a deep structure that is not the one the author used. Notice, for example, these two sentences:

      1) He was going to the store.[*2]

      2) He was going to go to the store.[*]

The reader may predict (2) while reading (1).

    c. The surface structure may be ambiguous with two possible deep structures:

      1) The doors are closed at 8 PM.

      2) Princess Anne will marry whom she pleases.

4. Lack Of, Or Variation In Meaning Input Readers may be unable to produce a deep structure, may produce a variant deep structure, or may be unable to derive meaning, if they lack experiential or conceptual input to bring to the task, or if the concepts they have are at variance with the writer's. Word meanings may be involved as well as idioms and special ways of using phrases. In many cases, however, the reader can handle the language if he has sufficient experience or conceptual background.

5. Choice of Alternate Grammatical Rules To Produce The Oral Surface Structure In oral reading, the reader encodes meaning as oral output. In doing so, he will tend to shift away from the writer's language choices towards his own.

    a. He may produce an alternate surface structure using optional rules. Example:

      1) to make it look new

    for

      2) to make it look like new

[2] * Starred examples are taken from Kenneth Goodman and Carolyn Burke *A Study of Oral Reading Miscues That Result in Grammatical Re-Transformations,* Final Report, USOE Project No. 7–E–219 June 1969.

or

1) Freddie didn't mind being compared with his uncle, who was a real chemist.*

for

2) Freddie didn't mind being compared with his uncle. He was a real chemist.*

b. He may shift to the rules of his own grammar.

1) You are just like Uncle Charles.*

for

2) You're just like Uncle Charles.*

c. The reader may shift to an alternate but equivalent way of saying the same thing.

1) He was going on nine.*

for

2) He was going to be nine.*

6. The Oral Output May Involve Alternate Phonological Rules

a. These can be rules in the dialect of the reader.

1. breakfases*

for

2. breakfasts*

b. They can be misarticulations.

1. alunimum

for

2. aluminum.

Listening and reading are the receptive aspects of language use, just as speaking and writing are the generative aspects. Much, therefore, that has been said of the reading process applies to listening as well, at least for literate language users.

Though oral language comes first in the natural history of both the individual and the tribe, when literacy is achieved, oral and written language become parallel alternate forms available to the user. Each has its own functions, strengths, and limitations. The language user chooses the one most appropriate for his communicative need. He may even use them in combination, exploiting the strengths of both, as when a speaker uses written notes.

In languages which use alphabetic writing systems, it may appear that the written language is a secondary representation of the oral language. This is because graphic patterns generally represent oral language patterns rather than each relating to meaning independently. Because of the system of relationships between graphic and phonological patterns, readers may even have the illusion that they are turning print into speech and then processing the aural input as in listening. But, if such were the case, reading would be seriously impeded, because the reader would be required to use graphic information to create sound patterns in a relatively complete sense in order to infer the underlying deep structure and assign meaning. That would make reading a slower and more tedious process than listening, since the listener is able to sample input and move directly to deep structure and meaning.

Written and oral language are alternate surface structures with the same underlying deep structure. In both listening and reading, the language user infers this deep structure from the surface structure without resorting to a shift from oral to written surface structure or vice versa.

In producing language, the user has alternate sets of rules for producing a signal *after* he has conceived his message. Phonological rules produce a signal which is an oral sequence. Orthographic rules produce a signal which is a graphic display. The reader's job is to get from the graphic display to meaning. It is only in the special case of oral reading that the reader is also interested in producing an oral signal and, even then, it appears that proficient readers decode graphic language for meaning and *then* encode (recode) an oral signal.

It is possible with alphabetic writing systems to recode graphic displays as oral sequences without recourse to meaning. Anyone literate in English can do so with *A marlup was poving his kump*. It is even possible to do so with a language that is foreign to the reader and which he neither speaks nor understands.[3] But this code to code shifting does not yield meaning; in fact, it still leaves the language user with a coded message.

In the recent literature, much has been made of this graphic to oral *recoding*. It has been mistakenly labeled *decoding*, which it cannot be, since it does not end with something other than code. Such *recoding* is not an essential part of the reading process. Even in beginning read-

[3] Editors' note: See Carolyn Burke's paper in Section I, pgs. 24–30, for detailed examples of a mature reader's ability to *recode*, as this term is employed by Goodman.

ing a focus on phonic *recoding* skills may interfere with the development of strategies for acquiring meaning from written language.

UNITS OF PROCESSING IN READING

Written language is a display of letters. Letters are composed of straight and curved line segments, and form letter groupings which are separated by white space. But meaning can be derived from written language only when underlying clauses and their interrelationships have been inferred. Thus, the most significant unit in reading is not the letter, word, or sentence, but the *clause*. The reader must be aware of what these clauses are in the deep structure and be able to handle the form in which they are represented in the surface structure. They may be reduced, embedded, combined, branched, conjoined, and subordinated in such a way that the surface structure represents the deep structure in a highly economical, information-loaded manner. A sentence is a clause or a set of interrelated clauses. The surface structure must be sampled to identify the deep structure clauses.

See Flip run is a common type of preprimer sentence, as was illustrated earlier. To get meaning from it, a reader must be able to deal with the following characteristics:

1. There are two verbs, each derived from a different deep structure clause.

2. *Flip,* the single noun in the surface representation, is the subject of *run* in an underlying clause *Flip runs* which serves as the object of the verb *see. See (Flip runs).*

3. This deep structure clause *Flip runs* is, therefore, embedded in another clause.

4. The subject of the other clause, *you,* was deleted in the surface structure *You see (Flip runs)* through a rule that requires it in command structure.

5. In the process of embedding *Flip runs,* rules have been applied which delete the *s* normally present in third person singular verb forms.

Even though it is composed of three short words, there is a great deal of complexity in this sentence. It requires a high degree of familiarity with the grammatical system of the language in order to be able to handle such complexity. Fortunately, since the grammatical system underlies oral language as well, the reader, even the beginner, has basic control over it.

The native language reader knows the system of his language so well that he predicts its surface structure and infers the deep structure on the basis of small samples of information actually processed. Two interrelated characteristics of language facilitate this prediction and sampling. One is *sequential constraint*. Given any single language element, the possibilities of which elements may follow are highly constrained: some may follow, some may not, some may but are unlikely. Given a string of elements, the constraints become much greater. Hence, language is highly predictable; particularly with regard to grammatical structures, since there are fewer grammatical structures than possible words that may fit within them.

Redundancy is the other factor that facilitates language processing. This term, derived from information theory, means the tendency in language for information to be carried by more than one part of the signal. Language is redundant to the extent that each element carries more than a single bit of information.

In the sentence *He was watching Mary, watching* has three cues to its function as a verb: its position in the sentence, the use of *was* with it, and its *ing* ending. Sequential constraint contributes considerably to redundancy. Since *q* must always be followed by *u*, no new information is provided by the *u*. Redundancy makes it possible to sample without losing information. It also provides a possibility of verification, since multiple cues must be consistent.

Two important principles emerge from these insights: (a) the *axiom of predictability:* a given sequence will be easy to read to the extent that what the reader is most likely to predict actually occurs; uncommon, unusual, or unlikely sequences will be harder to read than common, usual, or likely ones; (b) *length of passage:* since redundancy and sequential constraint build up as the reader progresses in a passage, short passages are harder to read than long ones, other things being equal. The first paragraph of a story will be relatively harder than the first page, for example. Tests composed of questions or short items are considerably harder to read than the more usual reading tasks.

TENTATIVE INFORMATION PROCESSING

Reading at its proficient best is a smooth, rapid, guessing game in which the reader samples from available language cues, using the least amount of available information to achieve his essential task of reconstructing and comprehending the writer's meaning. It can be regarded as a systematic reduction of uncertainty as the reader starts with graphic input and ends with meaning. The reader need not use all the graphic cues available in the printed page, nor is he restricted to them. As a user of language, he has both syntactic and semantic input to relate to graphic cues and interact with them. He uses graphic cues, perhaps supported by related phonological cues, to help predict grammatical sequences; he uses graphic and grammatical cues to trigger the search of his memory for related meaning; and he uses all, in turn, to predict subsequent input.

He is, then, *at all times* utilizing three sources of information interdependently:

1. Grapho-phonic information

2. Syntactic information

3. Semantic information

Even perception is constantly conditioned by expectation and prior input. What the reader thinks he sees is a fusion of what he actually sees and what he expects to see.

Letters are never really identified until the sequences in which they're found are identified. Words are never really recognized until the grammatical sequence is known. The grammatical pattern is never sure until the meaning is known. The view of reading as precise responses to letters and sounds is inappropriate. Everything is tentative until meaning results; and the reader is propelled toward meaning. As reading proceeds, he is constantly modifying both meaning and his tentative processing of language information.

Accuracy of identification or perception is not necessary. Rather, the reader needs:

1. Effective Strategies For Selecting The Most Useful Cues From The Three Kinds of Information Some cues carry a lot of information;

others are either undependable or redundant. Readers must learn to zero-in on the most useful cues while ignoring the others.

2. Effective Strategies For Guessing A Deep Structure So That He May Derive Meaning.

3. Effective Strategies For Testing Guesses   Essentially, the reader must be able to test the fit of his guesses against the grammatical and semantic constraints. He must ask himself whether what he thinks he has read makes sense within the semantic constraints. He also must ask himself whether it sounds like language; that is, whether it is grammatical within the syntactic constraints. These twin contexts are interdependent. There can be no meaning without grammar, though grammar without meaning is possible. Readers dealing with meaning beyond their comprehension can frequently give the illusion of understanding through their ability to manipulate grammatical patterns. Questions can often be answered by transforming them to statements and supplying the unknown elements from the text without knowing the meaning of the answer. The reader, of course, must learn not to be stopped short of comprehension.

4. Effective Strategies for Correcting   If the reader realizes he has made a miscue that needs correction, he must be able to recover, to gather and process more information, to reorganize his guesses, find alternate structures, and make sense out of what has eluded him. Regression, moving the eyes back over previously processed text, is often vital to the correction process, since the reader must literally re-view (see again) what he has processed ineffectively.

Figure 2 presents our model of the reading process.

TOWARD A THEORY OF READING INSTRUCTION

Eventually, the time will come when reading materials and methods will be solidly based in an articulated theory of reading instruction. This writer would like to present here some of the essentials of such an instructional theory:

1. Meaning must always be the immediate as well as the ultimate goal in reading. *Instruction must be comprehension centered.* This must be foremost in the mind of both the teacher and the learner. Every instructional activity must be organized around a search for meaning.

Figure 2 The Goodman Model of Reading

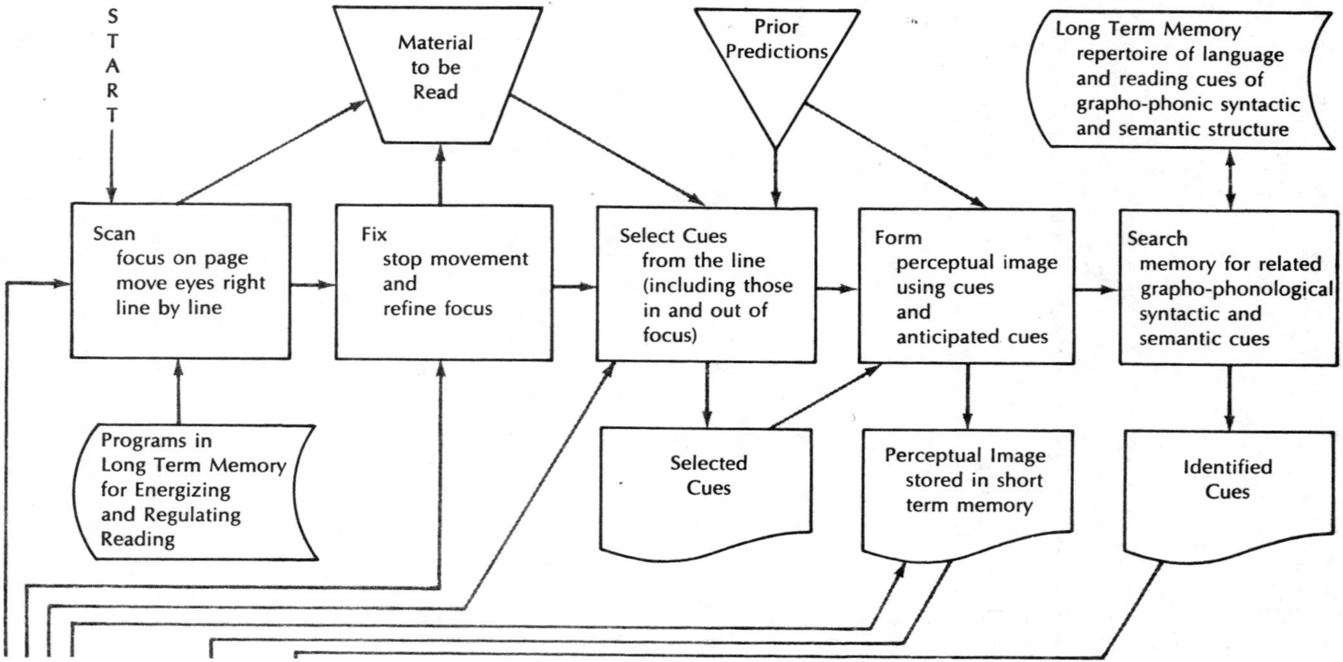

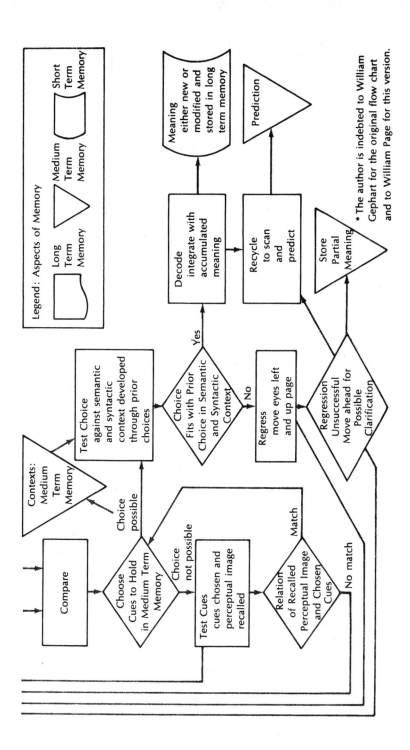

Legend: Aspects of Memory

Medium Term Memory

Short Term Memory

Long Term Memory

Compare

Choose Cues to Hold in Medium Term Memory

Choice not possible

Choice possible

Test Cues
cues chosen and perceptual image recalled

Relation of Recalled Perceptual Image and Chosen Cues

Match

No match

Contexts: Medium Term Memory

Test Choice against semantic and syntactic context developed through prior choices

Choice Fits with Prior Choice in Semantic and Syntactic Context

Yes

No

Regress
move eyes left and up page

Regression Unsuccessful Move ahead for Possible Clarification

Decode integrate with accumulated meaning

Recycle to scan and predict

Store Partial Meaning

Meaning either new or modified and stored in long term memory

Prediction

* The author is indebted to William Gephart for the original flow chart and to William Page for this version.

2. Language systems (phonology, grammar, lexicon) are interdependent and hence language is indivisible. Fractionating language for instructional purposes into words and word parts destroys its essential nature.

3. Language exists only in the process of its use. Instruction must view and deal with language in process. There is *no possible sequencing of skills* in reading instruction since all systems must be used interdependently in the reading process even in the first attempts at learning to read.

4. Children learning to read their native language are competent language users. This competence constitutes their primary resource for learning to read. This is a vital reason why instruction in reading must start "where the learner is."

5. Mechanisms which operate in the acquisition of oral language, whether we regard them as learned or innate, are available to the learner as he strives to master literacy. Though those mechanisms are not well understood yet, it is warranted to state that children will find it easiest to learn to read language which is meaningful and natural to them. Perhaps the key motivational factor to be exploited is *communicative need.* Children come to understand language which *they need* to understand. This is no less true in learning to read than it is in learning to understand oral language.

6. The reading process is the psycholinguistic guessing game we have described. Children must learn strategies for predicting, sampling and selecting information, guessing, confirming or rejecting guesses, correcting and reprocessing. Much research must be done on these strategies.

7. Special reading strategies must be developed for handling the reading of special forms of language. Literature is one such special form. It has a special set of constraints; for example, the strong tendency to avoid repetitive use of terms. Such a prohibition makes literary language less predictable. Each language form requires some special strategies which readers must develop to be able to read a broad range of language effectively.

8. Meaning is both input and output in reading. Any selection will be understood only to the extent that the reader brings to it the prerequisite concepts and experiences. Even in reading to learn, the new concepts can only be slightly beyond the reader's prior attainments, and he must

be able to relate vicarious experience to real experience in order to make any use of it.

Special materials for reading instruction, materials designed and prepared to facilitate learning to read, are perhaps a contradiction in terms, since such materials are likely to distort and fragment language. Eventually, we may come to the point where text materials for reading will be packages of selections with widely ranging content and levels of difficulty. These selections will be accompanied by extensive guidance to teachers on using the materials to increment the developing competence of the learners. In any case, materials for reading instruction must involve natural language; they must be highly predictable on the basis of the learner's language; and they must involve meaning within the learner's grasp; that is, they must be related to the reader's linguistic competence and his experience.

The time will come when we will know enough about the reading process and how it is learned to make the acquisition of literacy a universal extension of language learning.

QUALITATIVE READING MISCUE

ANALYSIS FOR TEACHER TRAINING

Yetta M. Goodman

For years, teachers of reading have been trained to teach children the physical components of reading print. The only argument about method concerned whether the input had to be words as a unit, or words broken into the constituent parts. Regardless, the view was to teach the youngsters either how to recognize words, or how to sound out letters or groups of letters. To be sure, there was concern with meaning, contextual clues, and so on; but the lack of understanding that reading is a language process allowed teachers to emphasize word attack skills, either "look-say" or "phonics." Children had to discover on their own the interrelationships of the language aspects which formed the communicative utterance they needed to grasp in order to read.

The use of principles and methodology from various social science disciplines has helped us to question many of the notions we used to have. Linguists, anthropologists, psychologists, sociologists, and other social scientists have learned that, in order to understand a group or an individual, it is necessary to describe his behavior—to attempt to understand his behavior, categorize it, and make hypotheses which are accepted or rejected through further research.

In the reading field, up to now, we have stated assumptions, placed a value judgment on them, and then described and prescribed based on the value judgment. We must help teachers move away from this unscientific way of viewing reading and readers to a more scientific approach.

THE TEACHER AS READING RESEARCHER

Teachers of reading have available to them the most basic source of reading research data—the child as he reads.

The best way to become aware of the reading process is to watch and listen to children reading orally. Their miscues, which have usually been thought of as reading mistakes, are extremely revealing. Instead of attacking the miscues children make when they read as something which must be eradicated, the teachers of reading must learn to describe overt reading behavior and then to understand this behavior by asking such questions as:

1. Why do readers make miscues?

2. What categories or patterns do the miscues make?

3. What is the significance of the miscues?

Teachers of reading and reading specialists can discover many aspects of reading if they examine the reading process through *qualitative miscue analysis*.

MISCUE ANALYSIS: THE TECHNIQUE

In order to provide data for qualitative miscue analysis, the reader is presented with something interesting to read which is entirely new to him. The selection of reading material is important and must be thought out carefully. It should neither be too easy, nor too difficult for the reader. The reader is then asked to read the selection, which is audio-taped. At the time of audiotaping, the teacher or researcher sits with a copy of the reading material and marks each miscue. The reader receives *no help* from the researcher, since important evidence is gained as readers discover ways to solve their own reading problems.

A miscue is an observed oral response which the researcher hears which does not conform to what is expected. The reader is asked to read orally since this is the only way miscues can be identified. After the miscues have been marked and subsequently rechecked by listening to the tape, each miscue is qualitatively analyzed. This is done by asking a series of questions related to psycholinguistic principles.

MISCUE ANALYSIS: MEANING

The first question might deal with how much the meaning of the text has been changed by the miscue. If the text meaning has been changed a great deal, the miscue is placed on a code sheet for further analysis, but when the following miscues are examined we may prefer another course:

Text: "Our kitten!" the Jones children said.
Reader: "Our kitten!" the Jones kids said.

Text: In a little while he was asleep.
Reader: In a little while he was sleeping.

Text: The three brothers went home.
Reader: The three brother went home.

There has been no change of meaning in the preceding examples. Since the major purpose in the teaching of reading is for meaning to be extracted from the printed page, there need be no concern with these miscues and such behavior should not be considered as weakness. Such miscues may, in fact, point to the strengths readers have as they move toward the ability of going directly from print to meaning. In the oral encoding, the reader in the examples has used an alternate surface structure. Most dialect miscues belong in this category and would suggest that reading is not the place to be concerned with changing a child's dialect. The ability to read in one's own dialect is a strength. The reader translates the language of the text into his own language for greater understanding. Correcting dialect while a child reads tends to confuse him and interferes with his development of reading proficiency. Examining the degree to which the miscue changes the meaning of the text often gives a good deal of insight into how important meaning is to the reader. Also, the experiential background of a child is often revealed through his miscues.

MISCUE ANALYSIS: GRAMMAR

After the miscues which do not change the meaning of the text are set aside, then the remainder of the miscues may be put through another group of questions. When miscues do change the meaning of the text to some degree, the next questions deal with the acceptability of the passage which resulted from the miscue, keeping in mind the child's language and experiential background. Children bring their understanding of grammar and meaning to the reading task and a large percentage of their miscues reflect this understanding. Children's miscues produce more grammatically acceptable sentences than meaningfully acceptable sentences.

Text: showing calmness and courage
Reader: showing climeness and congress

The reader in the preceding example came up with two words that semantically could not fit the passage. Yet, *climeness* has a morphemic ending which corresponds to *calmness;* and both *climeness* and *congress* are nouns as are the words they replaced—*calmness* and *courage.* Even beginning readers produce miscues which are the same functional part of speech as the expected response. This phenomenon increases as children become more proficient readers.

The grammatical system of a reader's language has great influence on the reading process. All readers, even at beginning stages, bring this strength with them to the reading task.

Text: I opened the dictionary and picked out a word that sounded good.

Reader: Ah opened a dictionary to pick out the word that sounded good.

Text: I mean I really yelled it.

Reader: I mean I'll really yell it out.

Value judgments will come into play in the examination of a child's miscues. Do the above examples make enough of a difference to the text to be concerned about? How important is the subtle difference between *a* and *the* to call attention to it? Is it very important to the whole story that at this particular point in time the reader put the second of the above examples into the present tense? Obviously, it is necessary to know more about the story, which means that this analysis cannot be done by looking at miscues apart from the context of the reading material. It may also suggest that reading cannot be taught apart from the context of reading materials.

When miscues result in passages which are fully acceptable within the child's language and experiential background and do not cause too great a change in the meaning of the text material, these miscues may also be put aside as ones which are not too important to be concerned with. Again, strengths are revealed in the reader rather than weaknesses.

MISCUE ANALYSIS: CORRECTION STRATEGIES

When miscues which do change the text to a great extent or which do not produce acceptable passages are examined, an additional question must be asked: Does the reader make any attempt to correct these particular miscues? The self-correction strategy is observed through the phenomenon of regressing, of looking back over text previously read. This is a strength that the reader learns as he becomes more proficient. Virtually every regression a reader makes is for the purpose of grasping better understanding of the reading material. Often correction strategies give insight into how much the reader is concerned with meaning or comprehension, as well as evidence that the child applies his sophisticated knowledge of the grammatical system to reading. When proficient readers use correction strategies, they are likely to correct miscues which result in semantically unacceptable passages, but even more likely to correct syntactically unacceptable miscues.

Children often correct during subsequent tries at the same word. Examining the different attempts at one try, or different attempts at different tries, can give insights into the reader's use of phonetic skills as well as his priorities in the reading task. Sometimes readers abandon a word which has close phonemic similarity to the expected response to move to a word which makes sense in the passage. This ability is a strength in reading.

Concepts of words or phrases are often developed through the reading of a story. In one story used in our research, the basic concept of the story was related to the fact that a "typical baby" turns into a baby who isn't so typical. Most of the readers had never heard or seen the word *typical* before. It was not pronounced correctly—most readers said *topical* or *typeical* for *typical*. Yet, at the end of the story, most of the children could explain that the baby was an ordinary baby, or a normal baby, or a usual baby.

Those miscues which are corrected by the reader either immediately or at subsequent tries can be set aside. Again, the child indicates an additional strength—his self correction strategy. This will serve him in good stead in his silent reading.

OTHER REASONS FOR MISCUES

The next questions deal with specific aspects of the reading process. Miscues are sometimes caused by something the child sees peripherally and which he draws into his reading, either inserting the word or phrase, or substituting it. This sometimes gives insight into the range the reader perceives as he reads. Young readers and less proficient readers sometimes associate words with an incorrect printed representation. For example, a child might read *happy birthday* every time the word *happy* appears in print. *Then* and *when, said* and *is* are some common habitual associations. These are problems that persist for some children over a long period of time. Special material may have to be written for an individual youngster to help him differentiate words like these from each other. Drilling on these out of context only tends to reinforce the association. Questions dealing with how the reader handles peripheral and habitual association miscues will give insights into a child's reading ability.

The last questions deal with the relationship of the miscue to the printed text in terms of the graphic system and the sound system. All readers pay attention to the graphic shape of what they read and miscues most often look like the words or phrases they replace. Knowledge of sound-letter correspondence is not highly sophisticated in early reading. Qualitative miscue analysis gives the teacher the opportunity to decide how close to the printed text the miscue is phonemically. *Men* for *man* is a much closer miscue than *monkey* for *man*. We need to find ways in the teaching of reading to help beginning readers zero-in on phonemic similarity and not have a model of perfection from the earliest stages. Children who overuse phonic and graphic clues often do this at the expense of comprehension.

CONCLUSIONS

Preservice and inservice teachers often become enthusiastic about the use of qualitative miscue analysis as they begin to make all types of discoveries about reading. Such analysis can produce:

1. Greater insight into the process of reading and the acquisition of reading proficiency.

2. Analysis of the strengths and weaknesses of the individual reader.

3. Knowledge to help readers use the reading process with greater awareness.

4. Focus on the important and significant aspects of the reading process.

Only when a preservice or inservice teacher gains insight into the reading process and is aware of the interrelatedness of the various aspects which qualitative miscue analysis provides can he begin to diagnose and plan programs for individuals within his class.

FOR FURTHER READING

Goodman, Kenneth S. "Analysis of Oral Reading Miscues: Applied Psycholinguistics," *Reading Research Quarterly*, 1969, 2 (February), 9–30.

A presentation of the system the author has developed for analyzing the unexpected oral reading responses of children.

Goodman, Kenneth S. and Niles, Olive S. *Reading: Process and Program*. Commission on the English Curriculum, National Council of Teachers of English, 1970.

This book concerns the relationship between language and reading, and between the content of written material and reading competence. It then develops a theoretical model of the reading process.

Goodman, Yetta "Using Children's Miscues for Teaching Reading Strategies," *Reading Teacher*, 1970, 23 (February), 455–459.

This article provides further discussion of how qualitative miscue analysis can give teachers insights into the strengths and weaknesses of readers and how it can be used to improve reading instruction.

SEVEN · LANGUAGE AND MEANING

Reading, as was pointed out in the previous section, is ultimately directed toward the reconstruction of meaning as contained in the writer's message. As Kenneth Goodman has remarked, and as his reading model indicates, reading must be comprehension centered. The present section contains two papers by authors whose main concerns are with meaning as it is conveyed through oral and written forms of language.

Professor Robert Ruddell of the University of California at Berkeley, and his associate, Mrs. Helen Bacon, also use a model to present their views of meaning in the reading process. Their *communication* model, which Ruddell developed, encompasses reading, listening, speaking, and writing. Ruddell devised this model on the basis of theory and research evidence derived from linguistics and psycholinguistics. His purpose was to provide classroom teachers and curriculum makers with a method for determining the kind of language instruction appropriate to pupils who are progressing or encountering difficulty in a particular learning situation.

Primarily, Ruddell's discussion of his model focuses on reading and on three processes employed by readers and listeners in comprehending oral and written messages: *decoding* strategies, *meaning* strategies, and *interpretation* abilities. Ruddell describes the model and illustrates its use, while Mrs. Bacon pays particular attention to the *interpretation* aspects of the communication model. Both authors regard interpretation as the process by which the reader (or listener) derives meaning from a communication; it is, they assert, a function of experience, memory, and the skills involved in critical and creative thinking.

Although Ruddell and Bacon have cast their discussion principally in theoretical terms, their aim is to indicate how theoretical frameworks can have relevance for the practical matter of classroom instruction. Inherent in Ruddell's communication model and Bacon's taxonomy of comprehension skills is much of the information presented in previous papers, particularly those pertaining to the writing system and to child language development.

Professor Ruddell is the Director of Project DELTA, an inservice teacher training program sponsored by the U.S. Office of Education. Mrs. Bacon is Associate Director of the project. She is also Supervisor of Reading and Language in the Novato, California school system.

Professor Pose Lamb of Purdue University has turned her attention to a discussion of definitions for the terms *language* and *meaning* as these relate to reading instruction. Using these definitions, she indicates how interpretations of linguistic and psycholinguistic evidence should be analyzed in respect to the theories from which they emanate. She also cautions against the tendency to apply such evidence in developing materials and plans for instruction without duly taking into account the consequences for children.

Lamb's focus is on the *child* in the language instruction setting. In her paper, she seeks to synthesize many aspects of language study—linguistics; language acquisition, writing, and sociolinguistics; and makes clear that meaning cannot be divorced from the language that is selected to convey it.

THE NATURE OF READING:

LANGUAGE AND MEANING

Robert B. Ruddell
Helen G. Bacon

Each hour of instructional time, in the kindergarten and elementary school classroom, demands numerous decisions related to reading-language instruction. These decisions may range from that of altering the level of abstraction as concepts in a space exploration story are introduced to an individual youngster, to the need to use individual literary selections rather than a group assigned story. During actual instruction, however, decisions must be effected in a split second if the learning activities of the children involved are to receive adequate guidance.

If effective and rapid-fire decisions are to be made, it is essential that we fuse two important instructional components—the instructional "why" and the instructional "how." That is, we must develop the ability to rapidly integrate our background knowledge of language and the way children learn with our applied classroom understandings. Of critical importance to this integrative ability and decision-making effectiveness is a conceptual framework, or model, of the reading-language process which will enable us to quickly identify the appropriateness of instructional experiences as we observe the specific progress and difficulty encountered by the individual child or group.

The following discussion is oriented toward the application of information about language and meaning to classroom reading-language instruction. In this discussion we will utilize a communication model, derived from a psycholinguistic research base (Goodman & Fleming, 1969; Ruddell, 1969, 1970; Singer & Ruddell, 1970), as we examine the communication process used in reading and comprehending a sample passage. Decoding strategies, meaning strategies, and interpretation abilities will be highlighted in the model. Mrs. Bacon will then examine the interpretation process in detail as we consider identification and recall, analytical, integrative, and evaluative levels. It is our purpose to emphasize the application of language information to the classroom reading-language program.

Figure 1 The Communication Model

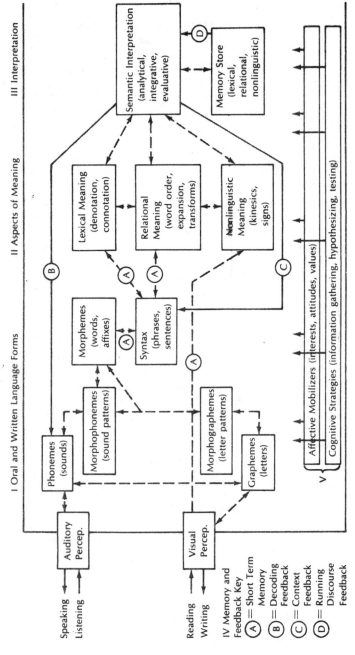

THE COMMUNICATION MODEL

The Communication Model presented in Figure 1 may be summarized by considering its five basic categories. The first category (I) is that of *Oral and Written Language Forms* and includes the phonological, graphological, morphological, and syntactical components. The second category (II), *Aspects of Meaning,* includes the meaning components—lexical, relational, and nonlinguistic; while the third category (III), *Interpretation,* integrates the various aspects of meaning through analytical, integrative, and evaluative thinking. The fourth category (IV) of *Memory and Feedback* provides for storing and transferring information from one part of the model to another as required in evaluating and formulating interpretations. The fifth and last category (V) is that of *Affective Mobilizers and Cognitive Strategies.* These dual components interact with and serve to direct all dimensions of communication as specific goals and objectives are identified and the individual directs his thinking processes to achieve the established goals and objectives, which culminates in the third previously mentioned category, *Interpretation.*

As the beginning reader approaches the printed page (see Figure 1), he is confronted with a representation of oral language—specifically, written language forms that are realized as letters, letter patterns, and punctuation symbols which provide intonation clues. His oral language system, in most instances, will be highly developed and realized through his production of sounds, sound patterns, sentences, and his utilization of lexical meaning, relational meaning, nonlinguistic meaning, and, to some extent, interpretation. He will have developed certain specific interests, attitudes, and early values; and he may have developed a strategy to approach decoding, meaning, and interpretative problems.

The following discussion which examines the nature of the reading process is graphically illustrated by the communication model in Figure 1. Progression through the model as it pertains to reading begins at the box labeled "Visual Perception."

ORAL AND WRITTEN LANGUAGE FORMS

An initial step in reading instruction is to aid the child in perceiving letters and letter patterns and building an understanding that these units represent his familiar sound system. We are interested in building letter-sound, and letter pattern-sound pattern relationships within the context of the word (see doubled-dash lines connecting these components in the model). In some instances, we will focus on a direct relationship between letter pattern sequence configurations and entire words or morphemes—commonly referred to as a sight vocabulary (see curved doubled-dash line connecting the letter pattern and morpheme categories). In other instances, a knowledge of root word and affix (prefix and suffix) boundaries can be a useful device for visual identification of letter units which are decodable on the basis of letter-sound and letter pattern-sound pattern clues. In addition, feedback from the interpretation of previous context in the reading material can serve to provide valuable decoding clues by narrowing the possible words to be decoded (see feedback line for evaluating decoding information). And still further, feedback information from the phrase and sentence structure can aid in limiting the possible words for decoding based on intuitive knowledge of word order and form class.

The process of communication becomes more meaningful as the act of reading is examined through the model components. First, read the following excerpt from the delightful story, *Charlie the Tramp*, written by Russell Hoban and illustrated by Lillian Hoban (1966). We will then discuss the process involved in decoding and interpreting the underlined sentence in this excerpt from the standpoint of the early reader—utilizing the communication model components.

The story is about Charlie, a young beaver, who decides that he would like to become a tramp and run away from home. At this point in the story, Father, Mother, and Grandfather have just noticed a new beaver pond which has been constructed near their home.

"That's funny," said Father. "I didn't make it. I wonder who did?"

"I did," said Charlie, waking up and coming out of the hollow tree. "That's my pond."

"That's your pond?" said Father.

"That's my pond," said Charlie.

"I thought you were a tramp," said Grandfather. "Tramps don't make ponds."

"Well," said Charlie, *"sometimes I like to tramp around, and sometimes I like to make ponds."*

"Any tramp that can make a pond like that is going to be some beaver one of these days," said Father.

"That's how it is now-a-days," said Grandfather. "You never know when a tramp will turn out to be a beaver."

Using the sample sentence italicized above, Table I illustrates the application of various decoding strategies used in assessing the decoding information available, formulating decoding hypotheses about each word and rapidly testing these hypotheses through context in an attempt to decode the sentence.

Table 1   Oral And Written Language Forms

"Well," said Charlie, "sometimes I like to tramp around, and sometimes I like to make ponds."

Strategy: Oral and Written Language Forms	Sample Words
Letter-sound relationship	Well—I—tramp—I—ponds
Letter pattern-sound pattern relationship	like—like—make
Sight word	said—Charlie—to—to
Root word(s) and/or affix plus preceding three steps	some*times*—sometimes— ponds—around
Root word and context	sometimes—ponds—around
Context, previous information	Charlie—tramp—ponds
Context, phrase or sentence structure	said—to—tramp—and—to
Intonation clues	" " — , — . —and capital letters
Nonlinguistic clues	illustrations in the text

It thus becomes obvious that a variety of strategies can be employed in decoding printed text. As adult readers, we rely heavily on our knowledge of letter pattern-sound pattern clues, a wide sight vocabulary, root words, and contextual constraints in decoding unfamiliar text. The instructional program will need to make provision for these strategies if the decoding ability of the child is to mature.

ASPECTS OF MEANING

As the reader moves toward an interpretation of the sentence, he begins to "chunk" the words into the larger units or phrases which are common in his developed oral language system. This is accomplished by using the syntax (phrase and sentence) component and a temporary syntactic structure is automatically assigned to the words and word groups—to be verified later by feedback information from the interpretation level (see feedback lines in model). The sentence is then processed through the various aspects of meaning. The lexical meaning component may be thought of as a "mental dictionary" of denotative and connotative meanings of words that have been determined by the nature and variety of the reader's past experiences. The relational meaning component will account for such features as word order, function words, and subordination, and provides for transforming the sentence for integration at the interpretation level. Information of a nonlinguistic nature, such as facial expression conveyed in an illustration accompanying the text, is available through visual perception and will also be used at the interpretation level. The lexical, relational, and nonlinguistic meanings may interact prior to the final interpretation of the sentence in order to define the types of meaning more completely. The sample sentence is used again (see Table 2) to illustrate the meaning components which are essential to a final interpretation.

Table 2   Aspects Of Meaning

"Well," said Charlie, "sometimes I like to tramp around, and sometimes I like to make ponds."

Strategy: Aspects Of Meaning	Words And Word Groups
Lexical	*Charlie*—little beaver—the main story character searching for his identity
	sometimes—at times or on occasion
	like—to enjoy or be fond of
	make—to build or construct

Relational	*Well*—an opener indicating that an explanation is to follow
	said—indicates Charlie is speaking
	I—refers to Charlie
	and—connects or relates the two sentence groups
Lexical And Relational	*to tramp around*—wandering about on foot from one place to another
	to make—building or constructing
Lexical, Relational, And Nonlinguistic	*ponds*—more than one small body of standing water formed by the beaver dam (picture clues may be used here)

INTERPRETATION, MEMORY, AND FEEDBACK

The final interpretation of the sentence takes place by integrating the lexical, relational, and nonlinguistic meanings the reader has developed thus far. As already noted, the reader's interpretation of the discourse will require that he account for previous information or events in the reading material. His interpretation will be greatly influenced by his level of conceptual maturity and his ability to handle concrete, functional, and abstract concepts. His interpretation ability will be directly related to his critical thinking skills—his abilities to analyze, to integrate, and to evaluate information—and will be influenced by his understanding of special language devices such as metaphor, simile, irony, and hyperbole.

Returning to the sample sentence again, Table 3 considers the base sentence interpretations and a final semantic interpretation.

Table 3   Interpretation

"Well," said Charlie, "sometimes I like to tramp
around, and sometimes I like to make ponds."

Base Sentence Interpretation	**Semantic Interpretation**
	ANALYTICAL SKILLS
Charlie tramps.	Separating fact from nonfact
Charlie likes tramping sometimes.	Recognizing cause and effect
Charlie makes ponds.	Separating fact from nonfact
Charlie likes making ponds sometimes.	Recognizing cause and effect
	INTEGRATIVE SKILLS
Charlie likes tramping sometimes and Charlie likes building ponds sometimes.	Identifying relationships
	Inferring beyond data
	Drawing conclusions, which in the running discourse results in the interpretation: Charlie, the little beaver searching for his place in life, enjoys wandering about from place to place on foot at times, and at other times enjoys building beaver dams which form small bodies of standing water.

This semantic interpretation is then categorized, probably in a form more similar to the base sentence interpretation above, and retained in memory where it can later be made available for immediate feedback in evaluating new running discourse or for later interpretative use.

AFFECTIVE MOBILIZERS AND COGNITIVE STRATEGIES

Throughout the various stages of the communication process, the reader's participation is directed by his interests, attitudes, and values—

what we have called his affective mobilizers (see bottom of model). These mobilizers may take the form of specific questions which the reader has raised (e.g., Why did Charlie think he wanted to become a tramp?) and which are of value in identifying specific content that can be useful in answering the question. On the other hand, his attitude toward the topic, or even toward the act of reading itself, may be extremely potent, positively or negatively, and thus can interfere with an objective interpretation of the material, or perhaps even terminate his participation in the reading process because of lack of motivation. His problem-solving abilities, which we call *cognitive strategies* (see bottom of model), are likewise involved in all stages of the model. These strategies not only provide for an approach to achieving the reader's objectives, such as answering any questions he has formulated (e.g., Did Charlie's parents and grandparents change their attitude toward his activities? If so, why?), but also readily direct a shift in that approach should initial attempts to achieve his objectives prove fruitless.

Now that an overview of the communication model has been developed, we can proceed to examine in greater detail the inter-pretation process. Mrs. Bacon will focus on the identification of the comprehension skills involved in interpreting spoken and written com-munication, skills whose development should, we assert, be a part of instructional programs.

INTERPRETATION

Interpretation accounts for the meaning which an individual derives from his abilities to think critically and creatively, and which has as its base, the domains of *cognition* and *affect*. Within the cognitive domain, we propose that two major areas can be identified: (1) *Experience and Memory*, which includes the skills of identification and recall, pre-requisites for the accumulation of knowledge and experiential data; and (2) *Critical Thinking*, which incorporates analytical, integrative, and evaluative skills, essential for the conduct of what Taba (1967) has designated as higher thinking processes.

In the affective domain, we include those responses and reactions which can be characterized as an individual's interest, attitude, feeling, motivation, and valuing toward events and ideas.

Table 4 Taxonomy of Comprehension Skills

	Experience and Memory	Critical Thinking Skills		
Comprehension Skills	Identification and Recall	Analytical	Integrative	Evaluative
	identifying and restating facts, events and ideas by: naming listing classifying categorizing sequencing	examining facts, events, and ideas by: separating fact from non-fact discriminating relevant from irrelevant information checking facts, events and ideas by: recognizing unstated assumptions recognizing propaganda recognizing cause and effect recognizing causal relations	explaining by: providing illustrations and examples making comparisons identifying relationships organizing facts, events and ideas summarizing by: inferring beyond given data forming generalizations drawing conclusions predicting outcomes	judging by: appraising validity and reliability of facts, events, ideas and purposes assessing the competence of writer/speaker on certain subjects rating a work or ideas according to standards in that field.
Problem Solving	recognizing and defining the problem, analyzing various sources of information,		synthesizing information, creating and generating ideas and hypotheses,	evaluating ideas and possible solutions, testing solutions.
Affective	interests	attitudes		values

It is in these regards that we have been attempting to devise a taxonomy of comprehension skills which can be applied to instruction. Similar models, such as Bloom's *Taxonomy of Educational Objectives* (1956), Guilford's model of the structure of the intellect (1960), and Taba's test of critical thinking (1964), have been widely used in various studies, and evidence indicates that directed instruction can enhance the critical thinking skills of elementary school children.

A few cautionary remarks should be made before proceeding to an explanation of the taxonomy shown in Table 4. First, we are aware that individuals may, but do not necessarily, proceed from one skill to another within this classification framework. For example, *sequencing ability*, listed at the bottom of the *Identification And Recall* category, is not predicated upon the earlier listed ability to *classify*. This premise remains constant for all skills in the other categories.

Second, individuals may, but do not necessarily, progress along a continuum from analytical, to integrative and, finally, to evaluative skills. We believe that individuals can, and do, utilize skills across all three areas. Specific use of one skill or another, such as *separating fact from nonfact*, will depend on several variables such as the materials or experiences under examination; the level of intellectual development of the student; and the availability of this skill in the student's repertoire.

EXPERIENCE & MEMORY

Turning to the first category of the taxonomy, *Experience & Memory*, we are concerned with the identification and recall of facts, events, and ideas. To recapitulate information from environmental stimuli, such as a field trip or the reading of a story, an individual utilizes one or more of the basic skills we have listed: naming, listing, categorizing, classifying, and sequencing.

For instance, having heard the nursery tale of *The Three Bears*, a young child may list or recite all the names of the characters in the story: Father, Mother, Baby Bear, and Goldilocks. An older student, on the other hand, may list all the specific details of the plays at his baseball game which resulted in his team's loss of the pennant.

Developmental reading series offer many opportunities to find and state the main idea of a passage; in fact, most reading comprehension tests measure this skill. However, in naming the main idea of a passage, a more complex operation is also involved, that of formulating a statement in which lexical and relational aspects must be coordinated into a creative expression. For example, upon completion of the reading of Marjorie Flack's book *Angus and the Ducks* (1930), children's responses may vary from a young child's, "It's about a puppy and two ducks," to a twelve-year-old's, "This is the tale of a puppy who restrains his curiosity after being frightened by the noise of two ducks." Notice that both students have named the main idea of the story, but that the older student's statement is more explicit. This difference can be attributed not only to level of mental maturity but also to alternative lexical and relational meanings available to and utilized by the twelve-year-old. These "aspects of meaning" are intricately interwoven into the interpretation component of oral and written communication.

Piaget (1963) has shown that one of the important functions of thinking is to order information into larger categories. A very young child may call all four-footed creatures by the name of the family dog, for example, "Sam" or "Rover." However, he soon makes distinctions, not only between his own pet and that of his neighbor, but ascertains that dogs differ from other animals, such as cats.

Within these larger categories, he learns to classify some cats as different also; for example, some are Persians, some are Manx, and some are Siamese. This differentiation process becomes more and more refined as students mature.

Noting sequence, in time, of events, ideas, and details is another essential feature of recalling experiential activities. For instance, retelling or dramatizing a folk tale requires an ability to place events in proper order.

By way of summary, it can be noted that all individuals employ the elementary functions of identification and recall with increasing finesse and skill as new information and experiences occur over time. It is these skills that serve as the basic ingredients for critical thinking.

CRITICAL THINKING

Moving to the next major category—*Critical Thinking*—we believe that three fundamental skills operate to assist in deciphering incoming oral and written messages; namely, (1) analytical, (2) integrative, and (3) evaluative skills. As we progress downward and across the hierarchy, these three skills become highly refined and integrated with the next major category, *Problem Solving*. Each of these fundamental skills will be discussed as we move from *Critical Thinking* into *Problem Solving*.

Analytical Skills   Incoming data are analyzed by examining facts, events, and ideas through the manipulation and interaction of information already stored in memory. An aptitude for collecting facts dealing with a wide variety of subjects—such as literary, historical, and geographical facts—occurs as children progress through the grades. As new experiences and information are received, children ordinarily begin to question and to separate fantasy and opinion from fact. They come to recognize the relevancy or nonrelevancy of information. This process can be aided and bolstered in small group discussions where students can receive immediate feedback from their peers and teacher regarding the factual basis and relevancy of information they share with the group. As a result of this sifting, sorting, and separating of old and new information, transformations occur in children's perceptions and concepts.

In the second phase, information can be checked further by recognizing in the information unstated assumptions, propaganda, cause and effect, and causal relations. For example, in a short story in which two elderly maiden ladies are rudely kept from taking their customary afternoon nap by the raucous noise of a small boy, the eldest of the two asks, "Why does that boy have to make so much noise?" The younger answers, "Just because he's a boy." Underlying this statement is the assumption that all boys are noisy just because they are boys. Being able to recognize unstated assumptions is an important skill which needs direction and training because, so often, only a thin line divides "a fact" from "an assumption."

Especially crucial to the development of cognitive skills is the ability to recognize widely employed propaganda techniques. Too often, the mass media subject us to the "testimonial" in an attempt to win our support for a special brand of toothpaste, detergent, or breakfast cereal. In addition to the testimonial, "generalities" and "name calling" have been used in political campaigns. As demonstrated by research conducted by Lundsteen (1963), lessons can be designed that are effective in developing critical listening skills of intermediate grade children in respect to analyzing and judging propaganda.

Moving to the other analytical skill areas listed in the taxonomy, we find that recognition of cause and effect and causal relations demands and requires that we constantly check facts, events, and ideas. When we read in one section of a novel that the hero is popular and well-adjusted to his peers, but later that, while making a bid for leadership of the football team, his behavior is selfish and ruthless, we may ask, "What has created this contradictory set of behaviors?" Searching for an answer may involve recognizing a number of factors; for instance, the effects of a deleterious family alliance, a need for prestige, or a latent desire for power. A simple cause and effect statement can be ruled out; for, intricate and diverse variables must be analyzed in order to determine the probable source of the hero's devious behavior.

Examining the taxonomy, it can be seen that the next step in the use of analytic skills is ordinarily that of *Problem Solving,* a process which logically would follow the checking of facts, events, and ideas. Humans, however, seldom behave in such a rational manner. The demarcation shown in the taxonomy between *Critical Thinking Skills* and *Problem Solving Skills* is only intended to imply that when an individual recognizes and defines a problem, he has actuated problem-solving processes.

The important point here is that the individual does recognize and formulate a problem, *not* that such recognition necessarily follows in the order of thinking represented in the taxonomy. For example, a major problem that presently exists on many university and college campuses is who will control campus decision-making policies—students, faculty, or administration. This conflict includes such areas as entrance and graduation requirements, the presence of ROTC on campus, hiring and firing of new faculty members, and the content of courses. Once this problem has been defined and delineated the next step is to analyze various sources of data such as research studies, historical documents, questionnaires, polls, and conference proceedings for the purpose of verifying the problem definition.

Integrative Skills   Two processes which identify the integrative category are (1) the ability to explain the data one has gathered, and (2) the ability to summarize that data. In explaining data, we are often confronted with situations in which it is necessary to provide examples of the topic about which we are communicating; for example, in explaining the significance of an editorial, a passage from a novel, or an experience at the theater. Examples and illustrations offer the listener or reader additional data with which to interpret the communication. This is especially applicable in the elementary school to written expository materials such as those found in social studies, science, and mathematics where a complex conceptual framework may be too intricate for the students to grasp without providing ample illustrations of the concept that is presented.

Part of the integrative process also involves the skill of *making comparisons*. Young children can easily compare likenesses and differences of characters, themes, plots, and endings of literary selections. As another example, Taba (1964) has indicated that students can utilize this skill in the study of social sciences as they compare and contrast the characteristics of differing cultures, such as contrasting the life styles of certain African tribes with the American Indians.

On the other hand, to *identify relationships* among factors is more complex than merely comparing them. To be able to identify the relationships among those factors that have been pertinent to the advancement of an industrial society, or to recognize the intricate web of relationships among factors in the ecological environment, for example, requires a higher level of thinking, one in which numerous variables are manipulated. The complicated nature of this skill necessitates that some adjustments be made in instructional procedures for primary children. It is necessary to locate situations and experiences which have a close correspondence to young children's intellectual development and experiential background. Their first experiences should involve identifying concrete and functional variables; later experiences can lead to the identification of abstract relationships.

Explanation requires one other skill, that of organizing facts, events, and ideas into a unified whole so that the listener or reader can follow the logic of the presentation. Through the use of oral explanation and discussions of firsthand experiences and reading selections, we can assist students in developing an ability to structure their information for their audience.

The second phase of integrative skills is *summarizing information*. This requires the ability to infer beyond the given data; that is, to deduce facts and ideas which are not explicitly stated. In addition, an indispensable attribute, especially for interpreting data, is the ability to form generalizations (Taba, 1967).

Finally, two other skills are involved in the summarizing process. These are the abilities to *draw tentative conclusions* while new premises are being tested and to *predict outcomes* on the basis of valid evidence. The research of Ripple and Rockcastle (1964), Lovell (1968), and Saadeh (1962) indicates that these critical thinking skills do not result merely as a consequence of intellectual development; rather, special training and direction is needed if the development of these skills is to occur at the elementary level. Students who have reached an intellectual level where they are capable of concrete and logical operations (Piaget & Inhelder, 1969) should benefit from lessons designed to develop these complex thinking skills.

Integrative skills extend, of course, into the problem-solving domain. An individual may synthesize several items of information simultaneously as new data are received, or, in some cases, subsequent to the accumulation of many different items of information. Combining data, individually or in concert with others who share the same problem, assists in uncovering a fresh and unique schema of ideas. Not only can new ideas be generated and created but also tentative hypotheses can be formulated for solutions to the problem. Crutchfield (1969) has demonstrated that problem solving can be effectively taught to fifth and sixth grade students. Ten- and eleven-year-old children are able to generate ideas, state hypotheses, and create a variety of solutions to the problems presented in a series of mystery stories.

Evaluative Skills Our taxonomy implies that as we proceed through the hierarchy, cognitive operations become increasingly complex. This is especially applicable to evaluative skills.

Evaluation involves one major operation, *making judgments.* We judge by appraising the validity and reliability of facts, events, ideas, and purposes; by assessing the competency of writers or speakers on certain subjects; and by rating a work or idea according to some set of standards in that field.

Developing skills in making judgments requires devising a set of criteria and standards and then providing numerous encounters with ideas, events, and facts so that students can assess and rate these experiences in the light of the predetermined criteria and standards.

It may justifiably be asked that, if all these components are essential for evaluation, how can young children be expected to participate in such complex activities? The following illustrations suggest procedures for developing these evaluation skills.

Evaluation processes can be introduced to young children through appraising the realistic qualities of familiar animate and inanimate objects. Second, criteria can be developed that are helpful in identifying these realistic features; for example, the shape and color of the animals and objects being analyzed. And third, these criteria can be used to appraise the qualities of abstractions of these objects as they are depicted in photographs and illustrations. Older students can be provided more sophisticated levels of instruction; as in the appraisal of the characteristics of literary characters, family relationships, language features, facts, events, or the purposes of various authors.

The two other evaluative skills are: assessing the competence of a writer or speaker on certain subjects, and rating a work or idea according to standards in that field. It is possible to develop students' proficiency in these two skills by delineating those essential elements that are to be judged and by defining the criteria and standards to be used for evaluation. Then, opportunities can be provided in applying these criteria in listening and reading situations.

Instruction in the use of these critical thinking skills, notably at the level of evaluation, can be effectively taught at the elementary level, as Wolf, King, and Huck (1968) have found in their study of the employment of critical reading skills by children in grades one through six. Students in their experimental group produced more evaluative responses than literal or memory responses as the result of teachers' questioning strategies.

Evaluative skills play an essential and vital role in problem solving. Just as ideas, events, and facts of other authors should be assessed for competency, validity, and reliability, so should these three evaluative skills be applied to the "newly" created ideas and solutions of the problem-solver. The task, however, is difficult to do objectively when applied to one's own creative effort. The final step in this process is to test the solutions which may reveal that the hypotheses, ideas, and solutions are adequate or should be revised. In the latter case, the problem-solver will have to devise more appropriate hypotheses and solutions.

AFFECTIVE DOMAIN

The affective sphere includes interests, attitudes, and values, and plays an important role in the thinking process.

Here, the concern is primarily with the reader's or speaker's identification of his reactions and responses to written and oral messages. If we could overhear the verbal interaction between students and teacher at any grade level, we might find that their discussion often encompasses the students' interest in a particular book, their attitudes toward the characters, and their feelings about specific incidents in the story, all of which are affective processes. Affective statements are commonly involved in a great deal of classroom instruction, as well as other daily routines and activities. Oftentimes, however, distinctions are not made between those statements which express our feelings and values and those which can be associated with the critical thinking and problem-solving skills. Since classroom instruction involves both the affective and the cognitive domains, we should be able to provide students with the discriminative ability to recognize messages which are founded on objective analysis and evaluation, and those which are based on personal attitudinal belief systems.

Drawing together the essential elements of the interpretation component of the communication model, we note that the affective domain accounts for expressions of feelings, attitudes, and values of individuals; while the cognitive domain explicates the analytical, integrative, and evaluative skills.

CONCLUSION

The communication model and taxonomy of comprehension skills just described and applied demonstrate that the process of communication is very complex. It should be obvious that the model and taxonomy that have been described represent one attempt to conceptualize the communication process. Future research data will demand revision of, and at the same time should support some relationships in, the model and taxonomy. Through such efforts, however, we are better equipped to formulate instructional goals, build instructional objectives, and design and implement our reading-language instructional programs as we establish a more complete understanding of the reading-language communication process. An awareness of the various components in the communication process provides a base for immediate and effective diagnosis and evaluation of reading-language achievement and a strategy for identifying difficulties which youngsters may be encountering. Such a model and taxonomy can also be of value in our examination of instructional approaches to reading-language learning in the elementary classroom, in the school district central office, and in undergraduate and graduate courses at the college and university.

REFERENCES

Bloom, Benjamin *Taxonomy of Educational Objectives.* New York: David McKay Co., 1956.

Crutchfield, Richard "Nurturing the Cognitive Skills of Productive Thinking," in Louis Rubin (Ed.), *Life Skills in School and Society.* Washington, D.C.: Yearbook of the Association for Supervision and Curriculum Development, 1969.

Flack, Marjorie *Angus and the Ducks.* New York: Doubleday & Co., 1930.

Goodman, Kenneth S. and Fleming, James T. (Eds.) *Psycholinguistics and the Teaching of Reading.* Newark, Del.: International Reading Association, 1969.

Guilford, J. P. "Basic Conceptual Problems in Psychology," in *Fundamentals of Psychology: The Psychology of Thinking,* annals of the New York Academy of Sciences, 1960, *91,* 9–19.

Hoban, Russell *Charlie the Tramp.* New York: Four Winds Press, a division of Scholastic Magazines, Inc., 1966.

Lovell, K. "Development Process in Thought," *Journal of Experimental Education,* 1968, *37,* 14–21.

Lundsteen, S. W. *Teaching Abilities in Critical Listening in the Fifth and Sixth Grades.* Unpublished doctoral dissertation, University of California, Berkeley, 1963.

Piaget, J. *The Psychology of Intelligence.* Totowa, N.J.: Littlefield, Adams & Co., 1963.

Piaget, J. and Inhelder, B. *The Psychology of the Child.* Translated by Helen Weaver. New York: Basic Books, Inc., Publishers, 1969.

Ripple, R. and Rockcastle, V. *Piaget Rediscovered.* A report of the Conference on Cognitive Studies and Curriculum Development. Ithaca, New York: School of Education, Cornell University, 1964.

Ruddell, Robert B. "Psycholinguistic Implications for a Systems of Communication Model," in Kenneth S. Goodman and James T. Fleming (Eds.), *Psycholinguistics and the Teaching of Reading.* Newark, Del.: International Reading Association, 1969.

Ruddell, Robert B. "Language Acquisition and the Reading Process," in Harry Singer and Robert B. Ruddell (Eds.), *Theoretical Models and Processes of Reading.* Newark, Del.: International Reading Association, 1970.

Saadeh, I. Q. *An Evaluation of the Effectiveness of Teaching for Critical Thinking in the Sixth Grade.* Unpublished doctoral dissertation, University of California, Berkeley, 1962.

Singer, Harry and Ruddell, Robert B. (Eds.) *Theoretical Models and Processes of Reading.* Newark, Del.: International Reading Association, 1970.

Taba, Hilda "Implementing Thinking," in Jean Fair and Fannie Shaftel (Eds.), *Effective Thinking in the Social Studies.* Washington, D.C.: Thirty-seventh Yearbook of the National Council for Social Studies, 1967.

Taba, H.; Levine, Samuel; and Elzey, Freeman *Thinking in Elementary School Children.* U.S.O.E. Cooperative Research Project No. 1574, U.S. Department of Health, Education, and Welfare. San Francisco: 1964.

Wolf, W.; King, Martha; and Huck, Charlotte "Teaching Critical Reading to Elementary School Children," *Reading Research Quarterly,* 1968, 3 (Spring), 435–498.

LANGUAGE, MEANING,

AND READING INSTRUCTION

Pose Lamb

One must surely be impressed with the great wisdom, the audacity, the naiveté, or the stupidity of a speaker, or writer, who attempts to deal with a topic as pervasive as "Language and Meaning" within such a limited time-space allotment as ours! This impression, whether positive or negative, must gain depth and breadth when one considers the controversy which surrounds our efforts to define the terms involved. What *is* language? Does it include a bee's signal concerning the location of a supply of nectar, or a dolphin's friendly noises? Or, is language a distinctly *human* characteristic, acquired without undue difficulty (in its oral form, at least) by most people of normal intelligence who are without incapacitating psychological and physical defects?

SOME VIEWS OF LANGUAGE

Lenneberg's treatment (1963) of communications systems in biological organisms other than man—chimpanzees, for example—has caused some to misinterpret his definition of language. He writes: "The empirically determined, primitive beginnings of language in man (in the 18 month-old infant or in feeble minded individuals) are behaviorally very different from the signals that animals emit for each other [p. 71]." Lenneberg cites data to suggest that physical deprivation (deafness) and psychological deprivation (institutionalization at infancy) need not, and typically do not, cause irreparable damage to language acquisition; and he notes that language is relatively independent of the quality or qualities loosely termed "intelligence." He remarks: "I see evidence for this view in the fact that children acquire language at a time when their power of reasoning is still poorly developed and that the ability to understand and to speak has a low correlation with measured I.Q. in man [p. 78]."

It would be deceptively easy, and nonproductive, particularly in terms of current and justified concerns for culturally and educationally disadvantaged children, to cite Lenneberg's views (1963) or Piaget's stages[1] that no really socialized language exists until age seven (Stauffer, 1969, p. 322) as excuses for doing nothing about the facilitation of language acquisition and language growth. If you wish further contradiction regarding the role of language, consider the following: Piaget writes (1967), "It is permissible to conclude that thought precedes language and that language confines itself to profoundly transforming thought by helping it attain its forms of equilibrium by means of a more advanced schematization and a more mobile abstraction [pp. 91–92]." Lenneberg (1963), however, seems to disagree, "Might it not be possible that language ability, instead of being the consequence of intelligence, is its cause [p. 78]?"

What is language? The structuralist's view that "Language is speech" will no longer suffice as an answer to that question. Speech obviously precedes writing, and an individual human being's language development parallels that of the human race in this respect. We are aware that many groups of human beings have communicated very effectively without a writing system; and it is certainly a fact that literacy is a privilege reserved for relatively few people in the world, while speech is not. The teacher of reading has to view language as more than speech, and print as more than "talk written down."[2] Language may be best defined as the interaction, at successively more sophisticated levels, of the phonological, morphological, lexical, syntactic, and semantic elements of a communications system. If this attempt at a definition is acceptable, then language must be viewed as a distinctly human process. Does language precede or follow thought? Is language structured? Or, does it structure the way one orders his experience? Is it possible that

[1] Editors' note: According to the renowned Swiss psychologist, Jean Piaget, intelligence develops from infancy to adolescence in four successive stages, each subsequent stage incorporating the previously developed stages. The final stage—the formal operational stage—is marked by the individual's ability to engage in propositional and hypothetical thinking. For an enlightening overview of the theories of Piaget, see Hans G. Furth, *Piaget for Teachers*, Englewood Cliffs, N.J.: Prentice-Hall, Inc., 1970.

[2] Editors' note: The reader is referred to Paul David Allen's paper in Section IV for an extended discussion of the view that writing is more than "talk written down."

both phenomena occur, perhaps simultaneously, certainly at different times, as the nature of the experience dictates or is dictated to?

It seems utterly negative, hopeless, and self-defeating to operate on the premise that nothing in the environment, human or otherwise, can effect much positive change on language. Man is more than a machine with a button, or switch, called "language" which is pressed or flipped at a certain crucial socio-psychobiological moment, setting into motion labeling, phrase-making, sentence-forming machinery which can neither be accelerated nor slowed down—at least not much. The shift of thought among linguists of a certain school which has resulted in the substitution of *infinite* for *finite* with respect to the number of phrase structure rules is a significant shift, indeed. There is much about man's language, its acquisition and use, which can be analyzed, charted, and even predicted. The several fields of scholarship subsumed under the label "linguistics" are based upon this belief. This is not to say, however, that language is cold, or mechanical, or nonhuman. Gesture "language" and kinesics are interesting facets of communication, and serve to enrich and add meaning to language; but man is never more human, more identifiable as separate from other biological organisms, than when he selects the words he wants to use, combines them to get the effect he desires, and utilizes the levels of pitch and stress which will most clearly convey his meaning, or when he attempts to use the means provided in our writing system to accomplish these goals.

LANGUAGE IN A SOCIAL CONTEXT

We are told that one of the major problems of the ghetto resident is the unlikelihood of his acquiring a language which will not penalize him, will not brand him as inferior when he is attempting to relate to people representing other facets of society. Those words were chosen very carefully. There was a time when the concept of "wardrobe of languages" or "market basket of languages" was generally accepted by linguists and teachers. This concept was most appropriate when referring to middle-class people using language in a somewhat limited variety of social contexts; for example, the linguistic behavior at home during an informal meal as contrasted with the language selected for use at a tea or reception. The "gap" isn't very wide in such situations. *He don't* or *Bof of us* are unlikely linguistic choices for the person or persons involved. In the informal home situation, endings may be dropped, one's idiolect will be more obvious, than in the more formal setting; but the language used will still probably be well within the confines of the term "standard English." The problem of the ghetto child, however, is concisely stated by Venezky (1970):

> The child whose language habits differ markedly from the so-cially acceptable *patois* of the school system faces both overt and covert discrimination in education. On the inter-personal level, he is an odd duckling—his kinder-peers, conservative and conformist (as all children tend to be) view *different* as *inferior*, with no exceptions given to what adults might class as prestige forms of speech; his teacher, as well meaning as she might be, may not comprehend all that he says, and worse, will have difficulty view-ing nonstandard as anything except substandard. On the less per-sonal level the situation is potentially more harmful; the educa-tional process and especially the reading programs are not equipped for him [p. 334].

It appears that the market basket, or the wardrobe, would have to be of gigantic size, perhaps too large for a young child to handle, to accommodate both the colloquial language of the ghetto and the language which is generally conceded to be a passport into the affluent world of the middle classes. The problem is a very complex one: Can one motivate a child to change his language (substitute *add to* for *change* if this makes you more comfortable) without causing him to doubt the validity and the credibility of the sources of his original language—sources which represented at least a tenuous hold on secur-ity? Can we tell a child we want him to acquire a language which in large measure is *future* oriented, when his current language is quite functional? Is the fact that most textbooks are written in WASP reason enough to demand a radical change in the child's oral language? If text-books aren't to be written in WASP, in whose dialect *are* they to be written? Bluntly, is the acceptance of a ghetto child's language, as is, a subtle and benevolent form of discrimination, or is *lack* of acceptance of his language synonymous with lack of acceptance of another human being, another way of life? Today's teacher, as well as today's teacher of teachers, must attempt to answer the question what *is* language; but perhaps even more crucial will be the answer to the question, *what* language?

A primary data source on this problem is *Teaching Black Children to Read*, edited by Baratz and Shuy (1969). Another excellent source is the N.C.T.E. publication, *Language Programs for the Disadvantaged* (1965). Obviously, there are no easy answers to the questions posed. Each teacher will find his own set of answers. Hopefully, these answers will not make the *different* child feel less human; and, hopefully, they will not cause teachers and pupils to accept that which *is*, linguistically, as all there ever will be. Our language programs must not be circular, beginning and ending in the same place!

CHILD LANGUAGE IN THE SCHOOL SETTING

It is also worth noting that the often repeated phrase "Children know a great deal about their language when they come to school" has been widely accepted, and has, in fact, become almost a truism. As a result of this recognition, reading programs which have focused on symbol-sound relationships are being scrutinized with somewhat more intelligence and care than previously. There have been such minor revolutions as the use of contractions in preprimers and an increasingly larger group of first grade teachers who believe that their pupils can understand complex concepts and don't have to be talked to as though they were pet kittens, puppies, or infants. However, overemphasis on the knowledge about language which children bring to school with them, can and has resulted in a rather subtle acceptance of the premise that not much more can, or needs to be, done in school, especially with oral forms of language. This situation is not improved by the textbook author who operates from the premise that oral language is relatively fixed and difficult to change, or that oral language is such a conglomerate of dialects that his efforts and those of the teacher and learner should be confined to examining those elements of language structure which bear the least resemblance to speech.

The artificial nature of much textbook language has been condemned so frequently and so strongly that little more needs to be said about this. It is possible to put textbook and school language, in general, in one category, and "playground language" in another; in fact, teachers have been doing this for some time. Exposing the child to, and making him cognitively aware of several kinds of language, each useful in different contexts, is realistic. We don't write as we talk; and we don't speak in precisely the same way in all social settings. For many children, this presents no problem—the major hurdle is in decoding (or recoding) those elements of his speech which rather closely relate to segments of our writing system. When the "match" is close, when there are few limiting psychophysical problems, the child makes a relatively easy entry into the process of becoming literate.

When the speech-print match isn't close, problems can occur. Perhaps Stewart's series of transition steps (1969), in which the child is gradually moved from nonstandard to standard language in print form, should be viewed as part of the answer.[3] Perhaps though, recording in print as accurately as possible elements of the child's phonological and syntactic system, and relying upon changes in oral language to result in changes in the written language used is a better way. However, what problems of transferring from oral to written language does this create? The eventual goal is that of independence in, and a positive attitude toward, reading. Does the use, even in initial reading stages, of a combination of letters representing a unit of the child's natural language that the child is unlikely to see again promote or inhibit the achievement of this goal? Can you reinforce what *is* without thwarting and delaying what you hope *will be*?

Research evidence is not very helpful. In our zeal to help the culturally different child achieve genuine literacy, we must be careful not to force him to overcome an obstacle which may be as overwhelming as the stilted middle-class language of yesterday's basal readers. Recording syntactic elements of a child's dialect, middle-class or non-middle-class, along with exposure, through trade and textbooks, to unfamiliar standard and literary forms, has some promise as an approach to beginning reading. Is recording elements of a child's phonological system merely a *logical* extension of this process? Perhaps. One frequently cited conclusion from the *First Grade Studies* (funded by the U.S. Office of Education) is that growth in writing *and* reading are both enhanced when the two processes are taught as related. A spoken "sentence" is frequently less structured than a written sentence. Can we expect a child to make this transfer at the same time he is learning to record "dey" for "they?"

---

[3] Editors' note: For a review of Stewart's and others' points of view on reading in the context of nonstandard English, see Roger Shuy's paper, pgs. 55–72, in Section III.

LANGUAGE AND MEANING

In a first grade inner-city classroom in a large midwestern urban area, a teacher was attempting to elicit an experience chart related to lions. The children had visited the zoo, lion pictures were displayed, and several books about lions had been read to the children. Obviously, the "March lion" concept had also been discussed. The following is the group chart which resulted:

TEENY TINY LION

He lived in a zoo
He lived with his mother
He wanted out
He looked outside
It looked fun
His mother was so big she could shake
the whole jungle
But she was a nice mother
He lived in a cage
When March came in he walked out
He walked between the bars
His mother was too big
She could not come
Where was he going?
He did not know
He looked around
He felt good
He blew a big air
He blew the kites into the air
The boys and girls laughed
It was fun
It was March—
Time to fly kites
He was nice
He grew up
But we still call him the Teeny Tiny lion
who makes March Winds.

Several concepts are obvious:

1. Children, even animal children, live with their mothers, but eventual independence is expected (He wanted out . . . His mother was too big. She could not come.).

2. Stories are to be pleasant and *always* have happy endings (But she was a *nice* mother . . . He was nice.).

3. Kites require wind, and wind is associated with March, as are lions. The rather tenuous hold on this concept is apparent: "He blew a big air . . . he blew the kites into the air."

These three concepts (and, of course, there are others in the rather lengthy story) were dictated and received emphasis in terms of the children's direct experience with the concepts.

Meaning refers to the assignment of labels to facets of experience. These children had had little experience with kite flying, and "March Winds" represented an abstraction, particularly since there was little wind on the morning this story was dictated. In contrast, relationship with mother, growing up, and achieving independence (at least briefly, in play) were concepts that held significance, especially for the child who was dictating at the time.

The linguist Leonard Bloomfield is frequently accused of having written that meaning is essentially unrelated to the reading process. The materials he prepared, beginning with the famous (or notorious) "Nan can fan Dan," would seem to support this accusation. Clarence Barnhart writes in the introduction to *Let's Read* (1961) that Bloomfield believed that reading involved nothing more than learning the relationship of the spoken to the written code. But no sentence from *Let's Read* (Bloomfield & Barnhart, 1961) can be found in which Bloomfield, *himself*, expressed such a belief.

Regardless of the position taken by Bloomfield and other pioneer structuralists who prepared so-called linguistic materials, it seems clear that reading is much more a simple decoding process, even in its beginning stages, although decoding may receive primary emphasis in the beginning. Most of the increasingly large and knowledgeable group of theorists who are interested in developing models of the reading process would agree that understanding the relationship of sound-to-letter is essential to maturity in reading. If this doesn't occur, comprehension can't. But if what is decoded lacks meaning, that is, lacks relevance to the child's previous experience, the effort to decode can hardly be considered worthwhile.

In the reading process, a child brings his previous experience with language, and with the efforts to communicate thoughts which language represents, to a segment or segments of print. He should *leave* the encounter with additional depth and breadth attached to each of the meaning-learning units he has encountered. An elevator is to ride in as well as to store grain in—or vice versa. To say that the writer and his reader never fully communicate is to repeat a truism—and one of not much consequence to the first grade teacher and her pupils struggling with "Tom said, 'Mother, where is Susan? It is time for school. Dick and I want to go now.' "

Meaning is brought *to* the page; it is also taken *from* the page; and hopefully, concept growth, in terms of quality and quantity, results from the interaction. The first-reader page just quoted seems fairly simple to interpret, which is true, at a superficial level. Obviously, a group of children plan to go to school together, and one member of the group is missing. But many teachers never help pupils probe more deeply than this; for example: why are Tom and Dick so eager to get to school; why is Susan missing; how important—or unimportant—is getting to school on time *to you*? These are just a few of the questions a teacher might ask. Returning to the chart about Teeny Tiny Lion for a moment, might not the teacher, without dominating the child's dictation, have changed "He blew a big air" to a series of words which would communicate more effectively? Perhaps the child was referring to the lion's roar, not the production of a kite-blowing gale?

Occasionally, one will see a distinction made between *reading* and the *uses of reading*. Critical reading, the probe for added meaning and reacting, would be placed in the latter category by those who make such a distinction. But if a particular piece of reading material has little use or value, it seems appropriate to ask, why bother making this distinction or even reading the material in the first place. *Meaning,* referring to author's purpose and reader's perceptions, can never be ignored by teachers of reading or readers. Nor can meaning be divorced from the language selected to convey it. Teachers, and pupils, develop countless lists of so-called synonyms without helping pupils to see the subtle differences which may be implied. The position of a term in a sentence, and the position of a sentence in a paragraph, lend a term at least part of its meaning. Both encoder and decoder (or recoder) are involved in the assignment of meaning, and both use language in all its interacting complexity (sound, sequence, lexical form) to attempt to communicate.

CONCLUSION

Reading is a complex process; and learning to read is of paramount significance to people in this age of upward social mobility and rising economic expectations. Marshall McLuhan may be right, but reading will continue to be important in the immediately forseeable future at least. A search for the clarification of the terms *language, meaning,* and *reading* (although this last term is rather well-defined once the other two are) may help us answer some of the questions which conclude this paper:

1. The textbook will be around for awhile; what function or functions can it serve to make it (a) more supportive of standard language patterns, (b) a better vehicle for developing higher level thinking skills, and (c) *less* representative of values not held by a significant proportion of our population?

2. How closely can and should the print a child reads represent his speech? Should the print represent all aspects of his speech, or just some? Which ones?

3. Can the child's initial reading materials accurately represent his speech and his thinking and still have a potential for producing growth —in *both* language and thinking?

REFERENCES

Baratz, Joan and Shuy, Roger (Eds.) *Teaching Black Children to Read.* Washington, D.C.: Center for Applied Linguistics, 1969.

Bloomfield, Leonard and Barnhart, Clarence *Let's Read: A Linguistic Approach.* Detroit: Wayne State University Press, 1961.

Language Programs for the Disadvantaged. Champaign, Ill.: National Council of Teachers of English, 1965.

Lenneberg, Eric H. "A Biological Perspective of Language," in Eric H. Lenneberg (Ed.), *New Directions in the Study of Language.* Cambridge, Mass.: Massachusetts Institute of Technology Press, 1963.

Piaget, Jean in David Elkind (Ed.) *Six Psychological Studies*. New York: Random House, 1967.

Stauffer, Russell *Directing Reading Maturity as a Cognitive Process*. New York: Harper & Row, 1969.

Stewart, William A. "On the Use of Negro Dialect in the Teaching of Reading," in Joan Baratz and Roger Shuy (Eds.), *Teaching Black Children to Read*. Washington, D.C.: Center for Applied Linguistics, 1969.

Venezky, Richard "Nonstandard Language and Reading," *Elementary English*, 1970, *47* (March), 334–345.

FOR FURTHER READING

Bloom, Benjamin *Taxonomy of Educational Objectives*. New York: David McKay Co., 1956.

Presents a hierarchical classification of cognitive skills consisting of six levels; knowledge, comprehension, application, analysis, synthesis, and evaluation. Each level is defined and examined with ample illustrations of how each skill may be tested.

Crutchfield, Richard "Nurturing the Cognitive Skills of Productive Thinking," in Louis Rudin (Ed.), *Life Skills in School and Society*. Washington, D.C.: Yearbook of the Association for Supervision and Curriculum Development, 1969.

Proposes that productive thinking skills can be taught to elementary school children, and that these skills can be taught in real classroom situations.

Smith, E. Brooks; Goodman, Kenneth S.; and Meredith, Robert *Language and Thinking in the Elementary School*. New York: Holt, Rinehart & Winston, Inc., 1970.

Provides a comprehensive survey of research related to children's acquisition of language and its relationship to cognition and perception. Presents the view that language is at the center of the curriculum, and that the primary purpose of school language programs is to help pupils expand their language effectiveness.

Taba, Hilda "Implementing Thinking As an Objective in Social Studies," in Jean Fair and Fannie Shaftel (Eds.), *Effective Thinking in the Social Studies*. Washington, D.C.: Thirty-Seventh Yearbook of the National Council for Social Studies, 1967.

Presents a rationale and a theoretical background for developing children's cognition, and includes a brief analysis of the teaching strategies which will enhance these cognition skills.

EIGHT · LANGUAGE AND THINKING

The reading process is undertaken to derive an author's meaning from his printed text. Obviously then, meaning and the thought processes that go into interpreting written words are central issues in theories of reading and in reading instruction. In the present section, Constance McCullough, Professor of Education at San Francisco State College, discusses the complexity of the reading process as it is related to language, meaning, and thinking. As Kenneth Goodman demonstrated in his paper, the structurally simple sentence *See John run* requires a quite sophisticated psychological and linguistic analysis on the part of the child. Professor McCullough's paper vividly illustrates this analytical thought process. Her detailed analysis of the kind of thinking involved in understanding two rather ordinary English sentences makes views of the reading process as a matter of "word recognition" or of "grapheme-phoneme correspondence learning" seem superficial.

Professor Edmund Henderson, Director of the McGuffey Reading Clinic at the University of Virginia, provides the concluding paper of this volume. In many ways, his paper summarizes the contributions to reading theory which have been presented here. He also briefly suggests the pedagogical implications of these contributions.

Henderson worked for a number of years with Russell Stauffer at the University of Delaware, and, along with Professor Stauffer, and others of his students, is well-known as a proponent of the "language experience" approach to the teaching of reading. In its survey of linguistic and psychological contributions to reading theory and the application of these contributions to the realities of the classroom, Henderson's paper provides a fitting capstone to the preceding papers.

WHAT SHOULD THE READING

TEACHER KNOW ABOUT

LANGUAGE AND THINKING?

Constance M. McCullough

Unlike a General Motors car, we do not come into the world with a manual explaining how we work or where we came from. Because of this, while part of our society simply lives with whatever is known, another part digs into the rocks for knowledge of the past, or explores outer space for a glimpse into the future, or studies the present behavior of man. Now, between linguists who tell us how language works, and psychologists who tell us how man thinks,—not to speak of neurologists who tell us how the thought messages are transmitted, or sociologists who describe the environmental influences on language and the damaging connotations of words alienating man from man—we reading teachers find ourselves faced with a new task.

MODERN CHALLENGES TO THE TRADITIONAL VIEW OF READING

Most of us learned a Latin grammar applied to English. In composition we were told to write what we meant. If the teacher didn't understand it, there were two possibilities: we didn't have a clear thought in the first place, or we hadn't used the language to express it clearly.

In learning to read, we were taught something about decoding word forms into the meanings associated with the spoken word we recognized. If we didn't know the word as a spoken word, we were told to look it up in a dictionary and to apply the meaning that made sense in the sentence. We learned the meanings of words in lists, and, thus equipped, we were ready to answer any question the teacher might ask about the meaning of what we had read.

King Alphonso of Spain chose my junior year in college to abdicate and surprise me with the amazing fact that history was still being made. It would have been even more jarring to my cocoon had I known at the time what linguists were up to: that a man named Fries (1951) had a serious intent when he wrote sentences like *The oogle aggled an oogle;* that a man named Whorf, studying Hopi, would shed new light on the nature of English (1964); that someday a Chomsky (1965) would transform our thinking with transformational grammar; and that a psychologist, Guilford, would present us with a new model of the intellect (1958).

Our goal, at present, is the development of a new way of looking at the teaching of reading by being aware of these new findings, of their relationships to each other, and of the bearing these relationships have upon reading comprehension. In addition, we are confronted by the problem of the relationship of these elements to the ways we teach and evaluate; for if, indeed, these elements are contributive to comprehension, diagnosis of reading difficulties must include an assessment of children's awareness of the operation of these elements when they are having difficulty in comprehension.

Whatever we do now toward the fulfillment of this goal will seem groping and fragmentary some years from now; but we can work only with what we now know, and can make progress only by being jarred by new ideas, which in themselves are never the whole truth. Various researchers are approaching the problem in different ways. Kenneth Goodman (1969) has developed a taxonomy of oral reading miscues and a model of reading through his investigations into the grammatical re-transformations which children create as they read aloud. Theodore Clymer has described other models of reading developed by reading specialists. Carl LeFevre (1964) views the sentence as the unit of meaning, disagreeing sharply with those who focus on the word as the unit of meaning. Lee Deighton has studied alterations in the selection of meanings for words in sentences as a reader reads the sentence from first to last. He has also commented on the fact that present tense is often used to describe an attribute rather than to present an event: *He smokes heavily* (habitual) versus *He smoked today* (past act). The National Society for the Study of Education Yearbook, part II, 1970, entitled *Linguistics in School Programs* is a precious document of information on the development of thought and language, and the contributions of linguistics to reading and spelling.

THE COMPLEXITY OF THE READING PROCESS

Drawing upon this knowledge, the teacher of reading can study the demands that printed material makes upon the reader, and can see that some adjustments must be made in the reading program and in the teacher's thinking and emphases. In our concern for decoding and for knowledge of the meanings of many words—both good things in themselves, we have created in children the idea that if they know the words and know what the words mean, they will know what the message is. The following quotation is excerpted from the first paragraph of a pamphlet, the name and source of which I do not remember. It goes like this:

> This bright blue marble that we call the earth is the third planet from the sun, a small star far from the center of a galaxy which is 50,000 light years across. A hundred billion other stars make up this system and there are untold numbers of such groupings.

What points of difficulty in this passage create hazards for reading comprehension?

The expression *this bright blue marble* in association with the clause which follows it requires that the reader select a meaning for *marble* suitable to the size and composition of Earth. The child who has been glued to the TV on the occasion of programs showing the appearance of Earth from the moon will have been reminded that Earth does look like a marble in a game of marbles; although we must keep in mind that Earth isn't bright-blue; that it looks blue from a distance when the sun is shining upon it; and that it is bright because of the sunlight.

We, it must be assumed refers to human beings who speak English; for, Earth is an English word, and, thus far, the author hasn't introduced his family or any other characters who, with him, might be *We*.

Call is used in the sense of naming, for the NVNN structure (*We call Earth marble*) suggests this meaning. We don't call Earth as we would call the police.

This marble, this earth, is a planet. In being called *the* planet, and the third planet from the sun, it is being located and associated with a particular sun. *The third planet from the sun* does not mean "order in time" or that it was the third planet to leave the sun. It is a planet third in position as measured from the sun. *From,* in this instance, has to do with position, not the action of departure.

The comma after *sun* could signal a number of relationships to follow; but when it is followed by a nominal expression, it suggests an appositive relationship with a previous noun. Unfortunately, an inexperienced reader could be bewildered by the four nouns he has now encountered: *marble, earth, planet,* and *sun.* Since the first three are all names for the same thing, it is a toss between the earth and the sun. Chances are that the nearest noun is the one we are looking for: *The sun is a small star.*

But, it is possible to think that the sun is not small at all; and we may know that the sun is larger than the earth. We may not know, however, that a planet is not a star.

Another condition which may cause the wrong choice of meaning is that the author has been stressing Earth, and may continue on that subject rather than branching to more comment on the sun.

Notice that the author does not say that the small star is *in* a galaxy or a *part* of a galaxy, but that it is far from the center of one. The reader may wonder what difference it makes where in a galaxy a star is. At any rate, *far from the center of a galaxy* is a location in space.

Which may refer to *galaxy* or *center* or *star,* and part of the decision rests with a knowledge of star sizes, galaxy sizes, center sizes, and light-year sizes. Would a small star be 50,000 light-years across? Are light-years the opposite of heavy years or dark years? Do light-years measure time or do they measure distance in terms of time? You can go *across* either time or distance.

What about the number relationships in the two sentences? The third planet from the sun must have whirling room. Are 50,000 light-years a generous accommodation for a hundred billion stars and one extra, or do we need star birth control, too? What are *untold* numbers? Are they uninformed, not yet counted, or unmentionable?

This system suggests that a system has been mentioned in the previous sentence. Is Earth a system? Is the sun? Is a star? Is a galaxy? If stars make up the system, then it might be called a system of stars. If the reader knows that neither the earth nor the sun could be called a system of stars, he may now suspect what a galaxy is, if he didn't know before.

In *such groupings,* the *such* implies that a grouping or *some* groupings have been mentioned before. As in the case of *This system,* the reader may again turn to the idea of *galaxy.* There are not only a hundred billion stars in this one system (or galaxy), but uncalculated or incalculable numbers of other galaxies in existence outside this one.

Now let us look for buried treasure in these two sentences. Are there definitions and classifications? Yes:

1. Earth is a planet.

2. The sun is a small star.

3. A galaxy is a system of stars.

4. A galaxy is a grouping of stars.

What can we learn from these two sentences? What questions do they answer:

1. The way the earth looks from outer space (moon-distance).

2. The location of Earth relative to the sun and two other planets.

3. The position of the sun in its galaxy.

4. The size of the galaxy in distance across and in number of star-units.

5. The number of galaxies in the universe (untold).

The "deep subject" of these two sentences may be the vastness of the universe.

What is the significance of the use of two terms in the classification of *galaxy?* What is the difference between being a *system* and being a *grouping?* The reader should appreciate the fact that a grouping is a cluster *in position,* while a system is a cluster *in interaction* or *operation.* This raises the question of how the components of a galaxy operate together. Mentioning Earth as the third planet raises the question of how many other planets there are; and so we have at least two good teasers for reference reading.

Why did the author use *and* in the second sentence? Does the reader see that the author is heaping 50,000 light-years and the hundred billion stars *and* perhaps zillions of galaxies into an impression of vastness?

Is the reader also aware of the author's progression from Earth to sun to galaxy to galaxies? Where will the author go from here? (For, part of the good reader's skill is expectation of possible directions for the thought to take.) Will he return to Earth, now that he has given its setting; will he proceed instead to a conception of the universe; will he report what is known of the operation and composition of galaxies; or will he discuss how earth-dwellers have discovered the facts now known about outer space?

What about the setting of these two sentences? If they had appeared in a religious magazine and if the author were a minister, rabbi, priest, or holy man, what might the rest of the article have presented? If they had appeared in a social studies book, what next? Or in a science book, what next?

The reader needs not only to look forward with expectations but backward to reconcile previous impressions, for the author's purpose in starting the article as he did will come clear only with what he does next. You can take the same two sentences and, in retrospect, find them serving different purposes.

1. Earth is so small, and yet God is mindful of it.

2. By rare chance, Earth is supportive of life; let us treasure its privilege.

3. We are alone in a vast, unfriendly universe; let us show consideration for each other.

4. The universe is so vast, Earth so small, and other planets still smaller, who are we to raise such a ruckus over our condition?

Of these four possibilities—of course, there could be others—notice that the first and last create a contrast, a contrary relationship which seems to defy logic ("In spite of the fact that"). The second and third present a cause-effect relationship ("Because").

The purpose of the author in the first contrast may have been to heighten the reader's appreciation of God; in the second, to quiet his outsized complaints by a reminder of his insignificance. In the first cause-effect relationship, the author may have been trying to impress the reader with his luck; in the second, with his need for friendship. Notice, too, how the word *unfriendly* provides a contrast with *consideration* while it lays the groundwork for the cause-effect relationship.

A reader who understands the basic relationships in our two sentences should be able to find plausible answers to the following items:

In these sentences,

The marble is
a. white and shining.

    b. bright blue.

    c. bright with light, and blue.

* The earth

    a. is a marble.

    b. is made of marble.

    c. looks like a marble.

We means

    a. English-speaking people.

    b. the author's family.

    c. all human beings.

* The third planet from the sun is called

    a. Earth.

    b. Marble.

    c. Star.

* The third planet is

    a. farther away from the sun than two other planets.

    b. traveling away from the sun.

    c. is a piece of the sun which was torn from it.

* The small star is

    a. the sun.

    b. the earth.

The small star is

    a. in the middle of a galaxy.

    b. not in the middle of a galaxy.

* Light years are

    a. the opposite of heavy years.

    b. measures of time.

    c. measures of distance.

* *50,000 light years across* describes

    a. the center of the galaxy.

    b. the breadth of the galaxy.

    c. the time it takes a galaxy to travel.

Other stars means

    a. stars other than the sun.

    b. stars other than the earth.

    c. stars of other galaxies.

Make up means
  a. color.
  b. form.
  c. package.

This system means
  a. a hundred billion other stars.
  b. stars traveling together in space.
  c. light years in a galaxy.

Such groupings means groupings of
  a. planets with a sun.
  b. galaxies with galaxies.
  c. stars with stars.

Untold means
  a. not mentioned.
  b. several.
  c. vast.

The starred items could have been answered by the reader without reading the two sentences at all, if he had known these facts about outer space. If he did not know them, he had to depend upon the relationships established in the two sentences. Thus, failure in the starred items suggests both lack of knowledge of the facts and inability to profit by whatever the relationships in the sentences indicate.

LEARNING TO COPE WITH LANGUAGE

How should we prepare children to cope with language beyond the skills of decoding, to grasp the thoughts and purposes of the author? The following are areas of possible concern. You will doubtless think of more.

1. English sentences present ideas in varied relationships within a given concept:
  a. sensory impressions (behaviors, qualities, uses)
  b. cognitive relationships [whole-part, cause-effect, sequence, comparison-contrast, subordination-coordination (hierarchies and parallels)]
  c. cognitive products (theories, laws, principles, generalizations, summarizations, definitions, classifications, procedures)

    d. practical extensions of cognitive observation (examples, elaboration, application)

2. The direction an author takes in developing his topic reveals the nature of his attack on it:

    "All men are liars.
    Socrates is a man.
    Therefore Socrates is a liar."

    "Some say the sky is blue.
    Some say the sky is black.
    Some say the sky isn't there at all.
    You can't believe anybody."

3. The direction an author may take in thought from one sentence to another is an individual matter:
    (1) Earth is the third planet from the sun.
    (2) Venus is the second, and Mercury the first. (sequence toward sun)
        or
    (2) It is the only one known to sustain life. (quality: condition)
        or
    (2) The sun is part of a galaxy we call the Milky Way. (location; part-whole relationship of Earth to galaxy, as well as sun to galaxy)
        or
    (2) Its light is only that reflected from the sun. (quality: brightness; cause-effect relationship)
        etc.

4. Different contexts dictate different selections of meanings for a given word:
    This bright blue marble *that we call the earth*
    third planet from *the sun* (distance)
    versus
    light from *the sun* (travel)

5. Connectives which have multiple meanings must be interpreted in context:
    (1) *Since* you left, things have been better.
    (2) Berkeley has a new freeway. (since-time)

or
(2) The boss doesn't get angry any more without you to fight with.
(since-cause)

6. Sentences of some complexity reveal relationships among the basic sentences embedded in them:

This bright blue marble that we call the
earth is the third planet from the sun.

We call this
       bright
       blue   *marble*
       the   *earth.*
       It is
    the third *planet*   from the sun

7. Although not infallibly, certain types of sentences tend to be associated with certain cognitive relationships:

Comparison
He is as ———— *as a* ————.
He ———— *like a* ————.
He ———— *more than a* ————. (less than, etc.)

Definition
A ———— *is a* ————.

Contrary To Logic
Although . . . , ...
In spite of . . . , ...

Cause-Effect
Because . . . , ...
If . . . , then . . . .
If ———— *had* ————, *then* ———— *would have* (could have) . . . .
Had the . . . , then . . . would . . . . (contrary to fact, cause-effect)

8. A sentence may play more than one role in the expression of cognitive relationships:

    "Earth rotates on its axis.
    It rotates around the sun.
    It travels with the sun."

(Each sentence describes a *behavior* of Earth. It offers one *part* of the *whole* concept of Earth. The three behaviors form a *class* of behavior. They also contribute to an unspoken main idea, that "Earth moves in three ways"; thus, each sentence contributes a fact to support a *generalization*.)

9. When the author does not offer structural supports for cognitive relationships, the reader must sense the cognitive relationships from the given:

It looked like rain. I took my umbrella.

(Because it looked like rain, I took my umbrella.)

In this case, the concepts must be familiar and their usual relationships known, or the reader fails to make the connection.

10. Noun determiners can suggest *classification:*

This marble (There are others: *that* marble.)

a star (There must be others.)

this system

such groupings

11. Facets of a concept are highlighted by modifiers:

blue marble (What color is it?)

morning chores (When are they done?)

skipping rope (What is it used for?)

barking dog (What can he do?)

prairie dog (Where does it live?)

prickly pear (How does it feel?)

pie crust (what kind? What is it a part of?)

(The marble is blue. The chores are done in the morning. The rope is used for skipping. The dog is barking. The "dog" lives in the prairie. The pear is prickly. The crust is part of the pie.) etc.

12. An author assumes that the reader possesses a certain body of knowledge about concept relationships:

Earth is not a marble.

Earth is not a star.

13. The role of a word in the syntax of a sentence dictates meaning:

Roast the chop versus *Chop the roast* (verb versus noun)

bright blue marble versus *bright blue marble statue* (noun versus adjective)

14. Word order dictates meaning:

   A hundred billion other stars versus *Another hundred billion stars*

   Songbird versus *birdsong*

15. Words used synonymously bear different relationships to one another, adding to meaning:

   earth . . . planet   sun . . . star (classification)

   marble . . . earth (comparison)

   galaxy . . . groupings . . . system (classification relative to position, operation)

16. The selection of meanings to be assigned to words requires awareness of their compatibility and incompatibility with other words associated with them:

   The earth ≠ a marble.

   The earth = a planet.

   The earth ≠ a star.

   The earth rotates on its axis.

   Does soil rotate on an axis? No.

   Does a planet rotate on an axis? Yes.

17. The figurative use of a word calls upon different skills and knowledge for its identification as figurative:

   This bright blue marble. . . .

   a. Is it a common expression like "Don't let the cat out of the bag," to be recognized by language experience?

   b. Is the earth made of marble stone? Is it shaped like a marble? (Which meaning of *marble* is compatible with the meaning of *earth* in the context of *earth . . . sun . . . planet?*)

   c. Have preceding sentences led you to expect a literal mention of *marble?*

   d. Does the book, the chapter heading, or type of assignment, suggest a literal *marble?*

   e. Have you seen the earth look like this? (experience)

18. Punctuation suggests relationships; so does lack of it:

   the sun, a small star

   a galaxy which is 50,000 light years across.

19. English is redundant in vocabulary, repeating the same idea in the same or different wording:

   marble . . . which . . . earth . . . planet

(The reader can use these observations as indications that the author is still on the same subject or dealing with the same action.)

20. English is sometimes repetitious in syntax, using the same sentence structure with as little as one variant. (The reader, observing the likenesses and differences, may detect comparison, contrast, cause-effect, continuation with a subject or change from it to something else, the items in an enumeration.)

21. English frequently practices economy by omission of "expected" elements:

> He gave me the keys, her the directions.
> a galaxy 50,000 light years across

22. English verb ideas are sometimes expressed in a verb and an adverb:

> other stars make up this system (create, comprise)

(Up should not be associated with this system as indicative of heavenly destination!)

23. The position of an adverbial modifier creates ambiguity when the modifier can apply to more than one of the concepts present:

> Steadily, I watched the train pull out.
> I watched the train pull out steadily.

24. Two or more adjectives preceding the noun can create differences in interpretation:

> bright-blue marble versus bright, blue marble

Since readers and authors never quite succeed in extricating their feelings from their thoughts, and often eagerly express their feelings anyway, it is useful to know that the considerations listed above have bearing on feelings, too.

Teachers should study the signals to meaning from the point of view of a reader who does not know all that an author knows about his subject, or know what a teacher knows about interpreting signals. This way, teachers can begin to assess the value of certain observations under certain conditions and determine strategies for teaching in all types of literature from preschool to the end of formal instruction. Thought processes must be cultivated and expressed in English. The versatility of English in expressing the same thought in numerous ways must be experienced in listening, in analysis, and by oral practice. Expectation of the directions the author may next take must provide readiness for whatever comes. Children must know that the ecology of literature, like the ecology of earth, is a matter of interrelationships. All of these considerations relate to what the author has presented. The reader's cognitive and affective reactions after that are something else again, and no small order!

REFERENCES

Carroll, John B. (Ed.) *Language, Thought, and Reality: Selected Writings of Benjamin Lee Whorf.* Cambridge, Mass.: Massachusetts Institute of Technology Press, 1964.

Chomsky, Noam *Aspects of the Theory of Syntax.* Cambridge, Mass.: Massachusetts Institute of Technology Press, 1965.

Fries, Charles C. *The Structure of English.* New York: Harcourt Brace Jovanovich, Inc., 1951.

Goodman, Kenneth *A Study of Oral Reading Miscues That Result in Grammatical Re-transformations.* Project No. 7–E–219, Contract No. OEG–0–8–070219–2806. June, 1969. U.S. Department of Health, Education and Welfare, Office of Education, Bureau of Research.

Guilford, J. P. "Three Faces of Intellect," *American Psychologist,* 1958, *14* (August), 469–479.

LeFevre, Carl *Linguistics and the Teaching of Reading.* New York: McGraw-Hill, 1964.

NSSE *Innovation and Change in Reading Instruction.* Part II, Chapter I. 67th Yearbook of the National Society for the Study of Education, Helen M. Robinson (Ed.). Chicago: University of Chicago Press, 1968.

NSSE *Linguistics in School Programs.* Part II. 69th Yearbook of the National Society for the Study of Education, Albert H. Marckwardt (Ed.). Chicago: University of Chicago Press, 1970.

LINGUISTICS, THOUGHT,

AND READING

Edmund H. Henderson

Thirteen or fourteen years ago, I think it was in the spring of 1957, Russell Stauffer taught a demonstration reading lesson with first grade children before a large audience at the University of Pittsburgh. The story was about children who were looking for a penny they had lost while playing in the park. Stopping the readers at this point in the story, Stauffer asked, "How do you think it will end?" All but one child, a boy, agreed that the penny would be found. Then they read to test their prediction. When all were finished, a girl spoke first, "We were right," she said. "They found the penny."

At once the boy who had challenged the prediction in the first place asked for the microphone and replied, "How do you know it was the same penny?"

"No. We were right," said the girl, "and I can prove it." She turned to the last page of the story and read aloud, "They found the penny." Then she added, "if it had been just any penny, it would have said a penny."

This teaching anecdote appears in Stauffer's text (1969); and it is such a delightful one that I feel it bears repeating. I can think of no more concrete way to illustrate the intellectual interplay that exists in reading, even in the reading of young children in very simple materials. It is my contention that this aspect of reading is the basis for a belief in the relevance of the study of thought and language for curriculum.

In what follows, I would like to review briefly the origin of the teaching strategy that led to this dialogue among first grade children. Then, I will suggest how different analyses of the thinking process yield some useful understandings or models that describe what these children were doing intellectually. Finally, I will consider some aspects of linguistics in order to see what this broad science suggests about the place of a reading lesson in the total language curriculum.

DIRECTED READING-THINKING ACTIVITY

It is of some interest to note that the beginnings of Stauffer's reading demonstration, which he terms a Directed Reading-Thinking Activity, preceded by some years the rediscovery of Piaget (Ripple & Rockcastle, 1964, pp. 7–20) and the major educational works of Jerome Bruner (1959, 1960), and preceded Guilford's "Three Faces of the Intellect" (1958) by a year. Stauffer's approach was founded in part on the ideas of men such as Edmund Huey, Ernest Horn, Alfred Korzybski, and I. A. Richards, and on the research of the emerging cognitive psychologists. His approach was also founded on an extended clinical examination of children reading individually and in small groups. This latter is a point, by the way, that I think is often missed by students of education. Rather than make gross field comparisons of relatively static but complex methods, it is more productive, in many ways, to vary an activity with children, in part systematically, in part intuitively, and then note the effects directly. In this way, pedagogical techniques can be forged from theory and modified rapidly to a level of function that is both relatively flexible and interpretable. What Stauffer was doing with reading instruction was very similar to Piaget's clinical method in the study of human thought. Thus, it is not surprising that the interaction schedules, like the episode narrated above, lend themselves to an analysis in Piaget's terms (1963).

LEVELS OF DISCOURSE

One notes, for example, that the children did not use the word "distributive" when they made the distinction between a *penny* and *the penny*. Clearly, they were not thinking *about* thinking. Rather, they were manipulating the facts and making judgments. This is in keeping with Piaget's ideas about a stage of concrete operations. The facts or words represented events and objects that were a part of these children's examined experience. They had been to parks or seen them. They had held pennies and probably even lost some. Eleanor Duckworth (1967) has emphasized the crucial role of experience by suggesting that reading, even at the adult level, can serve only to remind the thinker of what he knows. While I suspect she is nearly right in a sense, her position seems to me to be a little extreme.

I would argue with Bruner (1964) that language does provide the opportunity to command events in time and to permit symbolic reconstruction or conceptual growth. Stauffer's lesson, however, makes it clear that children can accomplish this kind of thinking about pennies and parks in elementary years. Only later on, and probably as a function of youthful exercise of this kind, will children be able to deal with principles of logic and symbolic logical argument.

INTELLECTUAL READINESS

It is worth noting also that the children in this lesson did perform various cognitive operations. For example, to predict a story outcome, on other than a memoriter basis, it is necessary to assume a "self-other" position with regard to the characters and words of the story. This is precisely the kind of cognitive trick that Piaget has found conspicuously absent in young children, between approximately two and seven years of age. These Pittsburgh first graders had attained a level of intellectual maturity that made possible idea testing as opposed to simple word association. Herein lies a powerful implication for the concept of reading readiness. It is unlikely that one can teach a three-year-old to read in the sense that these children were reading. It would appear, therefore, that the advent of reading between the ages of five and seven is neither an accident nor an oversight.

DISCOVERY READING

Because reading is a process rather than a subject, it is not surprising that Bruner's ideas, which he applied first to the science curriculum, are exemplified also in Stauffer's approach. One notes that here the children were not dully calling words, accumulating facts, and reciting them back —as Bruner (1959) has called it "passive knowledge-getting in pabulum readers." Rather, there was prediction, hypothesis testing, and substantiation judgment.

DIVERGENT-CONVERGENT MODEL

Guilford's (1958) model, too, is apparent in the reading lesson. The *production* of ideas about how the story would end prior to reading is a good example of divergent thinking. The final decision that the penny would be found was an example of convergent thinking. In one sense, the reading process can be described as an interplay of these two modes —creative inquiry and disciplined evaluation—to the end that past conceptual schema are affirmed or reformed. Our own research suggests both that facility in these critical thinking skills is related to reading efficiency (Tate and Harootunian, 1960; Henderson, 1965; Henderson and Long, 1968) and that extended exercise in this kind of reading approach influences the quality of children's thinking (Petre, 1969).

THE LINGUISTIC SETTING

Now I would like to turn to linguistics to see how the study of language has influenced this analysis of the reading-thinking process. At first glance, one might conclude that linguistics has little to offer such a view of reading because, until recently, the principal thrust of linguistic science in respect to the teaching of reading has been an explication of phoneme-grapheme correspondences and the recoding operation of printed to spoken words. It is my argument, however, that the more prominent linguistic approaches to reading represent but a minor aspect of linguistic theory, and that they are, in fact, somewhat at variance with much of the research in the study of language.

Regardless of Bloomfield's theoretical position in the field of linguistics (see Fries, 1963), it is my belief that the plan to apply principles of phoneme-grapheme regularity to reading instruction was an educational rather than a linguistic gambit. The question was not "Is such a correspondence the primary unit of language," but rather "Will intensive exposure to phoneme-grapheme correspondences facilitate learning to read?" Today, reading instruction materials run the gamut from those that maintain a strict linguistic control—the Bloomfield strategy—to those that replicate the traditional basal reader phonics program but substitute linguistic terms, that is, word attack-decoding, etc. It is, I think, pretty clearly a case of "let the buyer beware"; and one mitigates against the response of educators to much that is important in the study of language.

AN OVERVIEW

A hasty overview may help to support this point. A reading of Albert Baugh's *A History of the English Language* (1963) makes possible an understanding about the livingness of language that would provide teachers with a basis for curiosity about deviant form rather than a fear of its incorrectness.

The noted anthropologist, Levi-Strauss, in his book *The Savage Mind* (1966), interprets the dialectic of primitive men and finds in it an intellectual sophistication and elegance in every way the peer of that employed in modern analytic discourse. Such linguistic study enlightens our reading of myth and our understanding of the language of children, as well as shattering the misconception that man reached perfection in the form of a white Anglo-Saxon Protestant.

The writings of sociolinguists such as Roger Shuy, for example, inform us about dialect. From them, we learn that the mother tongue of the ghetto child has an integrity and potential of its own. Their work suggests not only that standard English readers are inappropriate for such children, but also that forced courses in a standard English are equally inappropriate. Since these are incapable of effecting instant change, they merely suppress the use of a child's natural language during a critical stage of development.

Lenneberg, a biologist, examines language as species-specific behavior and calls attention to the innate and developmental cognitive capacities underlying the acquisition of language in human children (1967). From such a work, one is persuaded that a narrowly conceived stimulus-response model is inadequate to describe language development or to serve as a basis from which to derive programs for teaching beginning reading.

Psychologists such as Roger Brown (1965) and his coworkers have presented many studies concerned with language acquisition in young children. Here, one notes the regularity, speed, and certainty of their mastery. A psycholinguist, John Carroll (1965), raises interesting questions about the possible parallel between the acquisition of speech and the learning-to-read process. Whereas the child learning to speak is exposed to the whole language, the child learning to read, in most programs, is given only one word at a time. Here lies a persuasive theoretical argument that would predict greater effectiveness for a beginning reading program in which the child's own language was used.

An experimental psychologist, Eleanor Gibson, has studied the word recognition process in adults and children for nearly a decade. Her report in the *American Psychologist* (1970) entitled "The Ontogeny of Reading" presents a series of findings about the development of children's abilities to discover graphic structures. Regarding the decoding process she states ". . . we do know it is not a simple matter of paired associate learning, either of a letter to a sound or a written word to a spoken one." Gibson's work, moreover, finds simultaneous and independent support in the research from Michigan, notably that of Wheeler (1970). Here are data that must indeed require educators to ponder common classroom practices. It calls into question the very acceptability of many word recognition skills programs, and suggests that those, in fact, may be "Do-It-Yourself" dyslexia kits.

During this century, a credulous public has continued to sponsor a sort of academic rodeo. One rider after another is wildly cheered, but each is eventually thrown by his snorting bias—whole word, phonics, diacritical marks, i.t.a., Royal Road Readers, Linguistic Readers, Programmed Readers. The costumes are becoming gaudier and the price of admission is going up, but conditions remain the same as they were when Huey (1908) described them sixty years ago.

Today, however, there is a difference. Society has confronted us with our 60 percent reading failure in the ghettos and among the rural poor. Scientists, as opposed to enthusiasts, have again turned their investigative skills to fundamental questions of language and thought. Further, the findings of these lines of hard research tend to uphold and to make sense of the work of educators who have based their procedures upon continuous clinical self-examination. These events suggest both the basis and the means of change.

It seems to me that there is a theme to be found in contemporary linguistics that makes some very clear implications for reading instruction. Moreover, I feel that this theme is supported by the major work of the decade in cognition and development.

I conclude that children should learn to read in their mother tongue, using that language in its unadulterated form. I think they should begin by seeing first their own communications written down. I believe that their learning should advance as a function of their opportunity and ability to examine printed language and attain functional concepts of its attributes. When an initial grasp of the fundamentals of printed language has been gained, instruction in reading should then proceed in real books by real authors under the direction of teachers who require a diligent and rewarding exercise of the mind.

REFERENCES

Baugh, A. C. *A History of the English Language.* New York: Appleton-Century-Crofts, 1963.

Brown, R. *Social Psychology.* New York: The Free Press, 1965.

Bruner, J. S. "Learning and Thinking," *Harvard Educational Review,* 1959, *29,* 184–192.

Bruner, J. S. *The Process of Education.* Cambridge, Mass.: Harvard University Press, 1960.

Bruner, J. S. "The Course of Cognitive Growth," *American Psychologist,* 1964, *19,* 1–15.

Carroll, J. B. *Some Neglected Relationships in Reading and Language Learning.* Paper presented at NCTE in Boston, November, 1965.

Duckworth, Eleanor Preconvention Seminar on Critical Thinking and Reading, IRA Conference, Dallas, 1967.

Fries, C. C. *Linguistics and Reading.* New York: Holt, Rinehart & Winston, 1963.

Gibson, Eleanor "The Ontogeny of Reading," *American Psychologist,* 1970, *25* (February), 136–143.

Guilford, J. P. "Three Faces of the Intellect," *American Psychologist,* 1958, *14* (August), 469–479.

Henderson, E. H. "A Study of Individually Formulated Purposes for Reading," *Journal of Educational Research,* 1965, *10,* 438–441.

Henderson, E. H. and Long, Barbara H. "Decision Processes of Superior, Average and Inferior Readers," *Psychological Reports*, 1968, *23* (December), 703–706.

Huey, E. B. *The Psychology and Pedagogy of Reading*. New York: Macmillan, 1908.

Lenneberg, E. H. *Biological Foundations of Language*. New York: John Wiley & Sons, Inc., 1967.

Levi-Strauss, C. *The Savage Mind*. Chicago: The University of Chicago Press, 1966.

Petre, R. *Quantity, Quality and Variety of Pupil Responses During an Open-Communication Structured Group Directed Reading-Thinking Activity and a Closed-Communication Structured Group Directed Reading Activity*. Unpublished doctoral dissertation, University of Delaware, 1969.

Piaget, J. "The Attainment of Invariants and Reversable Operations in the Development of Thinking," *Social Research*, 1963, *30*, 283–299.

Ripple, R. and Rockcastle, V. *Piaget Rediscovered*. A report of the Conference of Cognitive Studies and Curriculum Development. Ithaca, N.Y.: School of Education, Cornell University, 1964.

Shuy, R. "Some Language and Cultural Differences in a Theory of Reading," in *Psycholinguistics and the Teaching of Reading*. Proceedings of the International Reading Association. Newark, Del., 1969.

Stauffer, R. G. *Directing Reading Maturity as a Cognitive Process*. New York: Harper & Row, 1969.

Tate, M. W. and Harootunian, B. *Statistical Problems and Procedures in the Study of Differences between Good and Poor Problem Solvers*. Report American Educational Research Association, February, 1960.

Wheeler, D. D. "Process in Word Recognition," *Cognitive Psychology*, 1970, *1* (January), 59–85.

FOR FURTHER READING

Brown, Roger *Words and Things*. Glencoe, Ill.: The Free Press, 1958.
  An informative overview of language in a psychological context. Although many books on psycholinguistics have been published since, this volume still remains one of the most readable for a general audience.

NSSE *Linguistics in School Programs*. Part II. 69th Yearbook of the National Society for the Study of Education, Albert H. Marckwardt (Ed.). Chicago: University of Chicago Press, 1970.
  Presents a useful treasury of research evidence on language development in children and on children's learning difficulties with words of varied structure.

Stauffer, Russell (Ed.) *Language and the Higher Thought Processes*. Champaign, Illinois: National Council of Teachers of English, 1965.
  A Research Bulletin of the National Conference on Research in English in which articles by six scholars bring out the fundamental point that language is the essential medium in formal instruction.

SUMMARY

The contributors to this volume have conveyed their views on language and learning to read. Our introductions to their papers express many of our views on this topic. These introductions have been intended to add to the reader's perspective on the different papers in this volume; and in this summary statement we would like to state some more of our own views about language and learning to read—particularly in respect to teaching and to teacher education.

In respect to our knowledge of language and of learning to read, none of the authors represented here would contend that the "truth is all in." Also, even though not all of the contributors are in agreement about some of the substantive areas that have been discussed, we are impressed with the extent to which the various authors have generally reinforced what others in this volume have had to say. We recognize that each paper, in and of itself, is an independently valid statement of a major position and that different positions about language and reading can be found here. But, it is the cumulative and reinforcing effect of the totality of these papers that will have, we trust, the persuasive force to convince the reader of the importance of linguistic, psycholinguistic, and sociolinguistic study to his professional role as teacher of reading, administrator, curriculum specialist, or trainer of teachers.

The subtitle of this volume—*What Teachers Should Know About Language*—should not be taken to indicate that we have attempted to produce a textbook that covers all aspects of linguistic, psychological, or sociological disciplines and subdisciplines. One cannot, for example, become an expert in phonology by reading this book, nor a dialectologist, nor a psycholinguist (though we would hope a more knowledgeable person in these areas). Rather, what each author has attempted is to indicate the more important insights to be gained by a study of a particular area of specialization, and to identify the domains of knowledge which are necessary for the teacher of reading.

We wish, therefore, to emphasize in the subtitle the word *Should*. It is our assertion that teacher competence in the language and language-related disciplines which have been described throughout this book is not a luxury, but a *necessity* if the problem of illiteracy nationally, or in a given classroom, is ultimately to be solved.

What the authors in this volume have said, we believe, has profound implications for teacher training programs. A serious look needs to be directed at the teacher training curriculums in our universities and our colleges of education. How many teacher training programs, for example, now require a background in the nature and structure of language and writing systems as a prerequisite for methods courses in reading and in the language arts? Which *kinds* of psychology courses are required? Where does the prospective teacher gain experiences in the classroom or out of it that provide knowledge and understanding of the alternative cultures and subcultures which exist in our land? How many reading methods courses provide only a single strategy, or at the most a very few strategies, for carrying on reading instruction? How many of these strategies really consider the child, his background, his capabilities, or his needs? Other questions of a similar vein might well be asked.

While there may not be a necessary correlation, the recent concern for the improvement of reading instruction seems to be developing concurrently with some fresh looks at classroom organization and the role of the teacher in relation to the pupil. Under various labels, and with varying degrees of significant change, we are seeing numerous examples of, and a possibly significant trend toward, the revitalization of instructional practices in which *the child* is once again emerging (he tried in the 1930s and 1940s) as the center of the curriculum.

Though some have alluded to it,[1] no contributor to this book has explicitly discussed the structure of the classroom. Thus, it is clear that the significant aspect of changing views of classroom organization as it relates to the understanding of the reading process is not in the physical differences in classrooms which are beginning to appear (the absence of desks, the development of "interest" centers, and so on), but in the real recognition of the *child,* and of his background, capabilities, and needs. Although all of the contributors to this volume would not and do not agree completely upon one theory of grammar, one definition of language, one statement about the nature of the writing system, nor even one pedagogical solution to the reading problem, they do concur that reading instruction needs to be based upon an understanding of the

[1] See Dolores Mather's paper in Section II, pp. 44–51.

child and his language. For a teacher to do this—*to understand the child and his language*—he must first understand language; that was the rationale for the conference and this book.

Finally, let us return to the book's main title, *Language and Learning to Read*. Choosing a title for a book is not an easy task. A book title should, in the briefest form possible, characterize its content and intent. The title we have chosen is meant to emphasize *learning to read* rather than *teaching reading*. What many of the authors have suggested by the continual comparison between language acquisition and reading acquisition is that it is only in a trivial sense that we can *teach* a child to read, any more than we can *teach* him to speak. As teachers, and others who have responsibilities about reading, we must maximize the opportunities for the child to *learn* to read.

This statement, of course, is open to gross misinterpretation. It does not mean that we advocate a laissez faire atmosphere, where the teacher does little more than maintain a pleasant setting for his pupils. Exactly the opposite is the case. The teacher who is armed with knowledge about the reading process and about how children learn, and who takes each child's interests and needs seriously, multiplies his role, not just one to three times (depending on the number of reading groups there are), but possibly two dozen or more times (depending upon the number of *children* there are). The fact is, that if we take the relationship between learning a language and learning to read in its fullest sense, the deepest involvement of the teacher with the child is required. Language acquisition demands almost constant involvement with, and immersion in, language; but, for most children, this is a natural condition of human development. Similar involvement in the reading process must also be arranged, planned, and contrived by the teacher. For reading, unlike language, is not a necessary constant activity on the part of human beings.

The contributors to this volume are suggesting a major step toward the resolution of the reading problem: it lies not in the search for some new instructional method which will be a panacea for all the problems involved in learning to read, but in the preparation of a new kind of teacher and the acceptance of a new role for the teacher.

GLOSSARY

Affix: A word element that is attached to a base, stem, or root; a prefix or suffix. See **Morpheme.**

Allomorph: One of two or more forms of the same morpheme. For example, the endings of *boys, cats, boxes* are all members of a set of sounds that signal *plurality* when attached to nouns. Each ending, though differently pronounced, is an *allomorph* of the plural morpheme. See **Morpheme.**

Allophone: A variant of a class of phonetically similar speech sounds that constitute a phoneme. For example, the sound represented by the *k* in *kite* is produced slightly differently than the sound represented by *k* in *skate;* yet both are recognized as the "same" sound by English speakers. Both sounds are *allophones* of the phoneme /k/. See **Phoneme.**

Aspiration: The release of a puff of air following the articulation of a consonant sound, as in the initial consonant sounds of *pin, tin, kin.*

Biloquial: *adj.* To have control of two or more dialects of a language.

Cloze Test: A test procedure in readability studies in which words are deleted from sentences and the reader is scored on his ability to correctly replace the missing words of each sentence.

Connotative Meaning: A meaning that is suggested by, or associated with, a word or phrase apart from its explicit meaning or meanings. See **Denotative Meaning.**

Contentives: The meaning-bearing morphemes of a language as distinguished from function words, i.e., nouns, verbs, adjectives. See **Functors.**

Copula: A verb such as *seem, appear, remain, look,* and *to be* that takes a complement (an adjective or a noun) as in *Mary is beautiful, Mary is a child.* Also called *linking verb.*

Decoding: 1. A term commonly used in reading to refer to the process of rendering written or printed symbols into the speech forms that were originally recorded. 2. A term now also used to refer to the process of translating written or spoken messages to meaning. See **Recoding.**

Deep Structure: The abstract grammatical form presumed in generative-transformational grammar to underlie the surface grammatical form of a sentence. The deep structure contains the information necessary for a semantic interpretation of the sentence. See **Surface Structure, Generative-Transformational Grammar.**

Deletion: In generative grammar, a transformation rule which omits certain optional elements of a sentence; e.g., *Jack can't run fast, but Bill can run fast* can be expressed *Jack can't run fast, but Bill can.*

Denotative Meaning: The direct and explicit meaning or reference of a word or phrase.

Diachronic: *adj.* Pertaining to the historical study of the development of a language. See **Synchronic.**

Discourse: A group of sentences that are related in some sequential fashion.

Disyllabic Word: A word with two syllables.

Duality: The concept that language has two types of structure: (1) a phonological structure which of itself has no meaning, and (2) a morphological-syntactical structure which involves meaningful sequences of phonemes.

Expansion: A generative-transformational rule which enables a linguist to show how a sentence such as *I know Ann is happy* is derived from *I know Ann.*

Foot: In the prosodic features of speech, a metric unit consisting of a stressed or unstressed syllable or syllables.

Form Class: In structural grammar, any of the grammatical classes— noun, verb, adjective, adverb—to which words may be said to belong because of their particular characteristics in taking certain sets of affixes; e.g., in English, *nouns* take plural and possessive suffixes, *verbs* take past tense and participial suffixes, and *adjectives* take comparative and superlative suffixes. See **Contentives, Function word, Functors.**

Function Word: In structural grammar, a word with little or no lexical meaning whose main rule is to connect other words into syntactic structures, e.g., prepositions, conjunctions, auxiliary verbs. Also called *functor*.

Functors: Morphemes that signal relationships within a language; e.g., *than* in: Bob is taller *than* Joe. Also called *function words*. See **Contentives.**

Generative Grammar: A grammar whose set of rules would produce all the possible grammatical sentences of a language and no ungrammatical ones.

Generative-Transformational Grammar: A grammar in which all sentences in a language are viewed as either simple basic sentences (kernels) or combinations and permutations of these basic sentences by rules (transformations). The grammar assigns structural descriptions to sentences and relates their deep structures and meanings to their surface structures and sounds, and vice versa. See **Deep Structure, Surface Structure, Transformation.**

Genre: A distinctive class or category of literature.

Grammar: The set of rules by which a language operates.

Grapheme: A graphic symbol used in a writing system; e.g., the alphabet letters of English writing.

Grapheme-Phoneme Correspondence: The relationship between a grapheme of writing and a phoneme of speech.

Graphology: The study of a writing system. Also called *graphemics*.

Holophrase: The use of a single word to express an entire sentence, a characteristic of the early language development of children.

Homophone: One of two or more words that are pronounced alike

Homonym: Any of two or more words that are alike in spoken and/or written form, but are different in meaning.
but differ in meaning, derivation, and often in spelling.

Hyperbole: An exaggeration or extravagant statement used as a figure of speech, e.g., "I could eat a horse."

Iconic Memory: A stage of cognition in which visual impressions "persist" momentarily after the initial sensory stimulation.

Idiolect: A person's characteristic and individualized use of language.

Inflection: An affix, usually a suffix, that changes the form of a word though not its form class nor its basic meaning; e.g., plurals and possessives used with nouns, as in *cats* and *cat's*.

Intonation: The variation, or rise and fall, in pitch while speaking. See **Suprasegmental.**

Irony: An expression in which words are used to convey the opposite of their literal meaning.

Juncture: The transition from one speech utterance to another with either a pause or stoppage of the breath stream at the point of transition, as in *an aim* and *a name*. See **Suprasegmental.**

Kinesics: The study of the way people communicate through body movements and gesture, e.g., a raised eyebrow, a shift in posture.

Lexical Meaning: The "dictionary" meaning of a word; its meaning apart from the meaning it acquires in context of a larger unit of language, such as a phrase or sentence.

Lexicon: The stock of words of a language, i.e., a dictionary.

Metalanguage: In logic, a language that is used to talk *about* a language. The language that is talked about is called the *object* language.

Metaphor: An expression or statement which suggests an idea by comparison or analogy.

Miscue: An observed oral response to printed text that does not conform to what is expected.

Morpheme: The smallest unit of meaning of a language. A morpheme may be a complete word, as in *girl;* or it may be a unit of speech which has no meaning by itself but contributes to the meaning of words; e.g., the sound added to *girl* to produce the plural form *girls.*

Morphology: The study of the arrangement and interrelationships of morphemes in words; the "word-building" properties of a language.

Morphophonemic: Pertaining to the alternations of phonemes with a given morpheme; e.g., the alternation of /f/ and /v/ in *wolf* and *wolves.*

Nonlinguistic Meaning: The "sense" meaning of a word apart from its syntactic relationship with other words in a sentence.

Onomatopoeia: Naming a thing or action with the intention to reproduce the sound of the referent, e.g., the *buzz* of a bee.

Open Class: In early language development, words of infrequent use that may appear in more than one position in a sentence. See **Pivot Class.**

Orthography: A writing system.

Patois: Popular speech, usually construed as a dialect other than a standard dialect.

Phoneme: A set of phonetically similar speech sounds of a given language which are perceived by a native speaker of the language to be the same. See **Allophone.**

Phonetics: The study of speech sounds in terms of their physical properties (acoustical phonetics) or means of pronunciation (articulatory phonetics).

Phonics: A method of teaching reading in which the key units taught to children are letter-sound correspondences.

Phonology: The study of the sound structure of a language, including phonetics and phonemics. See **Phonetics, Phoneme.**

Phrase Structure: In generative-transformational grammar, the grammatical structure of a sentence before the application of transformations. See **Transformation.**

Pivot Class: In early language development, a small number of frequently used words which a child has learned to use in a fixed position in a sentence. See **Open Class.**

Pronominalization: In generative-transformational grammar, the transformation that produces a pronominal (pronoun) for a noun phrase; e.g., *that the dog barked* in *The dog barked, and that the dog barked made Bill angry* can be replaced by *this* in *The dog barked, and this made Bill angry.*

Psycholinguistics: The study of the interrelationships of psychological and linguistic behavior.

Recoding: The process of changing information from one code into another without recourse to meaning; for example, in reading, the process of changing graphic information into oral information.

Redundancy: A term used in information theory which refers to the duplication of information by more than one source. As applied to reading, redundancy is the property which enables a reader with experience and knowledge about the written code to know that only certain patterns of letters are possible out of all possible combinations.

Rule: As used in transformational grammar, a formal statement or direction for forming a sentence or part of a sentence.

Sequential Constraint: Restrictions placed on sequences of language elements; e.g., in English, the maximum permissible string of consonants is four (e.g., *sixths* = /siks θ s/) and only certain consonants can follow certain other consonants (e.g., /st/ may be followed only by /r/ as in *string*).

Simile: An expression or statement used as a figure of speech in which two unlike things are compared, e.g.: "Her hair is like silk."

Stratificational Grammar: A relatively recent theory of grammar whose mode of analysis describes the elements of language—phoneme, morpheme, etc.—in terms of a series of layers or strata.

Stress: The relative force or intensity with which a vowel is pronounced. See **Suprasegmental.**

Structure: In respect to language, the system of interrelated elements and their patterns that is distinctive to a language. See **System.**

Suprasegmental: Referring to the features of sound commonly called juncture, stress, and intonation. See **Juncture, Stress, Intonation.**

Surface Structure: The observed representation of a sentence—i.e., its lexicon and syntax—from which its phonetic or graphic realization is derived. See **Deep Structure, Transformation.**

Syllable: A sound unit composed of a vowel or vowel-like sound and usually one or more consonant sounds.

Synchronic: *adj:* Pertaining to the study of a language as it exists at a particular time without reference to its historical development. See **Diachronic.**

Syntax: The arrangement of words into grammatical phrases and sentences.

System: In reference to language, the notion that language elements —sounds, grammar, lexicon—have no independent validity, but are interacting and interdependent. Language is thus regarded as a *system of relations* among its elements; or more precisely, a set of interrelated systems.

Tagmemic Analysis: A theory of grammar which analyzes elements of language in terms of both their forms and their functions. The grammatical unit which is said to encompass both form and function is called a *tagmeme.*

Transformation: In generative-transformational grammar, a grammatical operation which rearranges, inserts, or deletes elements in the deep structure to produce the surface structure. See **Deep Structure, Surface Structure.**

Voiced: A speech sound in which the vocal cords vibrate during production of the sound, e.g., the initial sound of *ball, now, this*. See **Voiceless.**

Voiceless: A speech sound in which the vocal cords do not vibrate during production of the sound, e.g., the initial sound of *pal, far, thin*.

Zero Copula: The absence of a copulative (linking) verb in the surface (oral or written) production of a sentence; e.g., *He gone* for *He is gone.*

INDEX